SPANISH FOR CONVERSATION

A BLAISDELL BOOK IN THE MODERN LANGUAGES

CONSULTING EDITOR

Charles N. Staubach
UNIVERSITY OF ARIZONA

NORTHWESTERN UNIVERSITY   John Kenneth Leslie

SPANISH FOR CONVERSATION

A BEGINNING GRAMMAR   ■ ■ ■ ■   THIRD EDITION

BLAISDELL PUBLISHING COMPANY
A Division of Ginn and Company

WALTHAM, MASSACHUSETTS   /   TORONTO   /   LONDON

FOREWORD

Spanish for Conversation is a basic textbook for the first year of college Spanish. It is based on an oral-aural method which stresses the spoken language.

There are twenty-eight lessons, preceded by two preliminary lessons. Pronunciation is presented in the first preliminary lesson in such a carefully designed way that in any example, in addition to sounds already explained, the student hears only the one new sound which he is learning. In the first ten lessons, there are formal pronunciation reviews. New verb forms are introduced at the beginning of each lesson, not necessarily so that the student will learn them as paradigms, but in order that he may *hear* the new forms—*before studying them*—as spoken by his instructor. New vocabulary follows in the "Listening and Speaking" section, again so that the student may hear and repeat the new words and idioms before using them in context. The core of each lesson is a passage in Spanish based on a real-life situation or dealing with cultural aspects of Spain or Spanish America. The student listens to this as his instructor reads or as the accompanying tape is played in the laboratory. The minimum essentials of Spanish grammar are presented systematically in the Structure sections. Certain special constructions are indicated by superior numerals in the text and explained in the Notes which follow most of the situations. These Notes usually, though not necessarily, involve minor points that can best be understood and assimilated by referring directly from their occurrence in the text to the pertinent explanation.

Because the basis of each lesson is the Spanish situation, the student is asked to learn it thoroughly as a sequence of ideas but not to memorize it word for word. He must learn it well enough to be able to retell the story to himself, which he should do a number of times as part of his preparation. This constant practice leads to fluency on the part of the student—within the limited vocabulary range of some 1200 common words and idioms—

v

and builds up reflexes by which he can apply the principles of Spanish grammar to his own speaking and writing.

Exercise materials are of various types. After each situation there are questions to be answered orally. These are of such a nature that the instructor may easily adapt them to the student's personal experience. For instance, a question like "¿Cómo prepara Juan la lección de español?" may logically be followed by "¿Cómo prepara *usted* la lección de español?" At the end of each lesson is a "Test Yourself" exercise, which may be spoken or written. By means of this exercise, the student tests his mastery of the situation as part of his preparation. Composition exercises, for those teachers who wish to use them, are intended to give the student practice in writing, but only by having him write what he can say readily and easily. It has been the author's custom to ask the students to write short compositions, using every other line of one page of ordinary notebook-size paper. Under the heading "Práctica" in the verb and structure sections, there are highly useful drill exercises of several types: subject and item substitutions, tense and structure substitutions, patterned responses, pattern sentences to be expressed in Spanish, etc. These offer copious and rapid drill and should be done by the student as part of his preparation. In the classroom, with books closed, the students should repeat the models in chorus after the teacher, who then cues the responses as suggested in the exercises. For example, after the model "Es mi traje. Es mío," the teacher gives the cue "Es mi blusa," to which a student responds: "Es mía."

This book is designed for the modern teacher who believes that the class hour should be devoted largely to conversation based upon the material studied for the day and enlarged to include related experiences of the student's own. The instructor may wish to retell the story of the day to the class, varying the wording and the order of the details. He will find that the situations lend themselves to speedy recapitulation by the student either orally or in the form of compositions written on the blackboard. The ideas of the situations are so easily retained by the student that frequent impromptu reviews are feasible, with the result that the vocabulary and grammatical principles already studied can be kept fresh in mind and used throughout the course.

For many helpful suggestions for this or earlier editions the author wishes to thank his friends and colleagues: Professors Edwin B. Place, Joseph G. Fucilla, Frederick S. Stimson, Phares R. Hershey, Mabel Staudinger, and William T. Starr, all of Northwestern University; and Robert J. Bininger, of Arizona State University; Donald G. Castanien, of the University of California at Davis; Gabriel H. Engerrand, of North Georgia College; Harvey L. Johnson, of the University of Houston; and

José Sánchez, of the University of Illinois. A special word of appreciation is due to Professor Eduardo Neale-Silva, of the University of Wisconsin, who offered much constructive criticism, and to Professor Homero Castillo, of the University of California at Davis who kindly read the Spanish portions of the lessons.

J.K.L.

CONTENTS

TO THE STUDENT

Speaking Spanish is fun. Your instructor, aided by the materials in this book, can teach you to speak Spanish—within the range of the vocabulary here presented, of course.

Since the best way to learn a language is to imitate and repeat, imitation and repetition are the core of the method upon which this book is built.

You will prepare your lessons in a way that you may not have used previously in studying languages. First, you will listen to the new verb forms of each lesson as the instructor reads them. You will repeat each as you hear it pronounced. Then you will listen to the new words used in each lesson and repeat each one after the instructor. Next you will listen to the situation around which each lesson is built, either in the laboratory as the tape is played or in class as your instructor reads. You will repeat after the tape or after your instructor.

The main part of your work in preparing each lesson will be to repeat to yourself, preferably aloud, the situation. Tell yourself the story over and over again, until you can tell it as easily as if you were speaking English, but do not memorize the story word for word. Remember always to imitate the pronunciation and the inflection of your instructor. Pay particular attention to the word order in the phrases which you learn.

Study the Notes and Structure sections which follow each situation, for you need to know the basic grammatical structure which is explained in them in order to transfer the words and expressions you are learning to other circumstances—those of your own daily life, for example. Each point of structure is reinforced by practice exercises ("Práctica") which will help you to remember the basic structure of the language. Do the exercises assigned by your instructor.

Above all, keep speaking Spanish. Get into the habit of repeating to yourself and to your classmates the expressions which you learn. As you learn new words, keep using them to tell your classmates in Spanish what you are doing, what you are going to do, and what you have done recently.

SPANISH FOR CONVERSATION

FIRST PRELIMINARY LESSON

The basic sounds of Spanish

Consonants f, m, n, p

The consonants **f, m, n,** and **p** are pronounced as in English. However, there is no aspiration after Spanish **p** as there is in English p^hack. Examples are given below in the section on vowels.

Vowels

Each Spanish vowel is one single, pure sound. In English many vowel sounds are not single sounds. Instead we tend to drawl them out with a following glide sound. When we say the word *no,* for example, we usually say *no*ᵘ. But the Spanish-speaking person says **no/** and cuts the vowel short to one single sound. Beware of drawling your Spanish vowels as you do your English vowels.

The Spanish vowels **a, i,** and **u** have one sound each:

a as in *father:* **ama**	**mapa**	**fama**	**pan**	**pampa**
i as in *machine:* **mí**	**ni**	**mina**	**pipa**	**fina**

NOTE: The Spanish conjunction **y** (*and*) is pronounced like **i.**

u as in *rule:* **una**	**fuma**	**puna**	**puma**

1

Consonants l and t

L is pronounced as in the English word *leave,* with the tip of the tongue against the upper gums:

ala   Lima   luna   mula   al

T is pronounced as in English, but with the tip of the tongue against the upper teeth:

tan   tina   tuna   mata   lata

Vowels e and o

The Spanish vowels **e** and **o** have two sounds each.

e (1) like *a* in *mate,* when final in its syllable:

me   meta   nene   teme   lema

e (2) usually as in *let,* when followed by a consonant in the same syllable:

papel   felpa   inepta

o (1) as in *note,* when final in its syllable:

no   nota   toma   ola   tono

o (2) as in *nor,* when followed by a consonant in the same syllable:

con   completo   opta   olfato

Consonants with more than one sound

The following Spanish consonants have at least two pronunciations each, depending on the sounds which follow or precede:

1

g followed by **a, o, u**:

(1) as in *go* when initial after a pause or after **n**:

gato   gota   gula   tengo   un gato

(2) otherwise a fricative sound (the back of the tongue raised towards the soft palate but not touching it):

hago   lago   mago   pago

In the combinations **gue** and **gui** the **u** is silent, and the **g** has one of the above sounds, depending on its position:

(1) guía   un guía   (2) me guía   pague

g followed by **e** or **i**, like *ch* in German *ach* or in Scottish *Loch Lomond*:

gema   gente   página   imagino   agita

2

c followed by **a, o, u,** or a consonant, as in *cat*:

cama   cola   come   cuna   clima

c followed by **e** or **i**, like *th* in *think*:

celo   cinco   nace   cima   ciclo

NOTE: This is the pronunciation of Castilian Spanish. In some parts of Spain and in Spanish America, **c** before **e** or **i** is like *s* in *sent*.

3

d usually like *th* in *neither*:

cada   codo   nido   la duda   tomad

d initial after a pause and after **l** or **n,** like English, but with tip of tongue against upper teeth:

don   donde   el día   tilde   dando

4

B and **v.** These letters are pronounced alike. There is no difference between them. Note the pronunciation of English *b*. To form this consonant we dam the air up behind our lips and then suddenly and explosively release it:

Boy!   *Boston beans!*

That is, in English, *b* is an explosive sound. Spanish **b** and **v** are pronounced like English *b,* but less explosively, when they are initial after a pause or follow **m** or **n** (which, before **b** or **v,** is pronounced **m**):

bola   vaca   ambición   invita

But more frequently Spanish **b** and **v** are different from English *b*. Instead of closing the lips firmly, damming up the air and suddenly exploding it, you must keep the lips slightly open and allow the current of air to pass through continuously:

la vaca   la beca   Cuba   iba   el voto

NOTE: Never allow the upper teeth to touch the lower lip, as in the pronunciation of English *v*.

5

s usually like *s* in *sat*:

casa   mesas   sino   son   susto

s before a voiced consonant (**b, v, d, g, l, m, n**) like *s* in *rose*:

los besos   las vacas   desde   los gatos   los lunes   mismo

asno

6

r initial in a word (not necessarily after a pause), and after **l, n, s,** strongly trilled: two or more taps of the tip of the tongue against the upper gums:

romano   la rosa   el rato   un ramo   las rimas

Note that **s** before **r** is not pronounced as **s**; it is assimilated by the **r**. The result is about as if the **s** were dropped.

r otherwise, one single tap of the tongue against the upper gum ridge:

para   pero   barco   salir   brotar

7

x between vowels, like English *gs*:

taxi   exacto   éxito   exótico

x before a consonant, like *s* in *sat*:

excepto   excusar   extremo   explicar

Other Consonants

j like Spanish **g** in the combinations **ge, gi**:

tajo   lujo   jota   jinete   jamón

h is always silent:

heno   hilo   hoja   humano   hijo

y at the beginning of a syllable, like *y* in *yes*:

yo   ya   haya   tuyo

z is pronounced like Spanish **c** in the combinations **ce, ci**, that is, in Castilian Spanish, like the *th* in *think,* and, in the speech of parts of Spain and that of Spanish America, like the *s* in *sent*:

paz   vez   zapato   lápiz   caza

q occurs only in the combinations **que** and **qui**. It is pronounced like English *k*. The **u** is silent:

> **que   aquí   aquel   querer   quiso**

k is pronounced as in English: **kilo   kilómetro**

w occurs only in foreign words. It is usually pronounced like English *w*: **Wáshington.**

In addition to the twenty-six characters we know, the Spanish alphabet has four others, **ch, ll,** and **rr,** each of which counts as a single letter, and **ñ**. In dictionaries and vocabularies **ch, ll,** and **ñ** follow **c, l,** and **n** respectively.

ch as in *church*:

> **chico   muchacho   mucho   coche   chocolate**

ll like *lli* in *million*:

> **calle   halla   llama   llave   caballo   silla**

NOTE: In parts of Spain and in most of Spanish America **ll** is pronounced like *y* in English *yes*. In the region around Buenos Aires it is pronounced like *s* in *pleasure*.

ñ like *ny* in *canyon*:

> **señor   señorita   uña   leña   año**

rr strongly trilled:

> **perro   carro   parra   ferrocarril**

Diphthongs

Spanish vowels are classed as *strong* (**a, e, o**) and weak (**i,** or **y,** and **u**). Any combination of a strong and a weak vowel or of two weak vowels forms a diphthong. The vowels of a diphthong are pronounced as they would be if each stood alone, but they are run together into one syllable. Stress the *strong* vowel in a combination of strong and weak:

ai (ay): baile, hay, habláis
ia: gloria, patria
au: aula, causa, jaula
ua: Ecuador, cuaderno, suave
ei (ey): veinte, rey, treinta
ie: miel, cielo, cierto

eu: Europa, europeo
ue: suelo, bueno, vuela
oi (oy): boina, hoy
io: comió, bebió, idioma
uo: continuo, inicuo

Emphasize the *second* vowel in a combination of two weak vowels:

iu ciudad, viuda   **ui (uy):** ruida, cuidado, muy

NOTE: A combination of a strong and a weak vowel whose weak vowel bears a written accent, or a combination of two weak vowels the first of which bears a written accent, is not a diphthong. Neither is a combination of two strong vowels.

dí-a   rí-o   flú-ido   le-o   ca-e

Triphthongs

A triphthong is a combination of three vowels: a stressed strong vowel between two weak ones. Pronounce as one syllable.

iai: estudiáis   **uai, uay:** continuáis, Uruguay
iei: estudiéis   **uei, uey:** continuéis, buey

NOTE: A combination of a weak, a strong, and a weak vowel that bears a written accent on the first *weak* vowel breaks down into a vowel plus a diphthong.

vivirí-ais

Division of words into syllables

1. A Spanish word has as many syllables as it has vowels, diphthongs, and triphthongs:

bo-ni-ta   fue-ra   es-tu-diáis

Two strong vowels coming together are separated; so is a combination of vowels prevented by a written accent mark from being either a diphthong or a triphthong:

te-a-tro   rí-o   flú-i-do   ha-bla-rí-ais

2. A single consonant (including **ch, ll, rr**) between vowels goes with the following vowel:

pa-se-mos   mu-cha-cha   ha-lla-ron   ca-rro   se-ño-ri-ta

3. Two consonants are usually divided:

ac-ción   tar-dar   hon-ra   bur-lar   ob-je-to

But, with one exception, any combination of a consonant plus **l** or **r** which can begin a word in English goes with the following vowel in Spanish:

ha-bla-ron   sa-cro   so-bre   si-glo

The exception is s plus any consonant. This combination cannot begin a syllable. The s therefore goes with the preceding syllable.

is-la   Es-pa-ña   cons-tan-te   as-cen-sor

4. Three consonants are usually divided after the first one:

in-glés   im-pre-sión   sal-dré

Stress

Spanish words are usually stressed on the last or the next-to-the-last syllable.

1. Stress the *last* syllable of a word ending in any consonant (except **n** or **s**):

sa-lu-*dar*   na-tu-*ral*   ciu-*dad*   hon-ra-*dez*

2. Stress the next-to-the-last syllable of a word ending in a vowel (or a diphthong) or **n** or **s**:

her-*mo*-so	bo-*ni*-ta	in-te-re-*san*-te
glo-ria	es-*tu*-dian	ca-*ba*-llos

3. Any violation of the above two rules is indicated by a written accent on the stressed syllable:

lá-piz	*ár*-bol	mi-*ró*	bai-*lé*
na-*ción*	in-*glés*	*jó*-ve-nes	*dí*-ga-me

NOTE: There is only one written accent in Spanish, and it always means that the syllable which bears it is *stressed*. In addition, it distinguishes two words that would otherwise be spelled alike:

que	which, that	si	if	el	the
¿qué?	what?	sí	yes	él	he

Linking of words

Words are normally not pronounced in any language as isolated units but rather as breath groups. Within breath groups in Spanish, individual words will be linked to those following and preceding them according to the following principles:

1. A final vowel and the initial vowel of a following word tend to be pronounced as one syllable:

lindísima Amapola	mi amigo
Carlos está aquí	éste es mío
hablo español	su profesor y usted

2. A final consonant may be linked with an initial vowel of the following word:

es̮ella   un̮alumno   el̮español

■ Exercises

1. Copy the following words. Divide them into syllables and underline the stressed syllable. (EXAMPLE: **aeropuerto: a-e-ro-*puer*-to.**)

conoce	hablaré	instituir
saben	detrás	veintiséis
sillas	carro	soberbias
tarde	espero	compañía
sueltos	tranquila	Paraguay
trasto	leer	unión
supremo	caen	oiga

2. Explain why the following words have a written accent. (Without the accent the stress would be on a different syllable. Why?)

difícil	jamás	alemán
así	fábrica	baúl
frío	halló	célebre
canción	mártir	quizás

CONVERSATIONAL INTERLUDE

~~~~~~

En la calle

1

Buenos días. (Buenas tardes. Buenas noches.)
Good morning. (Good afternoon. Good evening.)

2

Buenos días. ¿Cómo está usted?
Good morning. How are you?

1

Muy bien, gracias. ¿Y usted?
Very well, thank you (thanks). And you?

2

Bien, gracias. ¿Cómo está la familia?
Well, thank you. How is the family?

1

Todos están bien, gracias.
All are well, thank you.

2

Adiós. Recuerdos a la familia.
Good-by. Regards to the family.

1

Gracias. Hasta luego.
Thank you. See you later (*literally,* Till later).

~~~~~~

SECOND PRELIMINARY LESSON

A. Verbs used in this lesson

es is
(yo) hablo I speak
usted habla you speak

son are
(ellos) hablan they speak
los españoles hablan the Spaniards speak

B. Listening and speaking

la* Argentina Argentina
el Brasil Brazil
¿cuál? (*pl. ¿cuáles?*) *interrog. pron.* which?
de of, from
donde *rel. adv.* where
¿dónde? *interrog. adv.* where?
dos two
en in
España *f.* Spain
el español Spaniard, Spanish (*language*)
los Estados Unidos United States
el francés Frenchman, French (*language*)
Francia *f.* France

hermoso beautiful, handsome
Hispanoamérica *f.* Hispanic America
hispanoamericano Hispanic American
Inglaterra *f.* England
el inglés Englishman, English (*language*)
interesante interesting
Italia *f.* Italy
el italiano Italian
la lengua language
Méjico *m.* Mexico
no no; not
el norteamericano American
otro another, other

---

* The definite article shows the gender of the noun it precedes. In most cases where it does not appear, *m.* (*masculine*) or *f.* (*feminine*) follows the noun. The definite article is not given in the English translation.

el **país** country
el **portugués** Portuguese
principal principal
que *rel. pron.* that, which
¿**qué?** *interrog. pron.* what?

¿**quién?** (*pl.* ¿**quiénes?**) *interrog.*
pron. who?
también also, too
un, una a (an)
y and

*Las lenguas**

En España los españoles[1] hablan español. En los Estados Unidos los norteamericanos hablan inglés. Un país donde hablan inglés también es Inglaterra. Los ingleses hablan inglés. La lengua que hablan los franceses, en Francia, es el[2] francés. En Italia, los italianos hablan italiano.

En Hispanoamérica hablan dos lenguas principales.[3] Las dos lenguas principales de Hispanoamérica son el español y el portugués. Hablan portugués en el[4] Brasil. En los otros países de Hispanoamérica hablan español. Hablan español en la[4] Argentina. Otro país donde hablan español es Méjico.

Yo hablo inglés. Hablo español también. El inglés es hermoso. El español es también una lengua hermosa. Otra lengua hermosa es el italiano. El portugués es una lengua interesante. Yo no[5] hablo portugués. ¿Qué[6] habla usted?[7]

■ Preguntas

Conteste (answer) *en español.*

a. 1. ¿Qué hablan los españoles?
   2. ¿Qué hablan los ingleses?
   3. ¿Qué hablan los franceses?
   4. ¿Qué hablan los italianos?

b. 1. ¿Quiénes hablan francés?
   2. ¿Quiénes hablan español?
   3. ¿Quiénes hablan inglés?
   4. ¿Quiénes hablan italiano?

c. 1. ¿Dónde hablan italiano?
   2. ¿Dónde hablan francés?
   3. ¿Dónde hablan español?
   4. ¿Dónde hablan inglés?
   5. ¿Dónde hablan portugués?

---

* The superior figures in the following text refer to corresponding figures in the section called Notes.

d. 1. ¿Qué lengua hablan en España?
  2. ¿Qué lengua hablan en los Estados Unidos?
  3. ¿Qué lengua hablan en la Argentina?
  4. ¿Qué lengua hablan en el Brasil?

e. 1. ¿Cuál es la lengua que hablan los españoles?
  2. ¿Cuál es la lengua que hablan los ingleses?
  3. ¿Cuál es la lengua que hablan los franceses?
  4. ¿Cuál es la lengua que hablan los italianos?
  5. ¿Cuál es la lengua que hablan los norteamericanos?

f. 1. ¿Cuáles son dos países donde hablan inglés?
  2. ¿Cuáles son dos países donde hablan español?
  3. ¿Cuáles son las dos lenguas principales de Hispanoamérica?

g. 1. ¿Es hermoso el español?
  2. ¿Es interesante el portugués?
  3. ¿Es el inglés una lengua hermosa?
  4. ¿Es el italiano una lengua interesante?

h. 1. ¿Habla usted inglés?
  2. ¿Habla usted español?
  3. ¿Habla usted francés?
  4. ¿Habla usted portugués?

NOTES

1. Only proper names and the first word of a sentence are capitalized in Spanish. Adjectives of nationality and names of languages are not capitalized.

   En España los españoles hablan español.   In Spain the Spaniards speak Spanish.
   Los ingleses hablan inglés.   The English speak English.

2. In general, the definite article is used more often in Spanish than it is in English. It is used, for example, with names of languages except after **hablar** and after **de** and **en**.

   El francés es interesante.   French is interesting.
   Yo hablo francés.   I speak French.
   la lección de español   the Spanish lesson

3. In Spanish a descriptive adjective generally follows its noun.

   dos lenguas principales   two principal languages
   una lengua hermosa   a beautiful language

4. The definite article is used with names of certain countries.

el Brasil   Brazil   **la Argentina**   Argentina

5. To make a verb negative in Spanish, place **no** before it.

Yo hablo español.   I speak Spanish.
Yo no hablo ruso.   I do not speak Russian.

6. Interrogative words bear a written accent to distinguish them from relatives and conjunctions with which they would otherwise be identical.

¿qué?   what?   **¿cuál?**   which?   **¿quién?**   who?

As pronouns, **¿qué?** means *what?* and **¿cuál?** means *which?* Both may be used as adjectives meaning *which?* though **¿qué?** is the more common.

¿Qué es esto?   What is this?
¿Cuál es la lengua que hablan los españoles?   Which is the language that the Spaniards speak?
¿Qué lengua hablan los italianos?   Which (What) language do the Italians speak?

7. In questions the subject usually follows the verb, as it does in the English sentence "Have you money enough?" Deviations from this general rule, for the sake of emphasis, euphony, etc., can be learned by observation. An inverted question mark is placed at the beginning of the actual interrogation.

¿Qué habla usted?   What do you speak?
Usted habla español, ¿verdad?   You speak Spanish, don't you?

C.   Structure

1. *Gender of nouns.* Spanish nouns are always masculine or feminine. Most nouns ending in **-o** are masculine; most nouns ending in **-a** are feminine.

estado *m.*   state   **lengua** *f.*   language

The gender of other nouns must be learned as observed.

español *m.*   Spanish   **país** *m.*   country

2. *Definite article.* The definite article has a masculine and a feminine form to agree with masculine and feminine nouns.

el inglés   the Englishman   **la lengua**   the language

3. *Indefinite article.* The indefinite article also has a masculine form and a feminine form.

un país a country   **una lengua** a language

4. *Plural of nouns.* The plural of nouns ending in a vowel is formed by adding **-s** to the singular. The plural of nouns ending in a consonant is formed by adding **-es** to the singular.

estados states   **lenguas** languages
españoles Spaniards   **ingleses** Englishmen

5. *Plural of definite article.* The definite article has a masculine plural **los** and a feminine plural **las**.

los países the countries   **las lenguas** the languages

■ Práctica

Cambie según se indica, siguiendo los modelos. (Change as indicated, following the models.)

a. **El español es la lengua de España.**

  1. el francés
  2. el inglés
  3. el italiano
  4. el español

b. **Los españoles hablan español.**

  1. los ingleses
  2. los franceses
  3. los italianos
  4. los portugueses

c. **Méjico es un país de Hispanoamérica.**
   El español es una lengua de Hispanoamérica.

  1. la Argentina
  2. el portugués
  3. el Brasil
  4. el español

6. *Adjectives.* Adjectives, like articles, agree in gender and number with the nouns they modify. Adjectives ending in **-o** in the masculine singular

change the **-o** to **-a** for the feminine. Most other adjectives are the same in both masculine and feminine.

otro país   another country
otra lengua   another language
una lengua hermosa   a beautiful language
la lengua interesante   the interesting language

The plural of adjectives is like the plural of nouns.

países interesantes   interesting countries
lenguas hermosas   beautiful languages
las lenguas principales   the principal languages

■ Práctica

Cambie según se indica, siguiendo los modelos.

a. **Méjico es un país.**
   España es otro país.
   Inglaterra y Francia son otros países.

   1. La Argentina es un país.
      el Brasil
      Italia y Méjico
   2. El francés es una lengua.
      el inglés
      el italiano y el español
   3. Inglaterra es un país.
      la Argentina
      Francia y el Brasil
   4. El portugués es una lengua.
      el italiano
      el inglés y el español

b. **El español es una lengua hermosa.**
   El español y el portugués son lenguas hermosas.

   1. El italiano es una lengua hermosa.
      el portugués y el español
   2. El italiano es una lengua hermosa.
      el francés y el inglés
   3. España es un país hermoso.
      España y Francia

4. El Brasil es un país interesante.
   Inglaterra y la Argentina

7. **Intonation.** Proper intonation—the rising and falling of voice pitch —is as important as correct pronunciation. Imitate your instructor's intonation as you imitate his pronunciation.

The most characteristic feature of Spanish intonation is the fairly uniform level of pitch between the first and last tonic stresses in a short declarative sentence. In a declarative sentence of one word group, the pitch rises until the first stressed syllable is reached, remains at the level of this syllable, and drops on the last stressed syllable.

Us*ted* habla espa*ñol*.

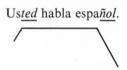

In a declarative sentence of two word groups, the pitch rises higher on the last stressed syllable of the first group; the second group has the pattern illustrated above.

En lo*s o*tros pa*í*ses/los hispanoameri*ca*nos hablan espa*ñol*.

In the commonest pattern for questions, the highest pitch is on the first stressed syllable. The pitch then falls, but rises again *after the last stressed* syllable, or on the last syllable, if stressed.

¿No *ha*bla usted espa*ñol*?

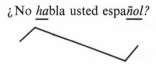

D. Writing

Test yourself. (If you can say and write the following without hesitation and without referring to the vocabulary, you know the lesson; if not, you must restudy the lesson carefully.)

1. What do you speak?
2. I speak English and Spanish.
3. I do not speak French.
4. In the United States they speak English.
5. England is another country where they speak English.
6. The Italians speak Italian.
7. The two principal languages of Hispanic America are Spanish and Portuguese.
8. They are beautiful languages, and they are interesting.
9. They speak Portuguese in Brazil.
10. In the other countries of Hispanic America and in Spain they speak Spanish.

LESSON I

A. Present indicative of regular verbs of the first conjugation

Spanish verbs are grouped into three conjugations according to the ending of the infinitive. The first-conjugation infinitive ends in **-ar,** the second in **-er,** and the third in **-ir.**

hablar to speak   **aprender** to learn   **vivir** to live

The present indicative of verbs of the first conjugation is formed by removing the infinitive ending and adding to the "stem" that remains the following personal endings:

	SINGULAR	PLURAL
1*	**-o**	**-amos**
2	**-as**	**-áis**
3	**-a**	**-an**

hablar to speak

yo hablo I speak   **nosotros (nosotras) hablamos** we speak
tú hablas you speak (*familiar*)   **vosotros (vosotras) habláis** you speak (*familiar*)
usted habla you speak   **ustedes hablan** you speak
él (ella) habla he (she) speaks   **ellos (ellas) hablan** they speak

Each form of the present tense has two other translations besides the simple translation given above:

Hablo. I speak. (I am speaking. I do speak.)
Hablan. They speak. (They are speaking. They do speak).

---

* The numbers here and in subsequent tables represent 1st, 2nd, and 3rd person.

Because the ending of the verb usually identifies the subject, subject pronouns (except **usted** and **ustedes**) are commonly omitted. They must be used, however, when the subject of a verb would not otherwise be clear or when they are to be emphasized.

Juan y María estudian. *Él* **prepara la lección y** *ella* **contesta a las preguntas.**
John and Mary are studying. *He* is preparing the lesson and *she* is answering the questions.
Nosotros **estudiamos, pero** *ellos* **conversan.** *We* are studying, but *they* are talking.

Notice that in Spanish there are two forms for *you speak* in the singular and two in the plural. In addressing most of the people with whom he comes in contact, the Spanish-speaking person uses **usted** or **ustedes** with the third person of the verb.

Usted habla, a student would say to his instructor.
Ustedes hablan, a professor would say to his students.

Usted is used with the third person of verbs because it is a contraction which originally meant "Your Grace." **Usted habla** originally meant "Your Grace speaks."
Spanish-speaking people reserve the second person singular and plural for use between members of a family, intimate friends, etc.

Tú hablas, a mother would say to her child.
Vosotros habláis, a boy would say to his chums.

However, in Spanish America the familiar second person plural (**vosotros habláis**) is generally replaced by the third person plural with **ustedes (ustedes hablan).**

■ Práctica

Cambie según el modelo. (Change according to the model.)

Yo hablo español.
Tú ____ (hablas) español.

1. Yo hablo español.
   tú / usted / ustedes / nosotros / vosotros
2. Ella no conversa mucho.
   yo / nosotros / vosotros / ellos / tú
3. ¿Estudian ustedes?
   nosotros / tú / yo / vosotros / usted

B. Present indicative of irregular verb *ser, to be*

soy I am	**somos** we are
eres you are (*familiar*)	**sois** you are (*familiar*)
usted es you are	**ustedes son** you are
es he (she, it) is	**son** they are

■ Práctica

Cambie según el modelo.

¿De dónde es usted?
¿De dónde ____ (son) ellos?

1. ¿De dónde ____ tú?
2. ¿De dónde ____ ella?
3. ¿De dónde ____ yo?
4. ¿De dónde ____ usted?
5. ¿De dónde ____ ellas?
6. ¿De dónde ____ nosotros?
7. ¿De dónde ____ ustedes?
8. ¿De dónde ____ vosotros?
9. ¿De dónde ____ Juan y Carlos?
10. ¿De dónde ____ el profesor?

C. Listening and speaking

alto tall
el alumno student
bajo short
la casa house
la clase class
como like, as
¿cómo? how?
contestar (a) to answer (to)
conversar to converse
delgado thin
escuchar to listen
estudiar to study
explicar to explain
gordo fat
hay there is; there are
inteligente intelligent
joven young
la lección lesson

moreno dark; brunet
la muchacha girl
el muchacho boy
mucho much; **muchos** many
pequeño small
la pregunta question
preguntar to ask
preparar to prepare
el profesor professor
rubio blond
señor Mr.; sir
uno, una one
viejo old

IDIOMS

en casa (at) home
en la clase in (the) class

PROPER NAMES

California California
Carlos Charles
Juan John

María Mary
Nueva York New York
Tejas Texas
Virginia Virginia

En la clase*

Hay muchos alumnos en la clase. Hay muchachos y hay muchachas.
Hay también un profesor. El¹ señor Martínez es el profesor.

Uno de los muchachos es Juan. Otro muchacho es Carlos. Una de las
muchachas es Virginia. Otra muchacha es María.

Juan es de Tejas. Es alto y moreno. Es delgado también.

Carlos no es moreno, como Juan; es rubio. No es alto y delgado; es
bajo y gordo. Carlos es de Nueva York.

Virginia es alta y rubia. Es hermosa también. Virginia es de California.

La otra muchacha, María, es de Tejas, como Juan. Ella no es rubia,
como Virginia; es morena. Y es pequeña. Las dos muchachas son
hermosas.

Los alumnos son jóvenes.² El señor Martínez es viejo. Él es inteligente,
y los alumnos son inteligentes también.

Yo soy otro alumno de la clase. Soy de Chicago.

No estudiamos en la clase. Preparamos la lección³ en casa. En la clase
el señor Martínez explica la lección. Nosotros escuchamos y contestamos
a⁴ las preguntas. Conversamos en la clase y hablamos en español.

—⁵¿De dónde es usted?—pregunta el señor Martínez.

—Soy de Chicago, señor—contesto.

—Yo soy de España—contesta el señor Martínez.

■ Preguntas

1. ¿Quién es el profesor?
2. ¿Quiénes son dos muchachos de la clase?
3. ¿Quiénes son dos muchachas de la clase?
4. ¿De dónde es Juan?
5. ¿Cómo es Juan?
6. ¿Cómo es Carlos?
7. ¿De dónde es Carlos?
8. ¿Cómo es Virginia?
9. ¿De dónde es Virginia?
10. ¿Cómo es María y de dónde es?
11. ¿Son viejos los alumnos?

---

* The superior figures in the following text refer to corresponding figures in the Notes section.

12. ¿Es joven el señor Martínez?
13. ¿Estudian ustedes en la clase?
14. ¿Dónde preparan ustedes la lección?
15. ¿Quién explica la lección?
16. ¿Habla usted inglés en la clase?
17. ¿De dónde es el profesor?

■ Práctica

Cambie según se indica. (Change as indicated.)

1. Yo estudio en casa.
   él / tú / nosotros / ella / vosotros / ellos
2. Ellas contestan a las preguntas.
   yo / usted / nosotros / tú / vosotros
3. Él no explica la lección.
   ustedes / vosotros / tú / nosotros / yo
4. Tú no escuchas.
   vosotros / él / ustedes / nosotros / yo / ellas

NOTES

1. The definite article is used with titles except in direct address.

   El señor Martínez es el profesor. Mr. Martínez is the professor.
   El profesor Martínez es viejo. Professor Martínez is old.
   But:
   —**Sí, señor Martínez.** "Yes, Mr. Martínez."

2. That syllable of a word which is stressed in the singular is stressed also in the plural. Words like **joven,** therefore, must add an accent in the plural **(jóvenes),** just as words like **inglés** drop their accent in the plural **(ingleses).**

3. Nouns ending in **-ión** are feminine: **la lección.**

4. Certain Spanish verbs are used with prepositions where their English equivalents take no preposition. Your attention will be called to such cases as they occur in the text.

   Contestamos *a* las preguntas. We answer the questions.

5. In Spanish dialogue a dash is used to introduce different speakers. It is not repeated at the end of each speech, unless narrative matter or words introducing the next speech follow in the same paragraph.

D. Structure

Uses of ser. Spanish has two verbs *to be*: ser, which you have already met, and estar, which you will learn later.

   a. Ser is used in expressing source or origin:

     Yo soy de Chicago. I am from Chicago.
     Juan y María son de Tejas. John and Mary are from Texas.
     El profesor es de España. The professor is from Spain.

■ Práctica

Haga preguntas (ask questions) *y conteste según el modelo.*

   ¿De dónde es usted?
   Soy de Nueva York.

1. ¿Y Virginia? California.
2. ¿Y Juan y María? Tejas.
3. ¿Y nosotros? Los Estados Unidos.
4. ¿Y ustedes? La Argentina.
5. ¿Y usted? Los Estados Unidos.
6. ¿Y ella? Méjico.
7. ¿Y el señor Martínez? España.
8. ¿Y tú? Chile.

   b. Ser is used with a predicate noun:

     El señor Martínez es el profesor. Mr. Martínez is the professor.
     Somos norteamericanos. We are Americans.
     Carlos es otro alumno. Charles is another student.

■ Práctica

Cambie según el modelo.

   ¿Qué es usted—italiano (italiana)?
   No, no soy italiano (italiana).

1. ¿Qué es Juan—español?
2. ¿Qué es Carlos—portugués?
3. ¿Qué es usted—argentino (argentina)?
4. ¿Qué son Juan y María—españoles?
5. ¿Qué es el señor Martínez—norteamericano?
6. ¿Qué son ustedes—ingleses?
7. ¿Qué eres tú—italiano (italiana)?
8. ¿Qué son ellos—franceses?

c. **Ser** is used with an adjective which indicates an essential characteristic:

Juan es alto y delgado.   John is tall and thin.
Las muchachas son hermosas.   The girls are beautiful.

■ Práctica

Cambie según se indica.

1. Carlos es inteligente.
2. Los alumnos ____.
3. ____ rubios y hermosos.
4. La muchacha ____.
5. ____ joven.
6. Los profesores ____.
7. ____ altos y delgados.
8. Las muchachas ____.
9. ____ pequeñas.
10. María ____.
11. ____ inteligente.
12. Nosotros ____.
13. ____ viejos.
14. El señor Martínez ____.

E. Writing

Test yourself

1. There are many students in the class.
2. Two of the boys are Juan and Carlos.
3. Juan is tall, dark, and handsome.
4. Carlos is short and fat.
5. The two girls are beautiful.
6. Virginia is from California; Juan and María are from Texas.
7. The professor and the students are intelligent.
8. I study and prepare the lesson at home.
9. Mr. Martínez explains the lessons.
10. The students converse in class and speak in Spanish.

Composition

Write a composition about the Spanish class. Tell about Juan, Carlos, Virginia, and María: what they are like and where they are from. Tell who the professor is and whether he is young or old. Tell where you prepare the lesson and what you do in class: you listen, you answer the questions, you speak in Spanish. Tell what Mr. Martínez does in class.

F. Pronunciation practice

When initial after a pause or after **l** or **n,** the Spanish **d** is like the English **d,** but articulated with the tip of the tongue against the upper teeth (phonetic symbol: [d]). In other positions **d** is like the *th* in *neither* (phonetic symbol: [đ]).

Pronounce the following series of words as you hear them.

[d]	[d]	[d]
dato	el dato	un dato
día	el día	un día
diario	el diario	un diario
daño	el daño	un daño
Dios	el dios	un dios
diente	el diente	un diente

[đ]	[d] and [đ]
cada	dado
nada	dedo
codo	delgado
la dama	despide
la duda	duda
la dicha	desdicha

LESSON 2

A. Present indicative of regular verbs of the second and third conjugations

The present indicative of regular verbs of the second and third conjugations is formed by removing the infinitive ending (**-er** and **-ir,** respectively) and adding to the "stem" the following personal endings:

	SECOND CONJUGATION		THIRD CONJUGATION	
	Singular	*Plural*	*Singular*	*Plural*
1	**-o**	**-emos**	**-o**	**-imos**
2	**-es**	**-éis**	**-es**	**-ís**
3	**-e**	**-en**	**-e**	**-en**

Notice that the endings of the second and third conjugations are identical except for the first and second persons plural.

aprender to learn

aprendo I learn
aprendes you learn (*familiar*)
usted aprende you learn
aprende he (she) learns

aprendemos we learn
aprendéis you learn (*familiar*)
ustedes aprenden you learn
aprenden they learn

vivir to live

vivo I live
vives you live (*familiar*)
usted vive you live
vive he (she) lives

vivimos we live
vivís you live (*familiar*)
ustedes viven you live
viven they live

■ Práctica

Cambie según se indica.

1. Yo aprendo mucho.
   tú / vosotros / él / ellas / yo / nosotros
   usted / ustedes / el muchacho / los alumnos
2. Nosotros vivimos en España.
   yo / ella / ellos / vosotros / tú / su padre
   ustedes / el señor Martínez / el profesor y yo

B. **Present indicative of irregular verb** *decir, to say*

digo I say	**decimos** we say
dices you say (*familiar*)	**decís** you say (*familiar*)
usted dice you say	**ustedes dicen** you say
dice he (she) says	**dicen** they say

■ Práctica

Cambie según el modelo.

Él dice que aprende mucho.
Yo digo que aprendo mucho.

1. el alumno
2. ustedes
3. tú
4. yo
5. las muchachas
6. nosotros
7. vosotros
8. los alumnos y yo
9. usted
10. el profesor

C. **Listening and speaking**

el abogado lawyer
bueno good
la cinta tape
el clima climate
comprender to understand
después *adv.* afterwards;
   después de *prep.* after
el día day
el ejercicio exercise
entrar (en) to enter
escribir to write

la familia family
la hermana sister
el hermano brother
el ingeniero engineer
leer to read
el libro book
luego then
la madre mother
el médico doctor
muy very
el padre father

pero but	IDIOMS AND OTHER EXPRESSIONS
el político politician	
porque because	**buenos días** good morning,
que *conj.* that	good day
un rato a while	**la sala de clase** classroom
la sala room	**toda la lección** all the lesson,
su his, her	the whole lesson

En la clase y después de la clase

El profesor entra en[1] la sala de clase.

—¡[2]Buenos días![3]—dice el profesor.

—¡Buenos días, señor!—dicen los alumnos.

Uno de los alumnos lee un libro. El profesor pregunta: —¿Qué lee usted en el libro? —El alumno contesta: —Leo la lección.

Luego el profesor pregunta: —¿No leen ustedes la lección en casa?—El alumno contesta: —Sí, señor Martínez, leemos la lección en casa, pero yo no comprendo toda la lección.

—¿Cómo preparan ustedes la lección?—dice el señor Martínez.

María contesta: —Escuchamos[4] la cinta, leemos la lección, contestamos a las preguntas del libro y escribimos los ejercicios. ¡Hay muchos ejercicios y muchas preguntas en el libro!

Después de la clase los alumnos conversan un rato.

Virginia dice que[5] es de California. Explica que su padre es médico y que es muy viejo. Su familia vive en California porque él es viejo y porque el clima[3] de California es bueno.

Carlos dice que es de Nueva York. Dice que su padre es abogado y que es político también.

—Es un político muy bueno—dice Carlos.

Juan explica que María es su hermana. Su familia vive en Tejas. El padre de Juan es ingeniero. No es norteamericano; es español. Pero su madre no es española; es norteamericana.

■ **Preguntas**

1. ¿Quién entra en la sala de clase?
2. ¿Qué dice el profesor?
3. ¿Qué lee uno de los alumnos?
4. ¿Qué no comprende el alumno?
5. ¿Cómo prepara María la lección?
6. ¿Qué hay en el libro?
7. ¿Qué es el padre de Virginia y dónde vive?
8. ¿Qué es el padre de Carlos?

9. ¿Quién es María?
10. ¿Dónde vive la familia de Juan?
11. ¿Es norteamericano el padre de Juan?
12. ¿Es médico el padre de Juan?

■ Práctica

Cambie según se indica.

1. Entramos en la sala de clase.
   yo / él / los alumnos / tú / vosotros
2. Usted lee toda la lección.
   los alumnos y yo / yo / ustedes / vosotros / tú
3. Escribo los ejercicios.
   él / vosotros / ustedes / tú / nosotros
4. Tú conversas un rato.
   nosotros / usted / vosotros / ustedes / yo

NOTES

1. When an object follows **entrar** the preposition **en** must be used with it.

   El profesor entra en la sala   The professor enters the room.
   Entro en la casa.   I enter the house.

2. An inverted exclamation point precedes an exclamation, just as an inverted question mark precedes a question.

3. Two nouns that are masculine, although they end in **-a,** are **el día** and **el clima.**

4. **Escuchar** may mean "to listen *to.*" It takes no preposition equivalent to English "to."

   Escuchamos la cinta.   We listen *to* the tape.

5. The conjunction **que** (*that*) may not be omitted in Spanish as its English counterpart often is.

   Virginia dice que es de California.   Virginia says (that) she is from California.

D. Structure

1. *Possession.* The Spanish possessive is expressed by **de** plus the name of the possessor.

el padre de Juan   John's father
el hermano de María   Mary's brother
los libros de los alumnos   the students' books

2. *Contraction* **del.** The preposition **de** contracts with the masculine definite article **el** to form **del.**

las preguntas del profesor   the professor's questions
los ejercicios del libro   the exercises of the book

It does not contract with **la, los, las.**

la madre de la muchacha   the girl's mother
la hermana de los muchachos   the boys' sister

■ Práctica

Cambie según los modelos.

a. **¿Quién es?**
   Es el padre de Juan.

   1. ¿Quién es? (la madre / María)
   2. ¿Quién es? (la hermana / el muchacho)
   3. ¿Quién es? (el hermano / la muchacha)
   4. ¿Quién es? (el padre / el profesor)
   5. ¿Quiénes son? (las hermanas / los muchachos)
   6. ¿Quiénes son? (los hermanos / el alumno)
   7. ¿Quiénes son? (las hermanas / el profesor)

b. **¿Qué libro es?**
   El libro de Virginia.

   1. ¿Qué clase es? (el profesor)
   2. ¿Qué clases son? (mi hermano)
   3. ¿Qué libros son? (María)
   4. ¿Qué médico es? (mi madre)

3. *Omission of the indefinite article.* The indefinite article is omitted with an *unmodified* predicate noun indicating profession, nationality, religion, political affiliation, etc.

Su padre es abogado.   His father is a lawyer.
El señor Martínez es español.   Mr. Martínez is a Spaniard.
Soy norteamericano.   I am an American.

But when the predicate noun is *modified,* the indefinite article is used, as in English.

Usted es un político muy bueno.   You are a very good politician.
Es un médico muy famoso.   He is a very famous doctor.

■ Práctica

Conteste según los modelos.

a. **¿Qué es usted?**
    Soy alumno (alumna).

    1. ¿Qué es usted? (médico)
    2. ¿Qué es usted? (ingeniero)
    3. ¿Qué es usted? (español)
    4. ¿Qué es el señor Martínez? (profesor)
    5. ¿Qué es Juan? (norteamericano)
    6. ¿Qué es su hermano? (político)

b. **¿Es médico?**
    Sí, es un médico muy bueno.

    1. ¿Es abogado?
       Sí, _____ muy inteligente.
    2. ¿Es ingeniero?
       Sí, _____ muy bueno.
    3. ¿Es político?
       Sí, _____ muy famoso.

4. ***More about the feminine of adjectives.*** Adjectives of nationality ending in a consonant add **-a** to form the feminine.

    Su padre es español.   His father is Spanish.
    Su madre no es española.   Her mother is not Spanish.

■ Práctica

Cambie según los modelos.

a. **Su padre es norteamericano. ¿Y su madre?**
    Mi madre no es norteamericana.

    1. Su padre es español. ¿Y su madre?
    2. Su padre es inglés. ¿Y su madre?

3. Su padre es italiano. ¿Y su madre?
4. Su padre es francés. ¿Y su madre?
5. Su padre es portugués. ¿Y su madre?

b. **Los muchachos son italianos. ¿Y las muchachas?**
Todas son italianas.

1. Los muchachos son franceses. ¿Y las muchachas?
2. Los muchachos son ingleses. ¿Y las muchachas?
3. Los muchachos son norteamericanos. ¿Y las muchachas?
4. Los muchachos son españoles. ¿Y las muchachas?
5. Los muchachos son portugueses. ¿Y las muchachas?

E. Writing

Test yourself

1. The professor enters the classroom and says, "Good morning."
2. One of the students is reading the lesson.
3. Mr. Martínez asks, "Don't you read the lesson at home?"
4. The student says that he does not understand all the lesson.
5. "How do you prepare the lessons?" asks the professor.
6. The students listen to the tape, they read the lesson, they answer the questions, and they write the exercises.
7. Virginia's father is a doctor.
8. He is old and lives in California, because the climate of California is very good.
9. Charles's father is a lawyer.
10. He is a very good politician, too.
11. John's father is a Spaniard and is an engineer.
12. His mother is not Spanish.

Composition

Tell how you prepare the lesson. (You listen to the tape, you read the lesson, you answer the questions, you write the exercises, you speak in Spanish a while, and you learn the whole lesson.)

Tell about the families of Carlos, Virginia, Juan, and María. (Tell where they live, what their fathers are, etc.)

F. Pronunciation practice

B and v have an explosive sound like the English **b** when initial after a pause or after **n** or **m** (phonetic symbol: [b]). Otherwise they have a fricative sound made with the lips slightly open (phonetic symbol: [ƀ]). Before **b** and **v, n** is pronounced like **m.**

Pronounce the following as you hear them:

[b]	[b]	[ƀ]
broma	en broma	la broma
venta	en venta	la venta
balcón	un balcón	el balcón
vino	un vino	el vino
burro	un burro	los burros
verso	un verso	los versos

[b] and [ƀ]	[ƀ] and [ƀ]
barba	la barba
boba	la boba
verbo	el verbo
bravo	el bravo
bebo	yo bebo
vivo	yo vivo

Castles in Spain: The Castle of Mombeltrán, Avila, with olive grove in the foreground. (Spanish National Tourist Office)

The Castle of Belmonte, Cuenca. (Spanish National Tourist Office)

Segovia: The Alcázar. (Philip D. Gendreau)

(Above) The Alhambra, Granada, with the Sierra Nevada in the background. (Spanish National Tourist Office)

(Left) The Bisagra Gate, Toledo. (Philip D. Gendreau)

Segovia: The Roman
Aqueduct.
(Philip D. Gendreau)

Moorish Spain: The
Giralda Tower, Seville,
built by the Moors in
the twelfth century as a
minaret for a mosque.
(Philip D. Gendreau)

The walls of Avila were built in the eleventh century. (Three Lions, Inc.)

LESSON 3

A. Present indicative of irregular verbs *estar* and *ir*

estar to be	ir to go
estoy I am	**voy** I go, am going
estás you are (*familiar*)	**vas** you go, are going (*familiar*)
usted está you are	**usted va** you go, are going
está he (she) is	**va** he (she) goes, is going
estamos we are	**vamos** we go, are going
estáis you are (*familiar*)	**vais** you go, are going (*familiar*)
ustedes están you are	**ustedes van** you go, are going
están they are	**van** they go, are going

■ Práctica

Cambie según se indica.

1. Estamos en casa.
    yo / tú / vosotros / usted / ustedes / mi hermano y yo
2. Ella no está en la clase.
    nosotros / vosotros / ustedes / tú / yo / el alumno
3. El profesor va a Cuba.
    ustedes / mi padre y yo / vosotros / tú / yo
4. Ustedes van a casa.
    tú / el alumno / yo / vosotros / mi hermana y yo / los muchachos

B. Listening and speaking

a to
¿adónde? (to) where?
ahora now
allí there
la amiga friend (*f.*)
el amigo friend (*m.*)
la biblioteca library
bien well
el café café
cansado tired
con with
contento happy
difícil difficult
enfermo ill
enojado angry
fácil easy
grande large, big
¿qué hacen? what do they do?
la historia history
más more
perezoso lazy
poco little; **un poco** a little

su, sus his, her, your, their
todos *pron.* all
trabajar to work
tu, tus your (*familiar*)

IDIOMS AND OTHER EXPRESSIONS

a casa (to) home
al contrario on the contrary
al fin finally
en broma jokingly
en efecto in fact
en todas partes everywhere
por eso therefore; that's why;
    for that reason
todos los días every day
tomar un refresco to have
    something to drink (*literally,*
    to take some refreshment)
¡vamos! let's go!
¡vamos a tomar ...! let's have
    ...! (*literally,* let's take ...!)

Estamos en la biblioteca

Ahora estamos en la biblioteca. La biblioteca es muy grande. Hay muchos libros en todas partes. Muchos alumnos van a la biblioteca todos los días. Allí leen sus libros y estudian sus lecciones.

Juan y María van a la biblioteca con su amigo Carlos y su amiga Virginia. Van a[1] preparar sus lecciones.

Carlos va a estudiar la lección de español.[2] Su lección es muy fácil. Por eso Carlos está muy contento.

María y Virginia van a aprender su lección de francés y Juan va a leer su libro de historia. María y Virginia están contentas, pero Juan, al contrario, está enojado. La lección de ellas es fácil, pero la lección de él es difícil.

Juan no está bien. Está un poco enfermo y por eso no trabaja mucho.

Al fin Juan dice: —No voy a trabajar más. Estoy un poco enfermo. Por eso voy a[3] casa.

—María—dice Carlos en broma—tu hermano no está enfermo. ¡Es perezoso y por eso no va a trabajar más! Yo, al contrario, no soy perezoso, pero estoy cansado. ¡Tú estás cansada también! En efecto, todos estamos cansados. ¡Vamos al café! ¡Vamos a tomar un refresco!

■ Preguntas

1. ¿Dónde estamos ahora?
2. ¿Cómo es la biblioteca?
3. ¿Qué hay en todas partes?
4. ¿Quiénes van a la biblioteca todos los días?
5. ¿Qué hacen los alumnos en la biblioteca?
6. ¿Qué va a estudiar Carlos?
7. ¿Cómo es su lección de español?
8. ¿Cómo está Carlos?
9. ¿Qué van a hacer María y Virginia?
10. ¿Qué va a leer Juan?
11. ¿Cómo están María y Virginia?
12. Al contrario ¿cómo está Juan?
13. ¿Cómo es la lección de Juan y cómo es la lección de María?
14. ¿Qué dice Juan?
15. ¿Adónde va?
16. ¿Qué dice Carlos en broma?
17. ¿Cómo están todos los alumnos?
18. ¿Qué más dice Carlos?

NOTES

1. The verb **ir** requires the preposition **a** before a following infinitive.

   Van a preparar sus lecciones. They are going to prepare their lessons.
   No voy a trabajar más. I am not going to work any more.
   ¡Vamos a tomar un refresco! Let's have something to drink!

2. In English, phrases like *a Spanish lesson* and *an English professor* may have two meanings. The latter may mean either a professor who is English or a professor who teaches English; and sometimes we are forced to phrase the idea in the longer way to make our meaning unmistakable. Spanish always differentiates between the two ideas, but more simply.

   un profesor inglés an English professor (a professor who is English)
   un profesor de inglés an English professor (a professor who teaches English)
   un libro español a Spanish book (a book written in Spanish, published in Spain, etc.)
   un libro de español a Spanish book (a book about Spanish)

3. The preposition **a** means "to." Except in certain idioms, do not use it to translate "at," which is **en.**

> **Vamos a casa.** We are going (to) home.
> **Estamos en casa.** We are at home.

■ Práctica

a. **Substituya según se indica.**

   1. Yo voy a estudiar.
   2. Ella ——— escuchar.
   3. Los alumnos ——— leer.
   4. Usted ——— hablar.
   5. Nosotros ——— escribir.
   6. Tú no ——— aprender.
   7. Juan no ——— trabajar.
   8. Yo no ——— contestar.

b. *Diga en español.*

1. Let's study.	4. Let's read.
2. Let's ask.	5. Let's go in (enter).
3. Let's learn.	6. Let's have something to drink.

c. *Diga en español.*

1. the Spanish lesson	5. the Spanish lessons
2. the history book	6. the history books
3. the French class	7. the French classes
4. the English professor.	8. the English professors.

C. Structure

   1. *Uses of* **estar.**

   a. **Estar** is used in expressing location:

> **Estamos en la biblioteca.** We are in the library.
> **Madrid está en España.** Madrid is in Spain.
> **Las muchachas no están en casa.** The girls are not at home.

   b. **Estar** is used with an adjective which denotes an accidental or temporary state or condition.

Juan está enfermo. John is ill.
Yo estoy bien. I am well.
María y Virginia están enojadas. Mary and Virginia are angry.

■ Práctica

Conteste según los modelos.

a. **¿Dónde está Pepe?**
 Está en casa.

 1. ¿Dónde está usted? (en la clase)
 2. ¿Dónde está Juan? (en España)
 3. ¿Dónde están los alumnos? (en el café)
 4. ¿Dónde estás? (en casa)
 5. ¿Dónde estamos? (en la biblioteca)

b. **¿Cómo está el profesor?**
 Está muy bien.

 1. ¿Cómo están los alumnos? (muy contentos)
 2. ¿Cómo está su hermana? (muy enferma)
 3. ¿Cómo estás tú? (muy enojado, enojada)
 4. ¿Cómo están ustedes? (muy bien)
 5. ¿Cómo estamos todos? (muy cansados)

2. *Possessive adjectives* **tu** *and* **su.**

 a. Possessive adjectives agree with the thing possessed. **Tu** and **su** have plural forms **tus** and **sus** to agree with plural nouns.

 tu lección your lesson (*familiar*)
 tus lecciones your lessons (*familiar*)
 su libro his (her, your, their) book
 sus libros his (her, your, their) books

 b. Since **su** and **sus** have several meanings each, there are times when they might not be clear. In such cases a substitute expression is used. The definite article replaces **su** or **sus** before the noun, to which is added **de** plus a pronoun, as follows:

	de él	his book
el libro	**de ella**	her book
	de usted (ustedes)	your book
	de ellos (ellas)	their book

$$
\text{las amigas} \begin{cases} \textbf{de él} & \text{his friends} \\ \textbf{de ella} & \text{her friends} \\ \textbf{de usted (ustedes)} & \text{your friends} \\ \textbf{de ellos (ellas)} & \text{their friends} \end{cases}
$$

La amiga de él es **española pero** *la amiga de ellos* es **francesa.** *His* friend is Spanish, but *their* friend is French.

■ Práctica

a. *Diga en español.*

1. Where is his father?
2. Where is their mother?
3. Where is your professor?
4. Where are your brothers?
5. Where are their exercises?
6. Where are her sisters?
7. Where are his doctors?
8. Carlos, where is your book?
9. Mary, where are your friends?
10. John, where are your lawyers?

b. *Diga en español empleando* (using) *dos formas, según el modelo.*

his book: **su libro; el libro de él**

1. his sister
2. her brothers
3. your father
4. your exercises
5. their house

6. their houses
7. her library
8. his lawyers
9. their class
10. your doctors

3. *Contraction* **al.** Just as **de** contracts with the masculine definite article **el** to form **del,** the preposition **a** contracts with **el** to form **al.**

¡Vamos al café! Let's go to the café!
al contrario on the contrary
al fin finally

■ Práctica

Substituya según el modelo.

Hablamos al profesor.
Hablamos a la señorita.

1. el médico
2. el abogado
3. la madre
4. la hermana
5. el ingeniero

6. el muchacho
7. los alumnos
8. las muchachas
9. el joven
10. la joven

D. Writing

Test yourself

1. Many students are in the library every day.
2. The library is large, and there are books everywhere.
3. Carlos is going to study his Spanish lesson.
4. He is happy, because his lesson is easy.
5. María and Virginia are happy, too, because their French lesson is easy.
6. Juan, on the contrary, is angry, because his history book is difficult.
7. Juan is ill, and is not going to work (any) more.
8. Carlos says jokingly that María's brother is lazy, and that's why he's going home.
9. In fact all the students are tired.
10. Let's go to the café and let's have something to drink.

Composition

Write a composition about going to the library. (You go to the library every day. You read and study there. Tell what the library is like. You are happy, because the Spanish lesson is easy, but other students are angry, because their lessons are difficult. Etc.)

E. Pronunciation practice

R when initial in a word or after **l, n** or **s** is strongly trilled (two or more taps of the tip of the tongue against the upper teeth ridges); **rr** is also strongly trilled (phonetic symbol: [r̄]). Otherwise **r** is a single tap of the tip of the tongue against the upper teeth ridges (phonetic symbol: [r]).

Pronounce the following words as you hear them.

[r̄]	[r̄]	[r̄]
radio	el radio	un radio
ramo	el ramo	un ramo
rayo	el rayo	un rayo
río	el río	un río

[r̄]	[r]
perro	pero
carro	caro
mirra	mira
corro	coro
parra	para
morro	moro

The sound of **s** is not heard before [r̄]:

las rosas	es rojo
las rimas	es rico

LAS ALTEÑITAS*

RANCHERA

Music and Spanish Lyric by J. J. ESPINOSA

Va - mos a Te - pa,   tie - rra so -

ña - da,   don - de la vi - da es un pri -

mor;_____ a - llá me es - pe - ra   mi cha - pe -

tea - da   la ú - ni - ca due - ña de mi a -

mor._____ Es tan bo - ni - ta, mi cha - pa -

rri - ta, que cuan - do va al tem - plo a re - zar_____

____ to - dos la lla - man_____ la vir - gen - ci - ta_____

____ de la bo - qui - ta de co - ral. Qué

lin - das las ma - ña - nas cuan - do sa - le el sol a -

sí son las Al - te - ñas de es - te al - re - de - dor. A -

le - gres y bo - ni - tas to - do el tiem - po es - tán las

lin - das Al - te - ñi - tas de Te - pa - ti - tlán.

LESSON 4

A. Present indicative of irregular verbs *querer*, *tener*, *poder*, and *ver*

querer to wish, want	tener to have
quiero I wish, want **quieres** you wish, want (*fam.*) **usted quiere** you wish, want **quiere** he (she) wishes, wants **queremos** we wish, want **queréis** you wish, want (*fam.*) **ustedes quieren** you wish, want **quieren** they wish, want	**tengo** I have **tienes** you have (*fam.*) **usted tiene** you have **tiene** he (she) has **tenemos** we have **tenéis** you have (*fam.*) **ustedes tienen** you have **tienen** they have
poder to be able	ver to see
puedo I can **puedes** you can (*fam.*) **usted puede** you can **puede** he (she) can **podemos** we can **podéis** you can (*fam.*) **ustedes pueden** you can **pueden** they can	**veo** I see **ves** you see (*fam.*) **usted ve** you see **ve** he (she) sees **vemos** we see **veis** you see (*fam.*) **ustedes ven** you see **ven** they see

■ Práctica

Cambie según se indica.

1. Nosotros queremos trabajar.
   él / tú / ustedes / vosotros / yo / Paco y yo
2. Yo tengo dos hermanas.
   usted / tú / ellas / vosotros / nosotros / yo
3. Él puede aprender mucho.
   ellos / yo / nosotros / usted / ustedes / vosotros
4. Veo al médico todos los días.
   Juan / tú / ustedes / vosotros / nosotros / yo

B. Listening and speaking

acompañar to accompany, go with
adiós good-by
bastante enough
el bistec steak, beefsteak
buscar to look for
el café coffee
¡caramba! confound it! gracious!
cerca de near
comer to eat
la cuenta bill, check
dejar to leave
el dinero money
exclamar to exclaim
¡gracias! thank you, thanks; **¡muchas gracias!** thank you very much
el gusto pleasure
hallar to find
invitar to invite
lavar to wash
mi, mis my
mirar to look at

nuestro, nuestra our
pagar to pay
las papas fritas fried potatoes
para to, in order to
el plato plate; **lavar los platos** to wash the dishes
pobre poor
¿por qué? why?
el reloj clock
el tiempo time
tomar to take; to have (*meals, foods, etc.*)
la universidad university

IDIOMS AND OTHER EXPRESSIONS

con mucho gusto with pleasure
la hora de la comida dinner time
no . . . más que only
tener calor to be warm
tener frío to be cold
tener hambre to be hungry
tener sed to be thirsty
tener que to have to

¡Vamos al café!

Carlos tiene calor y también tiene mucha sed.
—¡Vamos a tomar un refresco!—dice Carlos.
—Con mucho gusto—dice María.

Carlos quiere invitar a Virginia también, pero no ve a su amiga. No está en la sala donde estudian Carlos y María.

Carlos busca[1] a Virginia en otra sala y después en otra. Al fin halla a su amiga.

Pero Virginia dice que no puede ir con sus amigos. —No puedo— explica ella—porque no tengo tiempo. Tengo que[2] preparar otras lecciones. Mis otras lecciones son difíciles. No son fáciles como nuestra lección de español.

Por eso Carlos y María dejan a Virginia en la biblioteca. Van a un café muy bueno que está cerca de la universidad.

—¿Qué vas a tomar, María?—pregunta Carlos.

María no tiene sed, como Carlos. Al contrario tiene mucha hambre.

—Quiero un bistec con papas fritas—contesta María.

El[3] pobre Carlos no tiene mucho dinero. Él no toma más que café.

María come todo el bistec y las papas fritas. Después mira[1] el reloj. Luego mira a Carlos y exclama: —¡Caramba! Tengo que ir a casa porque es la hora de la comida.[4] ¡Muchas gracias, Carlos! ¡Adiós!

Y deja a Carlos en el café.

El pobre Carlos no puede acompañar a su amiga. No tiene bastante dinero para[5] pagar la cuenta. Y por eso tiene que lavar los platos en el café.

■ Preguntas

1. ¿Tiene Carlos mucha hambre?
2. ¿Qué quiere tomar Carlos?
3. ¿A quién busca Carlos?
4. ¿Qué dice Virginia?
5. ¿Cómo son las lecciones de Virginia?
6. ¿Adónde van Carlos y María?
7. ¿Dónde está el café?
8. ¿Qué pregunta Carlos?
9. ¿Tiene María mucha sed?
10. ¿Qué quiere María?
11. ¿Por qué no puede Carlos pagar la cuenta?
12. ¿Qué mira María?
13. ¿Adónde va María?
14. ¿Por qué?
15. ¿Qué tiene que hacer Carlos en el café?

NOTES

1. **Buscar,** *to look for,* and **mirar,** *to look at,* do not take prepositions equivalent to the "for" and "at" of their English counterparts.

   Juan busca sus libros.   John is looking for his books.
   María mira el reloj.   Mary looks at the clock.

   But when their direct object denotes a definite person, the "personal a" is used, as with other verbs. (See Section C: 1, p. 54.)

   Carlos busca al profesor.   Charles is looking for the professor.
   María mira a Carlos.   Mary looks at Charles.

2. The preposition "to" in *I* (*you etc.*) *have to* is translated into Spanish by **que.**

   Tengo que estudiar.   I have to study.
   ¿Tiene usted que pagar?   Do you have to pay?

3. The definite article is used before a proper noun modified by an adjective.

   el pobre Carlos   poor Charles
   la joven María   young Mary

4. Spanish has few true compound nouns. Notice that "dinner time" is **la hora de la comida** (literally, "the time of the dinner").

5. When "to" with an infinitive in English expresses purpose, it is usually translated into Spanish by **para.**

   Carlos no tiene bastante dinero para pagar la cuenta.   Charles doesn't have enough money to pay the check.
   Estudiamos para aprender.   We study to (in order to) learn.

Práctica

Substituya según se indica.

   1. Yo tengo que estudiar.
   2. Tú _____.
   3. _____ trabajar.
   4. Antonio _____.
   5. _____ aprender.
   6. Ustedes _____.
   7. _____ escribir.

8. Nosotros _____.

9. _____ leer.

10. Yo _____.

11. _____ contestar.

12. Vosotros _____.

13. _____ escuchar.

14. Usted _____.

C. Structure

1. *Personal* **a.** A noun direct object denoting a definite person is regularly preceded by the preposition **a.**

Carlos halla a su amiga.   Charles finds his friend.
Ustedes pueden invitar al profesor.   You may invite the professor.
No veo a Virginia.   I don't see Virginia.

The "personal a" is also used with **quién** to translate "whom."

¿A quién ve usted?   Whom do you see?
¿A quiénes buscan?   Whom are they looking for?

It is generally omitted after the verb **tener.**

Tenemos un profesor muy bueno.   We have a very good professor.

Práctica

Substituya según el modelo.

Veo a Juan.
María: Veo a María.
Busco: Busco a María.

1. Veo a Ramón	6. Isabel
2. la muchacha	7. hallo
3. busco	8. su hermano
4. el profesor	9. veo
5. invito	10. el médico

2. *Possessive adjectives.* You have already learned the possessive adjectives **tu** and **su.** Like them, **mi** (*my*) has its plural: **mis. Nuestro** and **vuestro** have four forms each: masculine and feminine, singular and plural.

SINGULAR	PLURAL	
mi	**mis**	my
tu	**tus**	your (*familiar*)
su	**sus**	his, her, your, its
nuestro, -a	**nuestros, -as**	our
vuestro, -a	**vuestros, -as**	your (*familiar*)
su	**sus**	their, your

In Spanish America the familiar second person plural (**vuestro, -a, -os, -as**) has been replaced by the formal third person **su, sus** (*your*).

Remember that these forms agree with the *thing possessed,* not with the possessor.

mi lección my lesson	**mis lecciones** my lessons
tu hermana your sister	**tus hermanas** your sisters
nuestra casa our house	**nuestras casas** our houses
su libro his (her, your, their) book	**sus libros** his (her, your, their) books

You have already learned the substitute construction for **su** and **sus** when the meaning of these words might not be clear.

la casa de ellos y la casa de él   their house and his house
el hermano de usted y el hermano de ella   your brother and her brother

■ Práctica

Substituya según los modelos.

a. **Yo quiero mi dinero.**
   Juan quiere su dinero.

   1. Ana
   2. tú
   3. nosotros
   4. ellos
   5. yo
   6. ella
   7. vosotros
   8. ustedes
   9. usted
   10. el abogado

b. **Teresa ve a sus hermanas.**
   Yo veo a mis hermanas.

   1. usted
   2. ustedes

3. tú
4. vosotros
5. yo
6. nosotros
7. Tomás
8. usted y yo

3. *Idioms with* **tener.** Some physical or emotional states in living beings are expressed by **tener** plus a noun.

Tengo calor.　I am warm.
Tienen sueño.　They are sleepy.
Carlos tiene miedo.　Charles is afraid.
Tenemos frío.　We are cold.

Since **calor, miedo,** etc. are nouns, they must be modified by the adjective **mucho,** not the adverb **muy.** Two common nouns used in such expressions, **sed** and **hambre,** are feminine. They must therefore be modified by the feminine form **mucha.**

Tenemos *mucha* sed.　We are *very* thirsty.
¿Tiene usted *mucha* hambre?　Are you *very* hungry?

■ Práctica

Diga en español.

1. I am very thirsty.
2. We are very hungry.
3. She is very sleepy.
4. He is not very cold.
5. The boys are not very warm.
6. They are not afraid.

D. Writing

Test yourself

1. Carlos says that he is very warm and very thirsty.
2. "Let's go to the café and let's have something to drink."
3. "With pleasure," says María.
4. Carlos wants to invite the other girl too.

5. But he does not see Virginia.
6. He looks for his friend in another room.
7. "I can't go to the café," says Virginia, "because I have to study my lessons."
8. "What are you going to have, María?"
9. "I want a steak and fried potatoes, because I am very hungry."
10. Carlos takes only coffee.
11. María looks at the clock and looks at Carlos.
12. Gracious! She has to go home, because it's dinner time.
13. "Thank you very much," she says, and leaves Carlos in the café.
14. Poor Charles doesn't have enough money to pay the check and has to wash the dishes.

Composition

Write a composition about an experience that you have in a café. (You are thirsty and want to go to a café to have some coffee. You invite two friends. Tell where the café is. You ask them what they are going to have. They say that they are hungry. They eat a steak and fried potatoes. They look at the clock and say that it is dinner time and that they have to go home. You do not have enough money to pay the check. For that reason you have to wash the dishes.)

E.   Pronunciation practice

The sound of **j** is like that of **ch** in German *ach* or Scottish *loch*. When followed by **e** or **i**, **g** has the same sound. Pronounce the following words as you hear them.

joven	gema	gime
jamón	gente	giro
jinete	general	gigante
tajo	genio	gimnasio
lujo	gesto	gitano

LESSON 5

A. Present indicative of irregular verbs *saber* and *conocer*

sé	sabemos	conozco	conocemos
sabes (*fam.*)	sabéis (*fam.*)	conoces (*fam.*)	conocéis (*fam.*)
Vd.* sabe	Vds.* saben	Vd. conoce	Vds. conocen
sabe	saben	conoce	conocen

Note that these verbs have only one irregular form, the first person singular.

Saber means *to know* in the sense of *to have in one's head, to be master of*: *to know* a fact, a theorem, a language, etc. **Conocer** means *to know* in the sense of *to be acquainted with* (persons, places, books, etc.).

Yo sé la lección. I know the lesson.
El señor Martínez sabe el español. Mr. Martínez knows Spanish.
Conozco a Virginia. I know Virginia.
¿No conoce Vd. al profesor? Don't you know the profesor?
Conozco esa ciudad. I am acquainted with that city.

■ Práctica

Cambie según se indica.

1. El alumno sabe la lección.
   yo / nosotros / tú / vosotros / los muchachos / él
2. Ellos conocen al señor García.
   tú / Vd. / vosotros / yo / Vd. y yo / Vds.

---

* Usted and ustedes are commonly abbreviated to **Vd.** and **Vds.** Hereafter, they will sometimes appear in this form.

B. Commands

There are two forms of command in Spanish: (a) the formal command and (b) the familiar command.

a. The formal command is used in addressing persons whom you would normally address as **usted (ustedes),** using the third person of the verb. It is derived, in all regular verbs and in many irregular verbs, from the first person singular, present indicative. The **-o** is dropped and the following endings are substituted:

First Conjugation: Singular **-e,** plural **-en.**

    hable usted   speak   **hablen ustedes**   speak

Second and Third Conjugations: Singular **-a,** plural **-an.**

    aprenda usted   learn   **aprendan ustedes**   learn
    escriba usted   write   **escriban ustedes**   write

Note that the pronoun **usted (ustedes)** follows the verb.

b. The familiar imperative is used in addressing persons whom you normally adress as **tú,** using the (familiar) second person of the verb. In all regular verbs and in many irregular verbs the singular of the familiar imperative is the same in form as the third person singular, present indicative.

    habla   speak   **aprende**   learn   **escribe**   write

Tú may be used for emphasis, in which case it follows the verb.

    ¡Habla tú, María!   *You* speak, Mary!

While there is a plural of the familiar imperative (see Lesson 28), the form most commonly used in Spanish America is the plural of the formal command with **ustedes,** as in ordinary polite conversation. This is the form which will be used in this book.

   ¡Hablen ustedes, niños!   Speak, children!
   Juan y María, escriban ustedes los ejercicios.   John and Mary, write the exercises.

c. A formal command is made negative by placing **no** before the verb.

   ¡No mire usted el reloj!   Don't look at the watch!
   No coman ustedes ahora.   Don't eat now.

The negative of the familiar imperative, however, is not formed in this way. It will be studied later.

■ Práctica

Conteste según los modelos.

a. **Quiero hablar.**
   Hable usted.

    1. Quiero aprender.   6. Quiero comer.
    2. Quiero escribir.   7. Quiero trabajar.
    3. Quiero escuchar.   8. Quiero comprender.
    4. Quiero leer.   9. Quiero estudiar.
    5. Quiero contestar.   10. Quiero preguntar.

b. **Vamos a escribir.**
   No escriban ustedes.

    1. Vamos a trabajar.   6. Vamos a preguntar.
    2. Vamos a comer.   7. Vamos a escuchar.
    3. Vamos a contestar.   8. Vamos a leer.
    4. Vamos a aprender.   9. Vamos a estudiar.
    5. Vamos a escribir.   10. Vamos a hablar.

c. **¿Quieres escuchar?**
   Escucha.

    1. ¿Quieres comprender?   6. ¿Quieres leer?
    2. ¿Quieres trabajar?   7. ¿Quieres escribir?
    3. ¿Quieres comer?   8. ¿Quieres estudiar?
    4. ¿Quieres contestar?   9. ¿Quieres aprender?
    5. ¿Quieres hablar?   10. ¿Quieres preguntar?

C.   Listening and speaking

además besides
aquí here
azul blue
bonito pretty
barato cheap; **más barato**
  cheaper
los calcetines socks
la camisa shirt
caro expensive
cincuenta fifty
comprar to buy
la corbata necktie, tie
el dólar dollar

examinar to examine
la ganga bargain
¿qué hace? what does he
  do?
hola hello
el hombre man
honrado honest
la lana wool; **de lana** of wool,
  woolen
la mañana morning; **mañana**
  tomorrow
necesitar to need
el precio price

pues well! then!
rebajar to lower
rojo red
la seda silk
siempre always
la tienda store
el traje suit
unos, unas some
ya already; indeed
el zapato shoe

IDIOMS AND OTHER EXPRESSIONS

aquí tiene Vd. here is, here are
ir de compras to go shopping
mucho gusto de verlos (I am)
  very pleased to see you
¿verdad? aren't you? don't
  you? isn't it? etc. (**Verdad** is
  really a feminine noun
  meaning *truth*.)

Los alumnos van de compras

Una mañana Carlos dice: —¡Hola, Juan! ¿Quieres ir de compras?
Yo quiero comprar un traje, unas camisas y una corbata. Voy a una tienda
que conozco. Es la tienda del señor García. Él me conoce y sé que siempre
rebaja un poco los precios. ¿No le conoces tú?

—¡Sí! Le conozco. Es de Puerto Rico y es un hombre muy honrado.

—Mucho gusto de verlos—dice el señor García. —Ustedes estudian el
español, ¿verdad?

—Sí, señor,—contesta Carlos—lo estudiamos.

—Pues ¡hablen ustedes en español!

—¡Sí, sí, Carlos, habla en español!—dice Juan.

Carlos dice en español que quiere comprar un traje azul.

—¡Mire usted!—dice el señor García. —Aquí tiene usted un traje muy
bonito. Es de lana.

—¿Cuál es el precio?—pregunta Carlos.

—Cincuenta dólares.

—Mira, Carlos, es una ganga—dice Juan. —¡Cómpralo!

—Ya lo sé—dice Carlos. Y lo compra.

Carlos necesita también una corbata. Ve una corbata roja. Es de seda.
La examina y la compra, porque es barata.

Carlos examina también unas camisas. Va a comprarlas, pero el señor
García dice: —No las compre usted. Son muy caras. Mañana voy a
tener otras más baratas.

Juan ve unos calcetines y unos zapatos que no son muy caros. Los
compra.

—¡Adiós, señor García!—dicen Juan y Carlos.

—¡Adiós, señores! Y muchas gracias.

—El señor García—dice Carlos—es un hombre muy honrado. Además
nos conoce y por eso siempre rebaja un poco los precios.

■ Preguntas

1. ¿Qué dice Carlos una mañana?
2. ¿Qué quiere comprar Carlos?
3. ¿Adónde va Carlos?
4. ¿Le conoce el señor García?
5. ¿Conoce Juan al señor García?
6. ¿Qué pregunta el señor García?
7. ¿Qué contesta Carlos?
8. ¿Qué dice luego el señor García?
9. ¿Cuál es el precio del traje de lana?
10. ¿Qué más necesita Carlos?
11. ¿Qué hace Carlos?
12. ¿Por qué no compra Carlos las camisas?
13. ¿Qué compra Juan?
14. ¿Cómo es el señor García?
15. ¿Qué hace siempre el señor García?

D. Structure

1. *Direct object pronouns.* The direct object pronouns are as follows:

me	me		**nos**	us
te	you (*familiar*)		**os**	you (*familiar*)
le	him; you (*m.*)			
lo	him; you, it (*m.*)		**los**	them, you (*m.*)
la	her; you, it (*f.*)		**las**	them, you (*f.*)

Notice that **le** refers to a masculine person (*him, you*) and that **lo** may refer to a masculine person or a masculine thing (*him, you, it*). In Spanish America and parts of Spain **lo** is used more frequently then **le** to mean *him* or *you*. Your instructor will tell you which form he prefers you to use.

Lo is also a neuter form (*it*) used in referring to an idea or an action:

Lo sé.   I know it.

The familiar plural **os** (*you*) has been replaced in Spanish America by the formal plural **los, las.**

Normally, object pronouns are placed immediately before the verb.

El profesor me conoce.   The professor knows me.
Carlos la compra.   Charles buys it.
Los conocemos.   We know them (*or* you).
No las compren Vds.   Don't buy them.

However, they follow and are attached to the infinitive and the *affirmative* command forms.

Quiero comprarlos.   I want to buy them.
Cómprelo usted.   Buy it.
Mírenla ustedes.   Look at her.
Cómpralas (tú), Juan.   (You) buy them, John.

Notice that, as in the last three examples, a written accent is required when an object pronoun is added to a command form of two or more syllables. The accent is placed over the syllable of the verb which was stressed before the pronoun was added.

■ Práctica

Conteste según los modelos.

a. **¿Compra Juan el traje?**
    Sí, lo compra.

    1. ¿Compra Juan la corbata?
    2. ¿Compra Juan los calcetines?
    3. ¿Compra Juan las camisas?
    4. ¿Compra Juan el libro?
    5. ¿Compra Juan las corbatas?
    6. ¿Compra Juan los zapatos?
    7. ¿Compra Juan la camisa?
    8. ¿Compra Juan los trajes?

b. **¿Vas a examinar los zapatos?**
    Sí, voy a examinarlos.

    1. ¿Vas a examinar el libro?
    2. ¿Vas a examinar los libros?
    3. ¿Vas a examinar la camisa?
    4. ¿Vas a examinar las corbatas?
    5. ¿Vas a examinar los calcetines?
    6. ¿Vas a examinar el ejercicio?
    7. ¿Vas a examinar la lección?
    8. ¿Vas a examinar las camisas?

c. **Quiero ver los calcetines.**
    Mírelos, pero no los compre.

    1. Quiero ver la camisa.
    2. Quiero ver el libro.

3. Quiero ver los zapatos.
4. Quiero ver las corbatas.
5. Quiero ver el traje.
6. Quiero ver las camisas.
7. Quiero ver los libros.
8. Quiero ver la corbata.

d. **¿Conoce usted al señor García?**
Sí, le (lo) conozco.

1. ¿Conoce usted a Dolores?
2. ¿Conoce usted al profesor?
3. ¿Conoce usted a las señoritas?
4. ¿Conoce usted a mi hermana?
5. ¿Conoce usted a los muchachos?
6. ¿Conoce usted al señor López?
7. ¿Conoce usted a las alumnas?
8. ¿Conoce usted a mis hermanas?

e. **Diga en español.**

1. He knows me.
2. They know us.
3. She knows you, señor.
4. She knows you, señora.
5. Does he know you, Pepe?
6. Does he know you, María?
7. Do they know you, boys?
8. Do they know us?

 2. **Ser** *with expressions of material.* **Ser** is used in naming the material of which a thing is made.

El traje es de lana.   The suit is of wool (woolen).
La corbata es de seda.   The tie is (of) silk.

■ Práctica

Diga en español.

1. It is a woolen suit.
2. It is a silk tie.
3. I need woolen socks.
4. I need silk ties.

5. Have you woolen suits?
6. Have you silk shirts?

E. Writing

Test yourself

1. "Hello!" says Carlos. "Let's go shopping!"
2. I know a store that is near the university.
3. It is Mr. García's store.
4. He knows me and always lowers the price a little.
5. "I know him, too," says Juan, "and I know that he is from Puerto Rico."
6. Carlos wants a blue suit. "Here it is," says Mr. García.
7. "What is the price of the suit?" asks Carlos.
8. It is a woolen suit, and he buys it because it is a bargain.
9. He needs a red tie, too, and he is going to buy it.
10. Carlos wants some shirts, but Mr. García says, "Don't buy them; they are very expensive."
11. Juan needs shoes and socks, but he does not buy them.
12. Mr. García is an honest man.

Composition

You and Juan go to a store that is near the university. Write a composition telling what you need and what you buy. Tell what Juan needs and what he buys. Tell what he does not buy, and why. Use as many direct object pronouns as you can.

F. Pronunciation practice

Spanish vowels must be pronounced clearly and distinctly—never slurred. Failure to pronounce unstressed vowels distinctly may sometimes make the meaning of words unclear.

Pronounce the following pairs of words as you hear them, paying particular attention to the unstressed vowels.

a vs. e		a vs. i	
basar	besar	casa	casi
estudia	estudie	alusión	ilusión
prepara	prepare	amago	imago
señoras	señores	manar	minar
españolas	españoles	pasada	pisada
pasó	pesó	anterior	interior

a vs. o		a vs. u	
vieja	viejo	paré	puré
altas	altos	lanar	lunar
alumnas	alumnos	pañal	puñal
pasar	posar	maleta	muleta
saltar	soltar	maceta	muceta
barbón	Borbón	añoso	uñoso

LESSON 6

A. Stem-changing verbs (sometimes called radical-changing verbs)

Many Spanish verbs change the vowel of the stem under certain conditions. There are three classes of these verbs.

Class I
Verbs of the first and second conjugations with stem vowel **e** or **o**.

pensar	to think, intend	**perder**	to lose
contar	to count	**volver**	to return, go back

Class II
Third-conjugation verbs with stem vowel **e** or **o**.

sentir	to regret	**dormir**	to sleep

Class III
Third-conjugation verbs with stem vowel **e**.

pedir	to ask for	**despedirse de**	to take leave of

B. Present indicative and command forms of stem-changing verbs of Class I and Class II

Stem-changing verbs of Class I and Class II change stem vowel **e** to **ie** and stem vowel **o** to **ue** wherever the stress falls on the syllable containing these vowels, that is, throughout the singular and in the third person plural. You have already learned these same changes in some irregular verbs **(querer, poder)**.

67

Class I: **pensar** to think		**volver** to return	
p*i*enso	pensamos	v*ue*lvo	volvemos
p*i*ensas	pensáis	v*ue*lves	volvéis
Vd. p*i*ensa	Vds. p*i*ensan	Vd. v*ue*lve	Vds. v*ue*lven
p*i*ensa	p*i*ensan	v*ue*lve	v*ue*lven

Class II: **sentir** to regret		**dormir** to sleep	
s*i*ento	sentimos	d*ue*rmo	dormimos
s*i*entes	sentís	d*ue*rme	dormís
Vd s*i*ente	Vds. s*i*enten	Vd. d*ue*rme	Vds. d*ue*rmen
s*i*ente	s*i*enten	d*ue*rme	d*ue*rmen

NOTE: There is only one other verb like **dormir: morir** (to die).

Not all verbs with stem vowel **e** or **o** are stem-changing. You must learn whether or not a verb is stem-changing when you learn the verb. Vocabularies indicate that fact, and at the same time the class to which a stem-changing verb belongs, thus: **pensar (ie), volver (ue), sentir (ie), pedir (i),** etc.

The command forms of stem-changing verbs have the same change as the present indicative.

> **piense usted**   **piensen ustedes**   **piensa (tú)**
> **duerma usted**   **duerman ustedes**   **duerme (tú)**

■ Práctica

a. *Cambie según se indica.*

　1. Yo pienso leerlo.
　　　Vd. / ellos / nosotros / tú / vosotros
　2. Juan no duerme bien.
　　　yo / nosotros / tú / vosotros / Vds.
　3. Vd. vuelve mañana.
　　　tú / yo / vosotros / Juan y yo / ellas
　4. Yo lo siento mucho.
　　　María / Vds. / Vd. y yo / vosotros / tú

b. *Cambie según el modelo.*
Quiero pensar.
No piense Vd.

1. Vuelvo mañana.
2. Quiero dormir.
3. Lo siento.
4. Pienso mucho.

C. Present indicative of irregular verb *dar, to give*

doy	damos
das	dais
Vd. da	Vds. dan
da	dan

Notice that **dar** has only one irregular form in the present indicative: the first person singular.

■ Práctica

Cambie según se indica.

1. Nosotros no damos dinero.
   ellos / tú / vosotros / yo / Vd. y yo
2. Virginia no me da el libro.
   Vds. / vosotros / tú / los alumnos / ella

D. Listening and speaking

blanco white
la blusa blouse
la compra purchase
contar (ue) to count
dar to give
el dependiente clerk
devolver (ue) to return, give back
diez ten
dormir (ue) to sleep
encontrar (ue) to find
la falda skirt
gustar (a) to be pleasing (to)
hoy today
las medias de nilón (*usually pronounced as if spelled* **nailon**) nylon stockings

morir (ue) to die
mostrar (ue) to show
mucho a lot, very much
el novio sweetheart
pensar (ie) to think; + *infin.* to intend
preferir (ie) to prefer
prestar to lend
sentir (ie) to regret, be sorry
la señorita young lady; Miss
si if, whether
el sombrero hat
la vendedora salesgirl
el vestido dress
volver (ue) to return, go back

IDIOMS AND OTHER EXPRESSIONS

me gusta I like it; **me gustan**   **por supuesto** of course
  I like them   **¡Qué vestido más hermoso!**
me parece it seems to me   What a beautiful dress!
¿Qué le (te) parece ...? How   **lo siento mucho** I am very
  do you like ...?   sorry

Las señoritas van de compras

—¿Qué piensas hacer hoy, Virginia?—pregunta María.

—Pienso ir de compras. Necesito un vestido y unas medias de nilón.

—Pues yo quiero comprar un sombrero, una falda y una blusa. ¡Vamos de compras!

Las dos señoritas van a una tienda muy buena que conoce María. La vendedora les muestra unos sombreros. Pero no les gustan los sombreros y no los compran.

Virginia quiere un vestido. La vendedora le muestra un vestido muy hermoso que le gusta.

—¡Qué vestido más hermoso!—exclama Virginia. —Me gusta mucho, pero es de lana y prefiero uno de seda.

—Es una ganga—dice María. —¡Cómpralo!

Pero Virginia no lo compra. Al contrario examina unas medias de nilón. Le gustan y las compra.

María ve una falda de lana que le gusta mucho.

—¿Qué te parece la falda, Virginia?

—Me parece muy hermosa. Es una ganga también.

—Voy a comprarla—dice María.

Ella quiere también una blusa de seda. La vendedora le muestra unas blusas.

—¿No les gustan a Vds. las blusas?—pregunta la vendedora.

—Sí, nos gustan—contestan las señoritas. —¡Qué blusas más hermosas!

—Prefiero la blusa blanca—dice María. —Pero no sé si tengo bastante dinero para comprarla.

—Cuenta tu dinero—le dice Virginia.

María cuenta su dinero, pero no encuentra bastante. —No puedo comprar la blusa—dice. —¡Lo siento mucho!

—Puedo prestarte diez dólares—le dice Virginia. Y le da el dinero.

María compra la blusa, pero dice: —Si no le gusta a mi novio, voy a devolverla.

—¡Por supuesto! Si no le gusta a su novio devuélvala—le dice la vendedora.

Luego las dos señoritas vuelven a casa. Están muy contentas, porque les gustan sus compras.

■ Preguntas

1. ¿Qué pregunta María?
2. ¿Adónde piensa ir Virginia?
3. ¿Qué necesita Virginia?
4. ¿Qué quiere comprar María?
5. ¿Qué les muestra la vendedora?
6. ¿Por qué no compran los sombreros?
7. ¿Qué le muestra a Virginia la vendedora?
8. ¿Qué exclama Virginia?
9. ¿De qué es el vestido?
10. ¿Qué prefiere Virginia?
11. ¿Por qué compra Virginia las medias de nilón?
12. ¿De qué es la falda que le gusta a María?
13. ¿Qué más les muestra la vendedora?
14. ¿Qué exclaman las señoritas?
15. ¿Cuál de las blusas prefiere María?
16. ¿Qué hace María con su dinero?
17. ¿Qué le presta Virginia?
18. ¿Va María a devolver la falda?
19. ¿Adónde vuelven las señoritas?
20. ¿Por qué están contentas?

■ Práctica

Substituya según se indica.

1. ¡Qué vestido más hermoso!
2. ¡_____ blusas _____ !
3. ¡_____ _____ caras!
4. ¡_____ sombrero _____!
5. ¡_____ _____ barato!
6. ¡_____ falda _____!
7. ¡_____ _____ hermosa!
8. ¡_____ medias _____!

E. Structure

1. *Indirect object pronouns.* The indirect object pronouns are as follows:

me (to) me	**nos** (to) us
te (to) you (*familiar*)	**os** (to) you (*familiar*)
le (to) him, her, you, it	**les** (to) them, (to) you

Notice that there is only one third-person form for the singular: **le;** and one for the plural: **les.** Furthermore, in Spanish America the familiar plural **os** (*to you*) has been replaced by the formal plural **les.**

Indirect object pronouns follow the same rules for position as the direct object pronouns. That is, they normally precede the verb, but they follow an infinitive and an *affirmative* command.

Me muestra el sombrero. He shows me the hat. (He shows the hat to me.)

¿Qué te parece la blusa? How do you like the blouse? (How does the blouse seem to you?)

Le doy a Vd. el dinero. I give you the money. (I give the money to you.)

No les preste Vd. el libro. Don't lend them the book. (Don't lend the book to them.)

But:

Voy a darle a Vd. el dinero. I am going to give you the money.

Muéstreme Vd. el sombrero. Show me the hat.

Since **le** and **les** have several meanings each, a redundant construction may be used to show which meaning is intended. This consists of the preposition **a** plus the appropriate prepositional object pronouns, as follows:

Le doy el libro	**a él.** **a ella.** **a Vd.**	I give the book	to him. to her. to you.	
Les doy el libro	**a ellos.** **a ellas.** **a Vds.**	I give the book	to them. to them. to you.	

The redundant construction is often used for emphasis, even when the meaning is otherwise clear. With **usted (ustedes)** it is frequently used merely for politeness. It may also be used, for clarity or emphasis, with direct object pronouns, as follows:

Le veo *a él*. I see *him*.

¿No le conocen *a Vd*.? Don't they know *you*?

■ Práctica

a. *Diga en español.*

1. They give him the money.
2. They give her the money.

3. They give me the money.
4. They give them the money.
5. They give us the money.
6. They give you the money.

7. He is going to show her the shoes.
8. He is going to show us the shoes.
9. He is going to show them the shoes.
10. He is going to show me the shoes.
11. He is going to show him the shoes.
12. He is going to show you the shoes.

13. Return the hat to him.
14. Return the hat to them.
15. Return the hat to her.
16. Return the hat to us.
17. Return the hat to me.

18. Don't show her the blouse.
19. Don't show us the blouse.
20. Don't show them the blouse.
21. Don't show me the blouse.
22. Don't show him the blouse.

b. *Cambie según se indica, siguiendo* (following) *el modelo.*
Le prestan el libro a Juan.
Les prestan el libro a ellas.

1. _____ (to you).
2. _____ (to her).
3. _____ (to them).
4. _____ (to him).
5. _____ (to Dorotea).
6. _____ (to the students).

2. *The* **gustar** *construction.* The expression **me gustan los zapatos** does not literally translate its common English equivalent, *I like the shoes.* The Spanish-speaking person is really saying, *to me are pleasing the shoes.* The English subject (the person) becomes the Spanish indirect object. The English direct object (the thing) becomes the Spanish subject and follows the verb.

Les gusta la tienda.   They like the store.
Nos gustan los sombreros.   We like the hats.

3. *Redundant* **le.** A redundant **le (les)** is used in Spanish in a sentence which contains a noun indirect object referring to a person.

Le **doy el dinero** *a mi hermano.*　I give the money *to my brother.*
A Virginia le **gustan los zapatos.**　*Virginia* likes the shoes.
A las muchachas les **gusta la blusa.**　*The girls* like the blouse.

■ Práctica

Diga en español.

a. 1. I like the store.
   2. He likes the store.
   3. They like the store.
   4. She likes the store.
   5. You like the store.
   6. You all like the store.
   7. We like the store.

b. 1. He likes the socks.
   2. I like the socks.
   3. You like the socks.
   4. You all like the socks.
   5. We like the socks.
   6. She likes the socks.
   7. They like the socks.

c. 1. María likes the shoes.
   2. Carlos likes the shoes.
   3. Mr. García likes the shoes.
   4. My father likes the shoes.
   5. My brother likes the shoes.
   6. My sister likes the shoes.

d. 1. How do you like the ties, señor?
   2. How do you like the ties, señora?
   3. How do you like the tie, señores?
   4. How do you like the tie, señoras?
   5. How do you like the tie, Juan?
   6. How do you like the ties, Virginia?

F.　Writing

Test yourself

1. María and Virginia intend to go shopping.
2. They need dresses, shoes, and blouses.

3. The salesgirls show them some hats.
4. Virginia sees some nylon stockings that she likes, and she buys them.
5. How do you like the woolen skirt?
6. She prefers one of silk.
7. The salesgirl shows her some blouses.
8. María is going to buy them.
9. But she does not know whether she has enough money to buy them.
10. Virginia lends her ten dollars.
11. She returns the purchases, if her sweetheart doesn't like them.
12. The young ladies return home.

Composition

Write a composition telling how you and Virginia go shopping. Tell where you go, what the salesgirl shows Virginia, what she likes, what you like, what she buys, what she does not buy, and why.

G. Pronunciation practice

Pronounce the following words as you hear them, paying particular attention to the pairs of unstressed vowels.

e vs. **i**		e vs. **o**	
pelar	pilar	escuche	escucho
pesó	pisó	puede	puedo
bebió	vivió	quiere	quiero
legué	ligué	pedido	podido
relegó	religó	prescrito	proscrito
case	casi	atentar	atontar

e vs. **u**	
melar	mular
regido	rugido
se pone	supone
se frió	sufrió
se vio	subió
se marcha	su marcha

En la tienda

Carlos (al entrar en la tienda).   Buenas tardes.

El dependiente.   Muy buenas tardes, señor.   ¿En qué puedo servirle?

Carlos.   Busco unas cosas típicas que regalar a mi familia.

El dependiente.   Tenemos muchas cosas bonitas. Hay carteras de cuero, ceniceros, artículos de plata.   Aquí tiene Vd. unos pendientes de plata muy preciosos.

Carlos.   ¿A cómo se venden?

El dependiente.   A tres pesos.

Carlos.   Bueno, me quedo con ellos.

El dependiente.   Hay también ceniceros de plata. Aquí los tiene Vd.

Carlos.   ¿A cuánto?

El dependiente.   A dos pesos.

Carlos.   Bueno, me llevo éste.   Es para mi padre.

The North is "Green Spain": Village scenes in Asturias. (Spanish National Tourist Office)

A granary near Oviedo. Notice the wooden shoes. (Spanish National Tourist Office)

A coastal town in Asturias. (Spanish National Tourist Office)

Sunny Spain is southern Spain: Views of streets in Vejer de la Frontera, Cádiz. (Spanish National Tourist Office)

Two scenes in the
Pyrenees, which long
kept Spain isolated from
the rest of Europe.
(Philip D. Gendreau)

LESSON 7

A. Stem-changing verbs, Class III

Stem-changing verbs of Class III are third-conjugation verbs with final stem vowel **e.** The **e** changes to **i** whenever it is in the stressed syllable—that is, throughout the singular and in the third person plural of the present indicative, and in the command forms.

pedir   to ask for

p*i*do	pedimos
p*i*des	pedís
Vd. p*i*de	Vds. p*i*den
p*i*de	p*i*den

p*i*da Vd. ask	**p*i*dan Vds.** ask	**p*i*de (tú)** ask

■ Práctica

Cambie según se indica.

1. Ellos piden un refresco.
    usted / usted y yo / Antonio / vosotros / tú / yo
2. Yo pido huevos fritos.
    nosotros / ellas / vosotros / tú / Héctor / tú y yo

B.   Reflexive verbs

Reflexive means "bending back." A reflexive verb is one whose action *bends back,* directly or indirectly, upon its subject:

80

me lavo   I wash myself (I wash)
me digo   I tell myself (I say to myself)

The object is a reflexive pronoun, of the same person and number as the subject; and it has the same form, whether direct object or indirect object. In vocabularies and dictionaries reflexive verbs appear with the pronoun **se** attached to the infinitive.

lavarse to wash		**vestirse** to dress	
me lavo	nos lavamos	me visto	nos vestimos
te lavas	os laváis	te vistes	os vestís
Vd. se lava	Vds. se lavan	Vd. se viste	Vds. se visten
se lava	se lavan	se viste	se visten

Note that the first two persons, singular and plural, of the reflexive pronouns are the same as the direct and indirect object pronouns for these persons. Only the third person differs: **se** (*himself, herself, itself, yourself, themselves, yourselves*).

Many Spanish reflexives may be translated by English reflexives:

Carlos se lava.   Charles washes himself.

But many others are not likely to be, or cannot be, translated by English reflexives:

Me acuesto.   I go to bed.
Usted se viste.   You get dressed.
María se sienta.   Mary sits down.
Ellos se despiertan.   They wake up.
Me llamo Juan.   My name is John. (I call myself John.)
Ella se va.   She goes away.

■ Práctica

Cambie según se indica.

1. Los muchachos se acuestan tarde.
     yo / usted / nosotros / tú / vosotros
2. Nosotros nos vestimos.
     vosotros / yo / tú / ella / ellos / usted y yo.
3. Ramón no se despierta.
     ellos / tú / vosotros / nosotros / yo / ustedes

4. La señorita se sienta.

   tú / Vd. y yo / yo / vosotros / usted / nosotros

C. Listening and speaking

acostarse (ue) to go to bed
bañarse to bathe
la cara face
el cuarto quarter (hour)
el desayuno breakfast
despedirse (i) de to take leave
   of, say good-by (to)
los dientes teeth
doce twelve
la fruta fruit
el huevo egg; **huevos fritos**
   fried eggs
irse to go off, go away
el jugo juice
levantarse to get up
limpiar to clean
la mano hand
medio *adj.* half
menos less
la mesa table
mientras while
la naranja orange
nueve nine
o or
ocho eight
pedir (i) to ask for; to order
   (*in a restaurant, etc.*)

peinarse to comb one's hair
poner to put; **ponerse** to put
   on
el restaurante restaurant
sentarse (ie) to sit down
servir (i) to serve; **servirse (i)**
   to serve oneself, to take (*at
   table*)
siete seven
tarde late
la tarde afternoon, evening
la taza cup
temprano early
las tostadas toast
vestirse (i) to dress, get dressed

IDIOMS AND OTHER EXPRESSIONS

a las siete y media de la mañana
   at seven-thirty in the morning
son las nueve menos cuarto it is a
   quarter to nine
por la mañana in the morning
por la noche at night
¿a qué hora? at what time?
¿qué hora es? what time is it?

Por la mañana

Yo no soy perezoso. Me levanto temprano por la mañana. Puedo
levantarme temprano porque me acuesto temprano por la noche y, además,
duermo bien. Juan y Carlos son perezosos. No se levantan temprano,
porque se acuestan tarde. Yo me levanto a las siete de la mañana. Ellos
se levantan a las ocho o a las ocho y media. Yo me acuesto a las diez o a
las diez y media de la noche. Ellos se acuestan a las doce o a las doce y
media.

Me levanto a las siete de la mañana. Me lavo las manos[1] y la cara.[2]
Me limpio los dientes. Luego me baño. Después me visto y me peino.

Me pongo[3] el sombrero y voy a un restaurante para tomar el desayuno.
Me sirvo fruta, tostadas y café.

Hoy, mientras tomo el desayuno, Juan y Carlos entran en el restaurante.
—¡Siéntense ustedes!—les digo.
Ellos se sientan a mi mesa. Juan pide jugo de naranja y huevos fritos.
Carlos pide café y tostadas. Yo pido otra taza de café. Me gusta el café.
—¿Qué hora es?—pregunta Juan.
—Son las nueve menos cuarto—contesta Carlos.
—Me parece—dice Juan—que nosotros nos levantamos tarde todos los
días.
—¡Es tarde!—exclamo yo, y me levanto de la mesa. Me despido de Juan
y Carlos y me voy a la clase.

■ Preguntas

1. ¿Se levanta usted tarde o temprano?
2. ¿Por qué puede usted levantarse temprano?
3. ¿Se levantan temprano Juan y Carlos?
4. ¿A qué hora se levanta usted?
5. ¿A qué hora se acuesta usted?
6. ¿A qué hora se acuestan Juan y Carlos?
7. ¿Qué hace usted por la mañana cuando se levanta?
8. Después ¿qué se pone usted y adónde va?
9. ¿Qué se sirve usted en el restaurante?
10. ¿Quiénes entran en el restaurante?
11. ¿Qué les dice usted?
12. ¿Dónde se sientan?
13. ¿Qué piden Juan y Carlos?
14. ¿Qué pide usted?
15. ¿Qué hora es?
16. Por eso ¿qué hace usted?

NOTES

1. Notice that **la mano** is feminine.

2. The definite article (instead of the possessive adjectives **mi, su, etc.**) is
   commonly used in Spanish with parts of the body and clothing actually
   being worn.

   Levanto *la* mano.   I raise *my* hand.
   María se pone *el* sombrero.   Mary puts on *her* hat.

   The possessor may be indicated by a reflexive or indirect object
   pronoun.

Me **lavo la cara.**   I wash *my* face.
Ella *le* **lava la cara.**   She washes *his* face.

3. **Poner (ponerse)** has only one irregular form in the present indicative: the first person singular.

> **pongo** I put   **me pongo** I put on

D. Structure

1. *Reflexive pronouns.* Reflexive pronouns follow the same rules for position as the other object pronouns. That is, they normally precede the verb. When they are the object of an infinitive or an affirmative command, however, they follow.

Me levanto a las siete.   I get up at seven o'clock.
Se sientan a mi mesa.   They sit down at my table.

But:
Voy a levantarme.   I am going to get up.
¡Siéntense ustedes!   Sit down!

■ Práctica

a. *Cambie según se indica.*

  1. Ellos se levantan a las siete.
       usted / tú / nosotros / ellas / vosotros / yo
  2. Marta se pone el sombrero.
       yo / usted y yo / ellas / vosotros / tú
  3. ¿Se despide usted ahora?
       tú / ustedes / vosotros / yo / nosotros / él

b. *Cambie según se indica.*

  1. Él quiere ponerse el sombrero.
       yo / ellos / usted y yo / tú / vosotros
  2. Ustedes tienen que vestirse ahora.
       él / vosotros / yo / nosotros / tú / ellas

c. *Substituya según se indica.*

  1. ¡Levántese usted!
       vestirse / sentarse / acostarse / despertarse

2. ¡No se acuesten ustedes!
   despedirse / sentarse / levantarse / bañarse
3. ¡Lávate!
   bañarse / despedirse / peinarse / vestirse

2. *Numerals one to twelve.* Notice that **uno** (*one*) has the feminine form
una, while the other cardinal numbers given below are invariable. **Uno**
becomes **un** before a masculine noun.

un(o), una	one	**siete**	seven
dos	two	**ocho**	eight
tres	three	**nueve**	nine
cuatro	four	**diez**	ten
cinco	five	**once**	eleven
seis	six	**doce**	twelve

■ Práctica

a. *Diga en español.*

1 más (*plus*) 1 son 2	6 + 2 = 8
2 + 1 = 3	7 + 2 = 9
3 + 1 = 4	8 + 2 = 10
4 + 1 = 5	9 + 2 = 11
5 + 1 = 6	10 + 2 = 12
6 + 1 = 7	11 + 1 = 12

b. *Cuente en español de 1 a 12.*

3. *Telling time.*

¿Qué hora es?   What time is it?
Es la una.   It is one o'clock.
Es la una y media.   It is one-thirty.
Son las dos.   It is two o'clock.
Son las dos y cuarto.   It is a quarter after two.
Son las tres menos cuarto.   It is a quarter to three.
a las cuatro y media de la tarde . . .   at four-thirty in the afternoon . . .
a las diez menos cinco . . .   at five minutes to ten . . .

Note the use of **la** or **las** in these expressions. **La** stands for **la hora**
and **las** stands for **las horas**; but the word **hora (horas)** itself is not expressed.
The singular verb is used in expressing one o'clock; from two o'clock on,

the plural verb is used. Minutes past the hour, up to the half-hour, are preceded by **y**; minutes before the hour are preceded by **menos.**

When the hour is specified, **de** must be used to translate *in* and *at* in the expressions **de la mañana** (*in the morning*), **de la tarde** (*in the afternoon, evening*), **de la noche** (*at night*). When no definite hour is specified, **por** is used for *in* or *at*: **por la mañana** (*in the morning*), **por la noche** (*at night*).

a las cinco de la tarde   at five in the afternoon
Me levanto temprano por la mañana.   I get up early in the morning.

■ Práctica

Conteste según se indica.

a. **¿Qué hora es? 2:15**
   Son las dos y cuarto.

   1. ¿Qué hora es?
      2:30 / 1:00 / 1:30
   2. ¿Qué hora es?
      3:15 / 5:30 / 6:05
   3. ¿Qué hora es?
      8:10 / 11:15 / 11:45
   4. ¿Qué hora es?
      6:50 / 8:55 / 3:45

b. **¿Se baña usted por la mañana?**
   Sí, me baño por la mañana.

   1. ¿Estudia usted por la noche?
   2. ¿Se viste usted por la tarde?
   3. ¿Se despierta usted temprano por la mañana?
   4. ¿Lee usted por la tarde?
   5. ¿Se acuesta usted tarde por la noche?

c. **¿A qué hora se despierta usted? 6 A.M.**
   A las seis de la mañana.

   1. ¿A qué hora se levanta usted? 6:30 A.M.
   2. ¿A qué hora se viste Vd.? 6:45 A.M.
   3. ¿A qué hora va Vd. a la clase? 8:50 A.M.
   4. ¿A qué hora come Vd.? 1:00 P.M.
   5. ¿A qué hora va Vd. a la biblioteca? 3:30 P.M.
   6. ¿A qué hora va Vd. al café? 5:00 P.M.

7. ¿A qué hora estudia Vd. la lección? 9:00 P.M.
8. ¿A qué hora escribe Vd. los ejercicios? 11:00 P.M.
9. ¿A qué hora se acuesta Vd.? 11:45 P.M.

E. Writing

Test yourself

1. We get up early in the morning, because we go to bed early at night.
2. We get up at seven in the morning, but they get up at eight-thirty.
3. She washes her hands and face.
4. They clean their teeth and bathe.
5. He gets dressed and combs his hair.
6. I put on my hat and go off to the restaurant.
7. He has fried eggs and orange juice every day.
8. My friends enter the restaurant and I say to them, "Sit down at my table."
9. They sit down and order coffee and toast.
10. It is a quarter to ten and I take leave of my friends.

Composition

Write a composition about what you do in the morning. Tell what you do when you get up, where you have breakfast, what you like for breakfast, etc.

F. Pronunciation practice

Pronounce the following pairs of words as you hear them, paying particular attention to the pairs of unstressed vowels.

i vs. **o**		**i** vs. **u**	
casi	caso	piñal	puñal
cursi	curso	pintura	puntura
trinar	tronar	pinchar	punchar
millar	mollar	avisar	abusar
mijar	mojar	vigía	bujía
tinillo	tonillo	tirón	turón

o vs. **u**	
osar	usar
moral	mural
tornar	turnar
borlar	burlar
moleta	muleta
torismo	turismo

LESSON 8

A. Preterit of regular verbs

Spanish has two simple past tenses, the imperfect, which you will learn later, and the preterit. The preterit is formed by adding to the infinitive stem the following endings:

FIRST CONJUGATION		SECOND AND THIRD CONJUGATIONS	
-é	-amos	-í	-imos
-aste	-asteis	-iste	-isteis
-ó	-aron	-ió	-ieron

hablar		aprender	
hablé I spoke		aprendí I learned	
hablaste you spoke		aprendiste you learned	
Vd. habló you spoke		Vd. aprendió you learned	
habló he (she) spoke		aprendió he (she) learned	
hablamos we spoke		aprendimos we learned	
hablasteis you spoke		aprendisteis you learned	
Vds. hablaron you spoke		Vds. aprendieron you learned	
hablaron they spoke		aprendieron they learned	

Note the written accent on the first and third persons singular.

■ Práctica

Cambie según se indica.

1. Vd. preparó la lección.
    yo / Vd. y yo / ellos / tú / vosotros / Tomás

2. Yo escribí el ejercicio.
   nosotros / ella / vosotros / ellas / tú / yo
3. Nosotros comimos bien.
   Vds. / tú / Vds. y yo / vosotros / yo / Pepe

B. Preterit of stem-changing verbs

Stem-changing verbs of Class I (that is, **-ar** and **-er** verbs) have no change in the preterit.

Stem-changing verbs of Classes II and III (that is, **-ir** verbs) have a change in the third person, singular and plural, of the preterit: final stem vowel **e** changes to **i**; final stem vowel **o** changes to **u**:

CLASS II		CLASS III
s*i*ntió	d*u*rmió	p*i*dió
s*i*ntieron	d*u*rmieron	p*i*dieron

■ Práctica

Cambie según se indica.

1. Tú dormiste bien.
   Nicolás / nosotros / ellas / yo / vosotros / él
2. Yo lo sentí mucho.
   Vd. y yo / vosotros / Vds. / yo / ella / tú / Vd.
3. Nosotros pedimos café.
   yo / Vd. / tú / vosotros / ellos / tú y yo / Vds.

C. Listening and speaking

agradable agreeable
argentino Argentine
asistir (a) to attend
asombroso astonishing, amazing
ayer yesterday
bastante rather, quite
la canción song
cantar to sing
clásico classic
la comida meal; dinner
la composición composition
la cordillera mountain range
la cosa thing
cubano Cuban
describir to describe

despertarse (ie) to wake up, awaken
divertirse (ie) to have a good time
la geografía geography
el guitarrista guitarist
hasta until
la leche milk
mejicano Mexican
la música music
la orquesta orchestra
la pampa pampa(s)
para for
pasar to pass, spend
popular popular
el programa program

quince fifteen	**tocar** to play (*an instrument,*
la selva forest	*song, etc.*)
Sudamérica South America	**tropical** tropical
la televisión television	**veinte** twenty
típico typical	**la vida** life

Ayer

Ayer pasé un día típico.

Me desperté bastante temprano. Me levanté a las siete y media. Me bañé, me lavé la cara, me limpié los dientes y me peiné. Luego me vestí. A las ocho y quince tomé un buen[1] desayuno con jugo de naranja, huevos fritos, café y tostadas.

Estudié un rato y después asistí a[2] la clase del señor Martínez.

El señor Martínez habló de cosas muy interesantes. Habló de la vida hispanoamericana. Describió la geografía asombrosa de los países de Sudamérica. Describió la cordillera de los Andes, la pampa argentina y la selva tropical.

Por la tarde trabajé tres horas. Estudié la lección de español y la aprendí. Luego escribí una composición para mi clase de inglés.

A las seis y quince comí con Juan y Carlos en un buen restaurante. Nos servimos bistec con papas fritas, leche y café. Me gustó mucho la comida.

Luego Juan, Carlos y yo volvimos[3] a mi casa para ver unos programas[4] de televisión. Vimos unos programas muy interesantes. Dos señoritas muy hermosas cantaron canciones cubanas. Cantaron media hora. Una orquesta mejicana tocó música clásica mejicana. Nos gustó mucho la música.

Juan y Carlos se despidieron a las once. Se acostaron y durmieron bien. Pero yo no me acosté. Escuché otro programa hasta las doce menos veinte. En el otro programa un guitarrista[5] español tocó canciones populares españolas que me gustaron mucho. A las doce me acosté y dormí bien.

Ayer pasé un día muy agradable. Trabajé mucho pero me divertí también.

■ Preguntas

1. Usted se despertó tarde ¿verdad?
2. ¿A qué hora se levantó usted?
3. ¿Qué hizo usted (*what did you do*) luego?
4. ¿A qué hora tomó usted el desayuno?
5. ¿Qué tomó usted?
6. ¿A qué clase asistió usted?
7. ¿De qué habló el señor Martínez?

8. ¿Qué describió?
9. ¿Qué hizo usted por la tarde?
10. ¿Qué escribió usted?
11. ¿A qué hora comió usted?
12. ¿Con quiénes comió?
13. ¿Qué se sirvieron ustedes?
14. ¿Qué vieron ustedes después?
15. ¿Qué cantaron las dos señoritas?
16. ¿Qué tocó la orquesta?
17. ¿A qué hora se despidieron Juan y Carlos?
18. ¿Cómo durmieron Juan y Carlos?
19. ¿Escuchó usted otro programa hasta las doce?
20. ¿Quién tocó canciones españolas?

NOTES

1. **Bueno** becomes **buen** before a masculine singular noun.
2. **Asistir** requires the preposition **a** before a following object.

   Asistí al teatro.   I attended the theater.
   Asistieron a la clase.   They attended the class.

3. When a plural subject includes the first person singular pronoun **yo,** the verb must be in the first person plural.

   Juan, Carlos y yo volvimos a mi casa.   John, Charles, and I returned to my house.
   Mis dos amigos y yo vimos el programa.   My two friends and I saw the program.

4. Note that **el programa** is masculine. Many Spanish nouns ending in -**ma** are masculine.

   el drama   the drama
   el poema   the poem
   el telegrama   the telegram

5. Note that **el guitarrista** is masculine. Nouns denoting living beings retain the biological gender, regardless of the ending **-o** or **-a**:

   el poeta   the poet
   la modelo   the model
   el novelista   the novelist

D. Structure

Use of the preterit

The preterit expresses an act completed in the past and delimited in time. The preterit is used:

a. When the time was instantaneous or nearly so.

Me desperté temprano.　I woke up early.
¿Entró Vd. en la tienda?　Did you go into the store?
Escribieron los ejercicios.　They wrote the exercises.

b. When the time was the conventional period of time for the act expressed.

Asistí a la clase del señor Martínez.　I attended Mr. Martínez's class.
Vimos unos programas de televisión.　We saw some television programs.
¿Comiste ayer en el restaurante?　Did you have dinner in the restaurant yesterday?

c. When the *duration* of the time is definitely stated.

Cantaron media hora.　They sang half an hour.
Por la tarde trabajé tres horas.　In the afternoon I worked three hours.
Mi padre vivió en España veinte años.　My father lived in Spain twenty years.

■ Práctica

a. *Substituya el singular por el plural, según el modelo.*

Estudié un rato.
Estudiamos un rato.

1. Canté media hora.
2. Describí la geografía.
3. Comí bien.
4. Me senté aquí.
5. No me vestí temprano.
6. Vd. se acostó tarde.
7. Vd. no durmió bien.
8. Vd. se despidió a la una.
9. Vd. se despertó a las nueve.
10. Vd. se vistió tarde.
11. Miraste el reloj.
12. No aprendiste mucho.
13. Te despediste luego.

14. Te acostaste a las once.
15. Te divertiste mucho.

b. *Substituya el plural por el singular, según el modelo.*

Entramos en la sala.
Entré en la sala.

1. Estudiamos la lección.
2. Escribimos el ejercicio.
3. Escuchamos al profesor.
4. No nos despedimos.
5. Nos vestimos pronto.
6. No visteis mucho.
7. Contestasteis bien.
8. Os divertisteis mucho.
9. Os sentasteis aquí.
10. Os despertasteis tarde.
11. Sus hermanos no murieron.
12. Sus amigos lo prefirieron.
13. Sus amigas no lo vieron.
14. Sus padres no durmieron bien.
15. Sus hermanas se divirtieron mucho.

E. Writing

Test yourself

1. Charles woke up at eight-thirty yesterday.
2. He got up, washed his face, bathed, dressed, and combed his hair.
3. At nine-fifteen he had a good breakfast and then attended Spanish class.
4. Mr. Martínez talked about the geography of South America.
5. In the afternoon Charles worked four hours and wrote a composition.
6. At six o'clock he had dinner with John in a good restaurant.
7. They went back to his house and saw some television programs.
8. Two young ladies sang Cuban songs, and an orchestra played Mexican classical music.
9. Charles went to bed at twenty minutes to twelve and slept well.
10. He worked a lot yesterday, but he had a good time, too.

Composition

Write a composition telling what Mary and Virginia did yesterday.

F.　Pronunciation practice

Between vowels Spanish **s** is pronounced like the **s** in *sat*. Pronounce the following words as you hear them.

casa	blusa	hermoso
mesa	uso	famoso
rosa	cosa	gracioso

Before a voiced consonant, however, Spanish **s** is voiced (like English **z**). Pronounce the following words as you hear them.

los besos	los gastos	los meses
las voces	las gangas	las mesas
los días	es lunes	es nuestro
las doce	es linda	es nuevo

ADIÓS, MUCHACHOS*

TANGO

Spanish lyrics by CÉSAR F. VEDANI　　　　　　　Music by SANDERS

A - diós, mu - cha-chos, com - pa - ñe - ros de mi vi - da, ba - rra que - ri - da de a - que - llos

*Copyrighted by Edward B. Marks Music Corporation. Used by permission.

tiem - pos,   me to - ca a   mí hoy em - pren-der   la   re - ti -

ra - da;   de - bo a - le - jar - me   de   mi bue - na   mu - cha -

cha - da.   A - diós, mu - cha-chos, ya me voy   y   me   re -

sig - no;   con - tra el   des - ti - no   na - die   la

ta - lla,   se ter - mi - na - ron pa - ra mí to - das las

Fine

fa - rras,   mi cuer - po en - fer - mo no re - sis - te   más.

A - cu - den a   mi   men - te   re - cuer - dos de o - tros

tiem - pos, de los be - llos mo - men - tos que an - ta - ño dis - fru -

té cer - qui - ta de mi ma - dre, san - ta vie -

ji - ta, y de mi no - vie - ci - ta que tan - to i - do - la -

tré. Se a - cuer - dan que e - ra her - mo - sa, más be - lla que u - na

dio - sa, y que e - brio yo de a - mor le di mi co - ra -

zón, mas el Se - ñor, ce - lo - so de sus en -

can - tos, hun-dién - do-me en el llan-to me la lle - vó. A-diós mu -

LESSON 9

A. Some irregular preterits

ser to be ir to go	dar to give	hacer to do, make
fui	di	hice
fuiste	diste	hiciste
Vd. fue	Vd. dio	Vd. hizo
fue	dio	hizo
fuimos	dimos	hicimos
fuisteis	disteis	hicisteis
Vds. fueron	Vds. dieron	Vds. hicieron
fueron	dieron	hicieron

estar to be		tener to have	
estuve	estuvimos	tuve	tuvimos
estuviste	estuvisteis	tuviste	tuvisteis
Vd. estuvo	Vds. estuvieron	Vd. tuvo	Vds. tuvieron
estuvo	estuvieron	tuvo	tuvieron

■ Práctica

Cambie según se indica.

1. El alumno fue a la biblioteca.
       yo / nosotros / ellos / vosotros / tú / ella
2. Ellos le dieron el dinero.
       Vd. / tú / vosotros / yo / Vd. y yo / sus amigos

3. Yo no lo hice.

   ellas / tú / vosotros / Vd. / yo / nosotros / Ana

4. Tú estuviste en el café.

   Juan / nosotros / yo / vosotros / ellos / él

5. Vd. tuvo que hacerlo.

   yo / tú / nosotros / ellos / vosotros / el médico

B.   Some preterits with orthographic changes

Some types of Spanish verbs have orthographic (spelling) changes. Such changes are made usually in order to preserve the sound of the final consonant of the stem where the addition of a personal ending would otherwise alter its sound.

In the first person singular of the preterit, verbs ending in:

-car change **c** to **qu**

-gar change **g** to **gu**

-zar change **z** to **c**

buscar (to look for):	**busqué**	**explicar** (to explain):	**expliqué**
pagar (to pay):	**pagué**	**llegar** (to arrive):	**llegué**
empezar (to begin):	**empecé**	**comenzar** (to begin):	**comencé**

In the preterit of verbs like **leer,** *to read* (whose infinitive ends in a strong vowel), the **i** of the ending changes to **y** in the third person singular and plural. In all other persons the **i** of the ending bears a written accent.

le**í**	le**í**mos
le**í**ste	le**í**steis
le**y**ó	le**y**eron

■ Práctica

Cambie según se indica.

1. Vd. buscó a los alumnos.

   tú / yo / Vd. y yo / ellos / vosotros

2. Mis amigos llegaron a las dos.

   Vd. / nosotros / tú / vosotros / yo

3. Tú comenzaste a trabajar.

   vosotros / yo / Vds. / tú y yo / él

4. Nosotros leímos la lección.

   yo / tú / Vd. / vosotros / ella / ellas

C. Listening and speaking

aceptar to accept
el actor actor
la actriz actress
anoche last night
el año year
casi nearly, almost
el cine movies
comenzar (ie) to begin
conocido well-known
¿cuánto? how much? ¿cuántos?
  how many?
dar to give; to show (*a movie*)
diecinueve nineteen
dieciocho eighteen
diecisiete seventeen
divertido amusing
empezar (ie) to begin
entretanto meanwhile
entretener to entertain
el examen examination
la flor flower
la gardenia gardenia
la invitación invitation
joven young; el joven young

man; los jóvenes young
  people
el lado side; al lado de beside
lindo pretty
llegar (a) to arrive, reach
mono cute
la película (moving) picture,
  film
pronto soon
se (to) him, her, you, them
sólo only
tan adv. so, as
tanto adv. so much
el teatro theater
la vez time

IDIOMS AND OTHER EXPRESSIONS

¿cuánto tiempo? how long?
no importa it doesn't matter
por fin finally
sobre todo especially
tener (veinte) años to be
  (twenty) years old
a veces at times, sometimes

El cine

A veces[1,2] el señor Martínez entra en la sala de clase y dice: —¡Buenos días, jóvenes!

Pero no somos tan jóvenes. María tiene diecisiete años. Carlos y Virginia tienen dieciocho años. Juan tiene diecinueve años y yo tengo veinte años.

Nos gusta mucho el cine. El señor Martínez dice que nos gusta porque somos jóvenes.

Anoche fui al cine. Busqué a mis amigos para invitarlos. Empecé a[3] buscarlos en el café, pero no los encontré allí. Fui luego a la biblioteca, donde por fin los encontré.

En la biblioteca Virginia me preguntó:—¿Quieres prestarme tu libro de español? Lo necesito. Préstamelo.

Tuve que prestárselo. —Te lo presto con gusto—le expliqué—porque voy al cine. ¿No quieren Vds. acompañarme?

Pero sólo María aceptó mi invitación. Los otros prefirieron estudiar, porque pronto empiezan los exámenes. Estuvieron tres horas en la biblioteca, donde leyeron y estudiaron mucho. Carlos leyó casi todo su libro de historia.

Entretanto María y yo fuimos al cine. Llegué al[4] teatro con ella a las ocho y media. En una tienda al lado del teatro vi unas gardenias muy lindas. Compré una y se la di a María. Pagué un dólar, pero no importa . . . ¡a ella le gustan tanto las flores!

En el teatro dieron una película de Cantinflas, el conocido actor mejicano. Cantinflas hizo cosas muy divertidas que nos entretuvieron mucho. Me gustó la película—¡sobre todo las actrices mejicanas muy lindas y muy monas!

■ Preguntas

1. ¿Adónde fue usted anoche?
2. ¿A quiénes buscó usted?
3. ¿Dónde comenzó a buscarlos?
4. ¿Dónde los encontró?
5. ¿Qué le prestó usted a Virginia?
6. ¿Qué le explicó?
7. ¿Qué les preguntó usted a sus amigos?
8. ¿Quién aceptó su invitación?
9. ¿Qué prefirieron hacer los otros?
10. ¿Por qué?
11. ¿Cuánto tiempo estuvieron sus amigos en la biblioteca?
12. ¿Qué hicieron?
13. ¿Qué hizo Carlos?
14. ¿A qué hora llegó usted al teatro?
15. ¿Qué compró usted?
16. ¿A quién se la dio?
17. ¿Qué dieron anoche en el teatro?
18. ¿Qué hizo Cantinflas?

NOTES

1. Nouns ending in **-z** in the singular change the **z** to **c** before adding the plural ending **-es.**

la vez	**las veces**
la actriz	**las actrices**

2. **La vez** means *time* in the sense of *instance.*

la primera vez   the first time
Siempre leo la lección tres veces.   I always read the lesson three times.

Time in the general or abstract sense is **el tiempo.**

No puedo hacerlo; no tengo tiempo.   I can't do it; I haven't time.
El tiempo vuela.   Time flies.

Time in the sense of *hour, the time of day,* is **la hora.**

¿Qué hora es?   What time is it?

3. Verbs of beginning require the preposition **a** before an infinitive.

Empecé a buscarlos.   I began to look for them.
Comenzaron a cantar.   They began to sing.

4. **Llegar** requires the preposition **a** before a following noun.

Llegué al teatro.   I reached the theater.
Ayer llegó a España.   He arrived in Spain yesterday.

D. Structure

1. *Two object pronouns.*

a. When both indirect and direct object pronouns are used in the same sentence, the indirect precedes the direct. Both normally precede the verb, but they follow an infinitive and an affirmative imperative.

Te lo presto.   I lend it to you.
¿Quieres dármelo?   Will you give it to me?
Préstemelos Vd.   Lend them to me.

b. When both pronouns are in the third person, the indirect object pronouns **le** and **les** change to **se.**

Se la di.   I gave it to him (to her, to you, to them).
Tuve que prestárselos.   I had to lend them to him (to her, to you, to them).

c. When the meaning of **se** might not be clear from the context, we use the same redundant construction that we used in Lesson 6 to clarify **le** and **les.**

Se los di a ella.   I gave them to her.
Se lo prestaron a Vd.   They lent it to you.

The redundant construction may be used also for emphasis.

No se lo dieron a él; se lo dieron a Vd.   They did not give it to him; they gave it to you.

■ Práctica

Substituya según los modelos.

a. **Me dieron el dinero.**
   Me lo dieron.

   1. Me prestaron el libro.
   2. Te dieron las flores.
   3. Os pidieron el traje.
   4. Nos prestaron la casa.
   5. Me pidieron los zapatos.
   6. Te dieron la gardenia.

b. **Van a darme la blusa.**
   Van a dármela.

   1. Van a darme los libros
   2. Van a darte el sombrero.
   3. Van a daros los calcetines.
   4. Van a darnos las camisas.
   5. Van a darme el dinero.
   6. Van a darte las corbatas.

c. **Préstele el libro a ella.**
   Présteselo.

   1. Préstele el dinero a él.
   2. Présteles las camisas a ellos.
   3. Préstele los zapatos a Juan.
   4. Préstele la falda a ella.
   5. Présteles las blusas a ellas.
   6. Préstele el traje a él.

d. **No le muestre el reloj a él.**
   No se lo muestre.

   1. No les muestre la casa a ellos.
   2. No le muestre los ejercicios a él.
   3. No les muestre el traje a ellos.
   4. No les muestre las medias a ellas.
   5. No le muestre la camisa a él.
   6. No les muestre los calcetines a ellos.

2. *Cardinal numerals thirteen to twenty.*

trece	thirteen	**diecisiete**	seventeen
catorce	fourteen	**dieciocho**	eighteen
quince	fifteen	**diecinueve**	nineteen
dieciséis	sixteen	**veinte**	twenty

■ Práctica

Diga en español.

$$12 + 1 = 13 \qquad 16 + 1 = 17$$
$$13 + 1 = 14 \qquad 17 + 1 = 18$$
$$14 + 1 = 15 \qquad 18 + 1 = 19$$
$$15 + 1 = 16 \qquad 19 + 1 = 20$$

3. *Expressions of age.* Age is expressed by **tener** followed by the number of years.

Mi hermana tiene trece años.   My sister is thirteen years old.
Yo tengo veinte años.   I am twenty years old.
¿Cuántos años tiene usted?   How old are you?

Sometimes the word **edad** (*age*) is used as follows:

¿Qué edad tiene Juan?   How old is John?
Tiene diecinueve años de edad.   He is nineteen.

■ Práctica

Conteste según el modelo.

**¿Cuántos años tiene su hermano?   20
Tiene veinte años.**

1. ¿Cuántos años tiene su hermana?   18
2. ¿Cuántos años tiene el muchacho?   13
3. ¿Cuántos años tiene la joven?   19
4. ¿Cuántos años tienen sus amigos?   16
5. ¿Cuántos años tienen las alumnas?   14
6. ¿Cuántos años tienen las muchachas?   17
7. ¿Cuántos años tiene Isabel?   20
8. ¿Cuántos años tiene Roberto?   15
9. ¿Cuántos años tiene usted?   19

E. Writing

Test yourself

1. I looked for María and Virginia last night in order to invite them to go to the movies.
2. I began to look for them in the café, and I found them in the library.
3. Virginia asked me for my Spanish book, and I had to lend it to her.
4. She preferred to study, because the exams begin soon.
5. She and Carlos were in the library three hours.
6. María accepted my invitation, and we went to the movies.
7. We reached the theater at eight-thirty.
8. I bought a gardenia and gave it to her.
9. They showed a Mexican picture.
10. The well-known Mexican actor, Cantinflas, did many amusing things.

Composition

We went to the movies last night. Tell who went with us, what time we reached the theater, how long we were in the theater, what picture they showed, who the actors and actresses were, whether you liked the picture, etc.

F.   Pronunciation practice

The sound of g followed by **a, o, u** is like **g** in *go* when initial after a pause or after **n** (phonetic symbol: [g]). Pronounce the following words as you hear them.

ganga	tengo	un gato
gato	vengo	un gusto
gota	rango	un guapo
gusto	mango	un guante

In other positions **g** followed by **a, o, u** is a fricative sound produced by raising the back of the tongue towards the soft palate, but without making contact (phonetic symbol: [g̶]). Pronounce the following words as you hear them.

la ganga	una gota	mi gusto
su gato	la gorra	sus gastos

In the combinations **gue** and **gui** the **u** is silent, and the **g** has one or the other of the above pronunciations, according to its position. Pronounce the following series of words as you hear them.

[g]	[g]	[g]
guerra	en guerra	la guerra
guerrero	un guerrero	otro guerrero
guía	con guía	mi guía
guitarrista	un guitarrista	otro guitarrista

LESSON 10

A. Imperfect indicative of regular verbs

The imperfect indicative is formed by adding to the infinitive stem the following endings:

First conjugation: **-aba, -abas, -aba, -ábamos, -abais, -aban;**
Second and third conjugations: **-ía, -ías, -ía, -íamos, -íais, -ían.**

hablar	aprender	vivir
hablaba	**aprendía**	**vivía**
I was speaking	I was learning	I was living
I used to speak	I used to learn	I used to live
I spoke	I learned	I lived
hablabas	**aprendías**	**vivías**
Vd. hablaba	**Vd. aprendía**	**Vd. vivía**
hablaba	**aprendía**	**vivía**
hablábamos	**aprendíamos**	**vivíamos**
hablabais	**aprendíais**	**vivíais**
Vds. hablaban	**Vds. aprendían**	**Vds. vivían**
hablaban	**aprendían**	**vivían**

Note the written accent over the first person plural of the first conjugation and throughout the second and third conjugations.

Only three Spanish verbs are irregular in the imperfect:

ir to go	ser to be	ver to see
iba I was going, etc.	**era** I was, etc.	**veía** I saw, etc.
ibas	**eras**	**veías**
Vd. iba	**Vd. era**	**Vd. veía**
iba	**era**	**veía**
íbamos	**éramos**	**veíamos**
ibais	**erais**	**veíais**
Vds. iban	**Vds. eran**	**Vds. veían**
iban	**eran**	**veían**

■ Práctica

Cambie según se indica.

1. Yo me levantaba tarde todos los días.
   Vd. / tú / vosotros / ellos / Vd. y yo
2. Nosotros no comíamos mucho.
   yo / ella / tú / ellas / vosotros / tú y yo
3. Tú siempre escribías todos los ejercicios.
   vosotros / Vds. / Ramón / yo / nosotros
4. Ellos siempre iban temprano a la clase.
   tú / tú y yo / Vds. / vosotros / Teresa
5. Yo veía muchas películas.
   Vd. y yo / ellas / mi padre / tú / vosotros
6. Vd. no era perezoso.
   tú / yo / vosotros / nosotros / los muchachos

B. Listening and speaking

el abuelo grandfather; **los abuelos** grandparents
el caballo horse
el campo country
la ciudad city
¡claro! sure! of course!
conmigo with me
cuando when **¿cuándo?** when?
enorme enormous

la fiesta celebration
la finca farm
había there was, there were
manso gentle
mejor best
el mes month
mí *after prep.* me
nadar to swim
el niño, la niña child

pescar to fish
el rancho ranch
el río river
el rodeo roundup
el trabajo work
triste sad
la vaca cow
el vaquero cowboy
veinticinco twenty-five
el verano summer

visitar to visit

IDIOMS AND OTHER EXPRESSIONS

¡claro que sí! of course (I did, we were, etc.)!
con frecuencia frequently
montar a caballo to ride horseback
de vez en cuando from time to time

La finca y el rancho

—¿Dónde vivías cuando eras niña, Virginia?—pregunta Carlos. —¿En California?

—No, vivía en Colorado. Fuimos a California cuando tenía nueve años. Y tú, ¿dónde vivías?

—En Nueva York, donde vivimos ahora.

—¿En la ciudad o en el campo?

—En la ciudad como ahora. Pero cuando era niño iba con frecuencia al campo. Visitaba la finca de mi abuelo. Iba con frecuencia porque me gustaba visitar a mis abuelos. Pasaba con ellos un mes o dos meses del verano.

—¿Era grande la finca?

—No, no era grande, pero había veinticinco vacas y tres caballos hermosos. Había un río cerca de la finca. Los muchachos de las otras fincas pescaban conmigo en el río casi todos los días. Y cuando teníamos calor, nadábamos en el río. Para mí los meses que pasaba en el campo eran los mejores del año. Siempre estaba muy triste cuando tenía que volver a la ciudad.

—María y yo—dice Juan—íbamos también a visitar a nuestros abuelos cuando éramos niños. Nuestro abuelo tenía un rancho enorme en Tejas. Había muchos caballos en el rancho.

—¿Montaban Vds. a caballo?

—¡Claro que sí! Montábamos con frecuencia porque siempre había caballos mansos para nosotros.

—Todos los días veíamos cosas muy interesantes—dice María. —El trabajo de los vaqueros era muy interesante. Había rodeos y de vez en cuando fiestas de los vaqueros mejicanos que trabajaban en el rancho.

■ Preguntas

1. ¿Dónde vivía Virginia cuando era niña?
2. ¿Cuándo fue su familia a California?
3. ¿Dónde vivía Carlos?

 4. ¿Adónde iba Carlos con frecuencia?
 5. ¿A quiénes visitaba?
 6. ¿Cuánto tiempo pasaba Carlos con ellos en el verano?
 7. ¿Cuántas vacas había en la finca de su abuelo?
 8. ¿Qué había cerca de la finca?
 9. ¿Quiénes pescaban en el río?
10. ¿Cuándo nadaba Carlos?
11. ¿Cómo estaba Carlos cuando tenía que volver a la ciudad?
12. ¿Adónde iban Juan y María cuando eran niños?
13. ¿Qué tenía su abuelo?
14. ¿Cómo era el rancho?
15. ¿Qué había en el rancho?
16. ¿Qué hacía Juan con frecuencia?
17. ¿Qué veían Juan y María todos los días?
18. ¿Quiénes trabajaban en el rancho?
19. ¿Cómo era el trabajo de los vaqueros?
20. ¿Qué había de vez en cuando en el rancho?

C. Structure

1. *Imperfect indicative.* The imperfect indicative expresses an act that
was not completed in past time. It tells what *used to happen* or what *was
happening*. Fundamentally it expresses:

a. Customary or repeated past action (English *used to, would*).

Visitaba a mis abuelos   I used to visit my grandparents.
Nadábamos en el río.   We would (used to) swim in the river.

b. An action which covered a relatively long period of time, but the
duration of which is never stated or delimited.

Cuando éramos niños, nuestro abuelo tenía una finca.   When we were
  children, our grandfather had a farm.
Había muchos caballos en el rancho.   There were many horses on the
  ranch.

b. An action that was going on when another act happened.

Yo leía cuando él entró.   I was reading when he entered.
Mientras estudiaban, ella fue al cine.   While they were studying, she
  went to the movies.

2. *Preterit and imperfect.* The preterit, delimited in time, tells what
happened, what incident occurred. It is a narrative tense.

The imperfect, not delimited in time, tells (1) what used to happen; (2) what was happening or what state of affairs existed, often as the attendant circumstances of some other act. It is a descriptive tense.

Observe the uses of these two tenses in the following sentences:

Abrí **la puerta.**   I opened the door. (Instantaneous act.)

Sonó **el teléfono.**   The telephone rang. (Instantaneous act.)

Mientras yo *abría* **la puerta, sonó el teléfono.**   While I was opening the door, the telephone rang. (What was happening, time not delimited, when something else happened.)

Pasé **las vacaciones en el campo, donde** *vivió* **mi abuelo cuarenta años.** I spent my vacation in the country, where my grandfather lived forty years. (**Pasé,** conventionally limited period of time; **vivió,** duration of time definitely stated.)

Pasaba **las vacaciones en el campo, donde** *vivía* **mi abuelo.**   I used to spend my vacations in the country, where my grandfather lived. (**Pasaba,** what used to happen, time not delimited; **vivía,** what state of affairs existed, time not delimited.)

■ Práctica

Diga en español.

1. They used to live in Spain.
   They lived there twenty years.
2. I was not looking for them.
   I looked for them last night.
3. He would always go to the movies in the evening.
   He went to the movies last night.
4. You were very thirsty.
   You had (took) something to drink.
5. They always ate in a restaurant.
   Yesterday they ate in a restaurant.
6. She was very tired.
   She was in class three hours.
7. We always saw interesting things.
   Yesterday we saw some interesting things.
8. I wanted to look for them.
   I began to look for them.
9. When he was young, he worked a lot.
   Yesterday he worked nine hours.
10. She would always listen to me.
    She didn't listen to me last night.

3. *Prepositional forms of the personal pronoun.* Except for **mí** and **ti,** the first and second persons singular, the personal pronouns used as the object of a preposition are the same as the subject pronouns. You have been using the third person forms in the redundant construction to clarify **le, les,** and **se.**

mí	me	**nosotros (-as)**	us
ti	you (*fam.*)	**vosotros (-as)**	you (*fam.*)*
usted	you	**ustedes**	you
él	him, it	**ellos**	them
ella	her, it	**ellas**	them

El libro es para mí.   The book is for me.
Siempre había caballos para nosotros.   There were always horses for us.
Pasaba mucho tiempo con ellos.   I used to spend a lot of time with them.

When the preposition is **con,** there are special forms for the first and second persons singular: **conmigo, contigo.**

Vivían conmigo.   They lived with me.
¿Fue al cine contigo?   Did he go to the movies with you?

■ Práctica

Conteste según el modelo.

¿Para quién es el traje?   (*him*)
El traje es para él.

1. ¿Para quién es el traje?   (*you*)
2. ¿Para quién es la falda?   (*her*)
3. ¿Para quién es el sombrero?   (*me*)
4. ¿Para quién es la corbata?   (*him*)
5. ¿Para quién son las flores?   (*her*)
6. ¿Para quién son las camisas?   (*us*)
7. ¿Para quién son las gardenias?   (*you all*)
8. ¿Para quién son los zapatos?   (*them*)
9. ¿Con quién trabajaban?   (*her*)
10. ¿Con quién comían?   (*him*)
11. ¿Con quién estudiaban   (*me*)
12. ¿Con quiénes vivían?   (*us*)
13. ¿Con quiénes conversaban?   (*you all*)
14. ¿Con quién hablaban?   (*with you, Juan*)

* In Spanish America the familiar second person plural has been replaced by the formal third person plural (**ustedes**). As this principle is true of all verbs, personal pronouns, and possessives, attention will not again be directed to it.

4. *Cardinal numerals—the twenties.* The twenties may be written as one word or as three, the form in one word being more common.

21	veintiuno, veintiún, veintiuna
	(veinte y uno, veinte y un, veinte y una)
22	veintidós (veinte y dos)
23	veintitrés (veinte y tres)
24	veinticuatro (veinte y cuatro)
25	veinticinco (veinte y cinco)
26	veintiséis (veinte y seis)
27	veintisiete (veinte y siete)
28	veintiocho (veinte y ocho)
29	veintinueve (veinte y nueve)

■ Práctica

Diga en español.

$21 + 1 = 22$ $25 + 1 = 26$

21 libros $+ 2 = 23$ $26 + 1 = 27$

21 blusas $+ 3 = 25$ $27 + 1 = 28$

24 clases $+ 1 = 25$ $28 + 1 = 29$

D. Writing

Test yourself

1. When I was a child, I lived in the city.
2. But I went to the country frequently to visit my grandparents.
3. They had twenty-five cows and three horses on their farm.
4. There were boys on the other farms, and I used to fish with them.
5. When we were warm, we could swim in the river.
6. John's grandfather had an enormous ranch in Texas.
7. John and I used to ride horseback nearly every day.
8. Mary would go with me, too.
9. We would see many interesting things.

Composition

Imagine that your grandfather had a farm when you were a child. Tell what you used to see there and what you used to do.

E. Pronunciation practice

In Spanish n is pronounced as m before b, v, p, f, and m. Pronounce the following words as you hear them.

en Vigo	un país	enfermo	un millón
en Barcelona	un padre	en febrero	un mejicano
un burro	en parte	en francés	en marzo
un vaso	en portugués	en Francia	en mayo

In Spanish n is like n in *think* before g and j. It has the same sound before qu, k, and c when pronounced as k. Pronounce the following words as you hear them.

un gasto	un joven	un queso
un gusto	un jueves	con quien
un guitarrista	con Juan	un kilo
un guisante	en julio	en casa
un guante	un gimnasio	un caballo
un guapo	un general	un café

ALLÁ EN EL RANCHO GRANDE*

Original Words and Music by SILVANO R. RAMOS

Spanish lyrics by J. del Moral

Music arranged by EMILIO D. URANGA

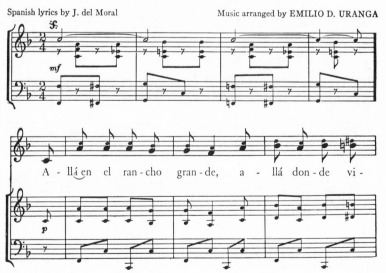

A - llá en el ran-cho gran-de, a - llá don-de vi-

*Copyrighted by Edward B. Marks Music Corporation. Used by permission.

ví - a,＿＿＿ ha - bía u -na ran - che - ri - ta que a -

le - gre me de - cí - a, que a - le - gre me de - cí - a.＿＿

rit.

Te voy a ha - cer＿＿ tus cal - zo - nes,＿＿
Nun - ca te fí - es de pro - me - sas,＿＿

p

＿＿ co - mo los u - sa el ran - che - ro;＿＿
＿＿ ni mu - cho me - nos de a - mo - res;

__ te los co - mien - zo de la - na,___ te los a -
__ que si te dan ca - la - ba - zas___ ve - rás lo

ca - bo de cue - ro.
que son ar - do - res.

D. S.

D. S.
varias veces

Everybody wants to win the *premio gordo* in the lottery. The northern Spaniard's *boina* is larger than the French beret. (Three Lions, Inc.)

Feria time in Seville. (Philip D. Gendreau)

Holy Week procession in Cuenca. Notice the picturesque hats of the
Guardias Civiles. (Spanish National Tourist Office)

University students
wearing white silk
collars used for
ceremonial occasions.
(Three Lions, Inc.)

Women making lace under the acacia trees in front of their homes.
(Philip D. Gendreau)

Bullfight posters are always fascinating. (Philip D. Gendreau)

LESSON 11

A. Past participle of the regular verb

The past participle is formed by removing the infinitive ending and adding to the stem the following endings: **-ado** for the first conjugation and **-ido** for the second and third conjugations.

hablar: hablado spoken
aprender: aprendido learned
vivir: vivido lived

B. Present perfect indicative

The present perfect indicative of a verb is formed by combining the past participle of the verb with the present indicative of **haber** (*to have*). It is normally used where we use the present perfect tense in English.

hablar	vivir
he hablado	**he vivido**
I have spoken	I have lived
has hablado	**has vivido**
you have spoken	you have lived
Vd. ha hablado	**Vd. ha vivido**
you have spoken	you have lived
ha hablado	**ha vivido**
he (she) has spoken	he (she) has lived
hemos hablado	**hemos vivido**
we have spoken	we have lived
habéis hablado	**habéis vivido**
you have spoken	you have lived
Vds. han hablado	**Vds. han vivido**
you have spoken	you have lived
han hablado	**han vivido**
they have spoken	they have lived

■ Práctica

Cambie según se indica.

1. Hemos contestado bien.
   yo / Vd. / vosotros / tú / tú y yo / los alumnos
2. No han vivido en España.
   tú / vosotros / yo / nosotros / mis padres
3. ¿Ha aprendido Vd. mucho?
   Vds. / tú / nosotros / yo / él / ellas

C. Irregular past participles

Some past participles are irregular. Among the verbs you have learned so far, the following have irregular past participles:

decir: dicho   said
escribir: escrito   written
hacer: hecho   done, made
morir: muerto   died (dead)
poner: puesto   put, placed
ver: visto   seen
volver: vuelto   returned, gone back
devolver: devuelto   returned, given back

■ Práctica

Conteste según el modelo.

¿Va Vd. a estudiar la lección?
Ya la he estudiado.

1. ¿Va Vd. a ver al profesor?
2. ¿Va Vd. a devolver el traje?
3. ¿Va Vd. a escribir la composición?
4. ¿Va Vd. a ponerse el sombrero?
5. ¿Va Vd. a hacer el trabajo?
6. ¿Va Vd. a decir la verdad?
7. ¿Va Vd. a volver?
8. ¿Va a morir el viejo?

D. Listening and speaking

brillante brilliant
caído *past. part of* **caer** fallen
el campeonato championship

el compromiso engagement, appointment
contra against; to (*in scores*)

cuarenta y nueve forty-nine
el domingo (on) Sunday
entonces then
el equipo team
la excursión de estudio field trip
el fútbol football
ganar to win
la geología geology
importante important
el jueves (on) Thursday
la jugada play (*in a game*)
jugar (ue) to play (*a game*)
el lunes (on) Monday
el martes (on) Tuesday
mejor better, best
el miércoles (on) Wednesday
el mío mine
el nuestro ours
el partido game (match)
perder (ie) to lose
recordar (ue) to remember
el sábado (on) Saturday

salir to go out, leave
el suelo ground
el suyo theirs (his, hers, yours)
tampoco neither
el tanto point (*in a game*)
treinta y seis thirty-six
el viernes (on) Friday
visto *past part. of* ver seen

IDIOMS AND OTHER EXPRESSIONS

la clase del miércoles the
  Wednesday class
hacer una excursión to go on a
  (day) trip, excursion
pasado mañana the day after
  tomorrow
por supuesto of course
¡qué (jugada)! what a (play)!
la semana que viene next week
tal vez perhaps

El fútbol

Carlos. —¿Qué hiciste ayer? No te vi.

Juan. —¿Ayer? Vamos a ver . . . ayer fue lunes . . . Ah, sí, fui al campo.
El domingo unos amigos que estudian geología me invitaron a[1] hacer una
excursión de estudio con ellos. La hicimos ayer.

Carlos. —¿Se divirtieron Vds.? ¿Fue interesante la excursión?

Juan. —Mucho.[2]

Carlos. —¿Quieres ir al cine conmigo?

Juan. —Hoy no puedo. Los martes siempre tengo que escribir una
composición para la clase del miércoles.

Carlos. —¿Pasado mañana, entonces?

Juan. —Tampoco. El jueves voy a salir con Virginia. Y el viernes
tengo un compromiso. Tiene que ser la semana que viene.

Carlos. —¿La semana que viene? Pues, ¿qué haces el sábado?

Juan. ¿No recuerdas? El sábado vamos al partido de fútbol. El partido
va a ser muy importante y quiero verlo.

(*El sábado*) *Juan.* —¡Qué jugada! ¿Has visto, Virginia? ¡Otros siete
tantos!

Virginia. —¿Quiénes van a ganar?

Juan. —Nosotros, por supuesto. Los dos equipos son buenos. El de
ellos ha jugado muy bien, pero el nuestro ha jugado mejor. El suyo no
puede ganar. ¿Te ha gustado el partido?

Virginia. —¡Sí, claro! Me he divertido[3] mucho.

Juan. ¡Mira, Virginia! Hemos ganado. ¡Cuarenta y nueve tantos contra treinta y seis! Los nuestros han ganado el campeonato.

Virginia. —Las jugadas han sido brillantes, ¿verdad?

Juan. —Brillantes y ... ¡caramba! He perdido el sombrero. ¿Lo has visto tú? Tal vez ha caído al suelo. No quiero perderlo.

Virginia. —No importa. ¡Te doy el mío!

■ Preguntas

1. ¿Qué hizo Juan ayer?
2. ¿Adónde fue?
3. ¿Con quiénes fue Juan?
4. ¿Adónde quiere ir Carlos?
5. ¿Qué día es hoy?
6. ¿Por qué no puede Juan acompañar a Carlos?
7. ¿Qué hace Juan los martes?
8. ¿Por qué no puede ir Juan el jueves?
9. ¿Qué van a hacer Juan y Carlos el sábado?
10. ¿Cómo son los dos equipos?
11. ¿Cuál ha jugado mejor?
12. ¿Quiénes han ganado?
13. ¿Con cuántos tantos ganaron?
14. ¿Qué han ganado además del partido?
15. ¿Qué ha perdido Juan?
16. ¿Qué le dice Virginia?

NOTES

1. **Invitar** takes the preposition **a** before a following infinitive.

   Me invitaron a hacer una excursión de estudio.   They invited me to go on a field trip.

2. Where English uses the word *very* standing alone, Spanish uses **mucho.**
3. Nothing may separate the auxiliary verb **haber** and the past participle. Object pronouns, including reflexives, therefore precede the auxiliary.

   Los he comprado.   I have bought them.
   Me he divertido.   I have had a good time.

   In questions, for the same reason, the subject follows the past participle.

   ¿Lo ha visto usted?   Have you seen it?

E. Structure

1. *Possessive pronouns.* The possessive pronouns in Spanish are as follows:

el mío	la mía	los míos	las mías	mine
el tuyo	la tuya	los tuyos	las tuyas	yours
el nuestro	la nuestra	los nuestros	las nuestras	ours
el vuestro	la vuestra	los vuestros	las vuestras	yours
el suyo	la suya	los suyos	las suyas	yours, his, hers, its, theirs

a. The possessive pronoun agrees in gender and number with the thing possessed, not with the possessor.

mi corbata　my necktie: *la mía*　*mine*
nuestra casa　our house: *la nuestra*　*ours*
sus padres　your (his, her, their) parents: *los suyos*　*yours (his, hers, theirs)*

b. The definite article is part of the pronoun and must always be used.

　　las mías　mine　　　**el nuestro**　ours　　　**los suyos**　yours

c. Since **el suyo (la suya, los suyos, las suyas)** may be ambiguous, the ambiguity is avoided by substituting as follows:

el de él　his　　　　　**el de ellos**　theirs *m.*
el de ella　hers　　　　**el de ellas**　theirs *f.*
el de usted　yours　　　**el de ustedes**　yours

El de él, etc., is changed to **la de él, los de él,** or **las de él, etc.,** depending on the gender of the thing possessed.

el sombrero de Vd. y el de ella　your hat and hers
mi casa y la de ellos　my house and theirs
nuestros libros y los de él　our books and his

These longer forms are also used for emphasis, in contrasts.

■ Práctica

Substituya según los modelos.

a. **Tengo mi corbata.**
　　Tengo la mía.

1. Vd. tiene su corbata.
2. Vd. tiene sus camisas.
3. Él tiene sus zapatos.
4. Él tiene su casa.
5. Tenemos nuestra finca.
6. Tenemos nuestro caballo.
7. Tenemos nuestras amigas.
8. Tú tienes tus ejercicios.
9. Tú tienes tu invitación.
10. Tienen su orquesta.
11. Tienen sus calcetines.
12. Vosotros tenéis vuestro libro.
13. Vosotros tenéis vuestras blusas.
14. Tengo mis sombreros.
15. Tengo mis ideas.

b. **¿Has visto el rancho de su abuelo?**
   ¿Has visto el de él?

1. ¿Has visto la casa de María?
2. ¿Has visto el sombrero de Tomás?
3. ¿Has visto la finca de su padre?
4. ¿Has visto el programa de las niñas?
5. ¿Has visto los trajes de mi hermano?
6. ¿Has visto las vacas del vaquero?

2. *Days of the week*

el lunes (on) Monday
el martes (on) Tuesday
el miércoles (on) Wednesday
el jueves (on) Thursday
el viernes (on) Friday
el sábado (on) Saturday
el domingo (on) Sunday

El jueves voy al cine.   On Thursday I am going to the movies.
Ayer fue lunes.   Yesterday was Monday.
Los sábados no trabajo.   On Saturdays I don't work.
Los martes tienen dos clases.   On Tuesdays they have two classes.

The names of the days of the week are masculine. They are not capitalized. Except after **ser**, they are used with the definite article. The English preposition *on* is not translated literally. **Sábado** and **domingo** form their plurals regularly. The names of the other days have the same form for both singular and plural.

■ Práctica

Conteste en español.

a. 1. ¿Cuántas clases tiene usted el lunes?
   2. ¿Qué hace usted el martes?
   3. ¿Siempre escribe usted una composición el miércoles?
   4. ¿Qué va usted a hacer el jueves?
   5. ¿Va usted al cine el viernes?
   6. ¿Tiene usted un compromiso el sábado?
   7. ¿Tiene usted clases los domingos?

b. 1. Si hoy es lunes, ¿qué día fue ayer?
   2. Si hoy es martes, ¿qué día va a ser mañana?
   3. Si hoy es jueves, ¿qué día va a ser pasado mañana?
   4. Si hoy es domingo, ¿qué día va a ser mañana?
   5. Si hoy es sábado, ¿qué día fue ayer?

3. *More cardinal numerals.* The thirties and forties follow the pattern
of the twenties, except that they are seldom written as one word.

31 treinta y uno	**48 cuarenta y ocho**
32 treinta y dos	**49 cuarenta y nueve**

■ Práctica

a. *Diga en español.*

30 + uno son 31	40 + dos = 42
32 + uno son 33	41 + dos = 43
34 + dos son 36	44 + dos = 46
35 + dos son 37	45 + dos = 47
38 + uno son 39	48 + dos = 50

b. *Cuente de 1 a 50 en español.*

F. Writing

Test yourself

1. Yesterday was Friday.
2. On Monday Juan went on a field trip with some students of geology.
3. "Was the trip interesting?" "Very."
4. Carlos invites him to go to the movies on Tuesday, but he can't go
   because he has to write a composition for his Wednesday class.

5. On Thursday he is going out with Virginia.
6. On Friday he has another engagement.
7. The football game has been very interesting; we have seen some brilliant plays.
8. The two teams have played well, but ours has been better.
9. Theirs is not going to win.
10. Ours has won—with forty-nine points!
11. And they have won the championship, too.
12. Virginia has had a very good time.
13. Juan has lost his hat.
14. Virginia says that she is going to give him hers!

Composition

We have been attending a football game. Write a composition telling who has accompanied us, how the two teams have been, which has played better, which has won, whether we have won the championship, whether we have had a good time, etc.

LESSON 12

A. Future indicative of regular verbs

The future indicative is formed by adding to the whole infinitive the following endings: **-é, -ás, -á, -emos, -éis, -án.**

hablar

hablaré I shall speak	**hablaremos** we shall speak
hablarás you will speak	**hablaréis** you will speak
Vd. hablará you will speak	**Vds. hablarán** you will speak
hablará he (she) will speak	**hablarán** they will speak

aprender	vivir
aprenderé I shall learn	**viviré** I shall live
aprenderás	**vivirás**
Vd. aprenderá	**Vd. vivirá**
aprenderá	**vivirá**
aprenderemos	**viviremos**
aprenderéis	**viviréis**
Vds. aprenderán	**Vds. vivirán**
aprenderán	**vivirán**

Note the written accent over each of the endings except the first person plural.

130

B. Future indicative of irregular verbs

The future of many irregular verbs is regular: **seré,** *I shall be*; **estaré,** *I shall be*; **iré,** *I shall go*; etc. The future of some others is not; but the irregularity always occurs in the infinitive stem, never in the endings.

hacer	decir	salir	tener

haré
    I shall do, make
	diré
	    I shall say
		saldré
		    I shall leave
			tendré
			    I shall have

harás	**dirás**	**saldrás**	**tendrás**
hará	**dirá**	**saldrá**	**tendrá**
haremos	**diremos**	**saldremos**	**tendremos**
haréis	**diréis**	**saldréis**	**tendréis**
harán	**dirán**	**saldrán**	**tendrán**

■ Práctica

a. *Cambie al plural, según el modelo.*

Estaré aquí mañana.
Estaremos aquí mañana.

1. Bailaré con ella.
2. Leeré el libro.
3. Escribiré el ejercicio.
4. Tú estudiarás.
5. Tú comprenderás.
6. Tú se lo dirás.
7. Vd. hará una excursión.
8. Vd. estará contento.
9. Él saldrá mañana.
10. Ella tendrá miedo.

b. *Cambie al singular, según el modelo.*

Ellos me contestarán.
Él me contestará.

1. Iremos a Méjico.
2. Trabajaremos mucho.
3. Seremos buenos.
4. Vosotros lo veréis.
5. Vosotros lo haréis.

6. Vosotros lo leeréis.
7. Vds. saldrán temprano.
8. Vds. tendrán frío.
9. Ellas lo harán.
10. Ellos lo dirán.

c. *Continúe según el modelo.*

Tú quieres estudiar y _____.
Tú quieres estudiar y estudiarás.

1. Yo quiero hacerlo y lo _____.
2. Ellos quieren decirlo y lo _____.
3. Tú quieres salir y _____.
4. Queréis tenerlo y lo _____.
5. Queremos bailar y _____.
6. Queréis hablar y _____.
7. Tú quieres volver y _____.
8. Ellos quieren sentarse y _____.
9. Juan quiere acostarse y _____.
10. Quieren ir y mañana _____.

C. Listening and speaking

bailar to dance
bajar to go down
cien, ciento a hundred
el comedor dining room
la cubierta deck
descansar to rest
habrá *3d pers. sing., fut. of*
  haber there will be
la medianoche midnight
el mediodía noon
la merienda light lunch, picnic
  lunch
mío my, of mine
muchísimo very much
noventa ninety
nuestro of ours
el paisaje landscape
pasearse to stroll

por for; around
¡qué (linda)! how (pretty)!
sobre on
subir to go up
suyo of his (hers, yours, theirs)
tanto so; so much
el vapor steamer, boat

IDIOMS AND OTHER EXPRESSIONS

a bordo on board
a la luz (light) **de la luna** (moon)
  by moonlight
¡Dios mío! my goodness!
otra vez again
río arriba up the river
si las hay if there are any

Una excursión en vapor

Carlos ha dicho que un amigo suyo ha hecho una excursión río arriba
en vapor. Fue muy agradable, y mañana nosotros también haremos la
excursión.

Tendremos que salir de la casa a las siete de la mañana. Virginia, Juan y su hermana María irán con nosotros. También irán otros amigos nuestros. Irán muchos alumnos de la universidad. Habrá tal vez noventa o cien personas.

Saldrá el vapor a las ocho y cuarto. Pasaremos la mañana paseándonos por la cubierta y mirando el paisaje. Al mediodía comeremos una merienda. Luego descansaremos un rato y como nos gusta tanto hablar español, lo hablaremos. Nos gustan las canciones españolas y las cantaremos.

Pasaremos la tarde divirtiéndonos en la cubierta, cantando y hablando.

A la hora de la comida bajaremos al comedor. Después de comer subiremos otra vez a la cubierta. Habrá una buena orquesta a bordo y bailaremos a la luz de la luna.

Yo me pasearé con una amiga mía y bailaré con ella.

—¡Dios mío!—le diré—¡qué linda eres y qué bien bailas!

Compraré unas flores, si las hay a bordo, y se las daré.

¡Qué agradable será la excursión!

Estaremos a bordo hasta medianoche o hasta la una divirtiéndonos muchísimo.

■ Preguntas

1. ¿Qué ha dicho Carlos?
2. ¿Cómo fue la excursión?
3. ¿Qué haremos nosotros?
4. ¿Quiénes irán con nosotros?
5. ¿Cuántas personas habrá a bordo?
6. ¿A qué hora saldrá el vapor?
7. ¿Cómo pasaremos la mañana?
8. ¿Qué haremos al mediodía?
9. ¿Qué haremos después?
10. ¿Qué lengua hablaremos?
11. ¿Qué cantaremos?
12. ¿Cómo pasaremos la tarde?
13. A la hora de la comida ¿adónde iremos?
14. ¿Qué haremos después de la comida?
15. ¿Qué haremos por la noche?
16. ¿Qué habrá a bordo?
17. ¿Con quién se paseará Vd.?
18. ¿Qué le dirá Vd.?
19. ¿Qué comprará Vd., si las hay?
20. ¿Hasta qué hora estaremos a bordo?

D. Structure

1. *Possessive adjectives—stressed forms*

mío, mía, míos, mías	my, mine, of mine
tuyo, tuya, tuyos, tuyas	yours, of yours
nuestro, nuestra, nuestros, nuestras	our, ours, of ours
vuestro, vuestra, vuestros, vuestras	yours, of yours
suyo, suya, suyos, suyas	yours (his, hers, theirs), of yours (his, hers, theirs)

The stressed forms of the possessive adjective follow the noun. Their forms are the same as those of the possessive pronouns (see Lesson 11), but they are used without the accompanying definite article. Like the other possessives, they agree in gender and number with the thing possessed.

a. Their commonest meaning is *of mine, of yours, etc.*

un amigo suyo   a friend of his (hers, yours, theirs)
unas amigas mías   some friends of mine

b. They are used after the verb **ser** to denote possession.

¿De quién es la corbata? Es *mía*.   Whose tie is it? It is *mine*.
¿De quién es el sombrero? Es *suyo*.   Whose hat is it? It is *yours (his, hers, theirs)*.

c. **Suyo,** like **su** and **el suyo,** may be ambiguous. When it is, the phrases **de él, de ella, de usted, de ellos, de ellas,** or **de ustedes** are substituted for it.

un libro de usted   a book of yours
un tío de ellos   an uncle of theirs
¿Son de ustedes los libros?   Are the books yours?

d. **Mío,** *my,* and **nuestro,** *our,* are used in direct address and exclamations.

Hijo mío, ¿qué haces?   Son (my son), what are you doing?
Padre nuestro que estás en los cielos ...   Our Father which art in Heaven ...
¡Dios mío!   My goodness!

■ Práctica

a. *Substituya según el modelo.*

Son mis zapatos.
Son unos zapatos míos.

1. Es mi vestido.
2. Es su hermana.
3. Son tus amigos.
4. Son tus libros.
5. Es vuestro profesor.
6. Es nuestra amiga.
7. Son nuestros caballos.
8. Son mis corbatas.

b. *Substituya según el modelo.*

Es mi traje.
Es mío.

1. Es mi blusa.
2. Son mis calcetines.
3. Es su tienda.
4. Son sus ranchos.
5. Son tus ejercicios.
6. Es nuestra finca.
7. Son vuestros libros.
8. Es vuestra casa.

c. *Diga en español, empleando dos formas, según el modelo.*

an uncle of his
un tío suyo
un tío de él

1. a tie of his
2. books of theirs
3. flowers of hers
4. a suit of yours
5. a farm of theirs
6. friends of his
7. a house of theirs
8. a brother of hers
9. a sister of yours
10. sisters of his

2. *The gerund.* The Spanish gerund, corresponding to the English present participle (*speaking, learning, etc.*) is formed by adding **-ando** to the infinitive stem of all regular and irregular verbs of the first conjugation and **-iendo** to the infinitive stem of all regular and most irregular verbs of the second and third conjugations.

hablar: habl*ando* speaking	**estar: est***ando* being
aprender: aprend*iendo* learning	**ser:** *siendo* being
vivir: viv*iendo* living	**ver:** *viendo* seeing

Stem-changing verbs of Classes II and III (**-ir** verbs) change **e** to **i** and **o** to **u** in the gerund.

sentir: sintiendo   regretting
morir: muriendo   dying
pedir: pidiendo   asking

Verbs like **leer** (whose stem ends in a strong vowel) change the **i** of the ending to **y: leyendo**   reading.

The following irregular verbs which you already know have irregular gerunds:

decir: diciendo   saying
ir: yendo   going
poder: pudiendo   being able

Object pronouns, including reflexives, follow and are attached to the gerund. A gerund with a pronoun attached requires a written accent.

Puesto que me gusta estudiar el español, pasé la tarde *estudiándolo.*
Since I like to study Spanish, I spent the afternoon *studying it.*
Pasaremos la mañana *paseándonos* **por la cubierta.**   We shall spend the
morning *strolling* around the deck.
Estarán a bordo hasta la una *divirtiéndose muchísimo.*   They will be on
board until one o'clock *having a very good time.*

■ Práctica

Conteste según el modelo.

¿Cómo pasarás la tarde? ¿Vas a estudiar?
Pasaré la tarde estudiando.

1. ¿Vas a aprender?
2. ¿Vas a escribir?
3. ¿Vas a leer?
4. ¿Vas a pasearte?
5. ¿Vas a divertirte?
6. ¿Vas a dormir?
7. ¿Vas a vestirte?
8. ¿Vas a cantar?
9. ¿Vas a comer?
10. ¿Vas a bailar?

3. *More cardinal numbers.* The fifties through the nineties follow the same pattern as the thirties and forties.

51 cincuenta y uno   **88 ochenta y ocho**
62 sesenta y dos   **99 noventa y nueve**
73 setenta y tres   **100 ciento (cien)**

Ciento drops the final **-o** before any noun.

cien hombres a hundred men   **cien personas** a hundred persons

■ Práctica

a. *Lea en español.*

1. Habrá 50 muchachas.
2. Habrá 60 libros.
3. Habrá 70 vapores.
4. Habrá 80 caballos.
5. Habrá 90 alumnos.
6. Habrá 100 personas.

b. *Diga en español.*

1. 53 más uno son 54.
2. 55 más uno son 56.
3. 67 más dos son 69.
4. 68 más dos son 70.
5. 76 más uno son 77.
6. 84 más uno son 85.
7. 87 más dos son 89.
8. 91 más dos son 93.
9. 98 más dos son 100.

E. Writing

Test yourself

1. Tomorrow I shall go on a boat trip up the river.
2. Some friends of mine and some friends of yours will go with me.
3. I shall leave at nine-thirty.
4. I shall spend the morning strolling around the deck and looking at the landscape.
5. At noon I shall eat a picnic lunch.
6. In the afternoon we shall sing Cuban songs.
7. After dinner we shall go up on deck again.

8. There will be a good orchestra on board which will play in the evening.
9. Our sweethearts will be with us and we shall dance by moonlight.
10. We shall be on board until midnight having a very good time.
11. My goodness! How interesting it will be!

Composition

Write a composition about a boat trip which you (*singular*) will take tomorrow.

LA GOLONDRINA

Arranged by EMILIO de TORRE

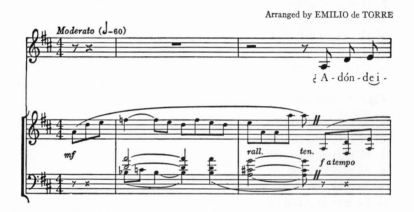

dri - na que de a-quí se va, _____ o si en el
sión _____ que me mi - ró na - cer, _____ mi vi - da es

vien - to se ha-lla-rá ex - tra-via - da bus-can-do a -
hoy _____ e - rran-te y an - gus - tia - da y ya no

bri - go y no lo en-con - tra - rá? _____ Jun-to a mi
pue - do a mi man-sión vol - ver. _____ A - ve que-

le - cho le pon - dré su ni - do en don - de
ri - da, a - ma - da pe - re - gri - na, mi co - ra -

pue - da___ la es - ta - ción___ pa - sar;___ tam - bién yo es -
zón___ al tu - yo es - tre - cha - ré,___ oi - ré tu

toy___ en la re - gión per - di - do ¡oh, cie - lo
can to, tier - na go - lon - dri - na, re - cor - da -

san - to!y sin po - der vo - lar.____ De - jé tam -
ré   mi pa-tria y llo - ra -   ré.

LESSON 13

A. Conditional tense of regular verbs

The conditional tense, like the future (see Lesson 12), is formed by adding certain endings to the whole infinitive. The endings are: **-ía, -ías, -ía, -íamos, -íais, -ían.**

hablar

hablaría I would speak	**hablaríamos** we would speak
hablarías you would speak	**hablaríais** you would speak
Vd. hablaría you would speak	**Vds. hablarían** you would speak
hablaría he (she) would speak	**hablarían** they would speak

aprender	vivir
aprendería I would learn	**viviría** I would live
aprenderías	**vivirías**
Vd. aprendería	**Vd. viviría**
aprendería	**viviría**
aprenderíamos	**viviríamos**
aprenderíais	**viviríais**
Vds. aprenderían	**Vds. vivirían**
aprenderían	**vivirían**

Note the written accent on the first **i** of the ending throughout.

142

■ Práctica

Cambie según se indica, siguiendo el modelo.

Sabían que él cantaría.
Sabían que Vds. cantarían.

1. Sabían que él cantaría.
   yo / tú / vosotros / Vd. / Vd. y yo / ellos
2. Parecía que Vd. volvería.
   nosotros / Vds. / yo / tú / vosotros / ella
3. Expliqué que nosotros escribiríamos.
   yo / Vd. y yo / ellos / tú / vosotros / él

B. Irregular conditionals

Whenever the stem of the future is irregular, the same irregularity is to be found in the conditional. The conditional of each of the four irregular verbs whose futures you learned in Lesson 12 is therefore as follows. (Only the first person singular of each is given.)

INFINITIVE	FUTURE	CONDITIONAL
hacer	**haré**	**haría** I would do, make
decir	**diré**	**diría** I would say
salir	**saldré**	**saldría** I would leave
tener	**tendré**	**tendría** I would have

■ Práctica

Cambie según se indica, siguiendo el modelo.

Explicaron que yo lo haría.
Explicaron que tú lo harías.

1. Explicaron que yo lo haría.
   tú / Vd. / nosotros / vosotros / ellas
2. Sabían que tú lo dirías.
   yo / ellos / Vd. / Vd. y yo / vosotros
3. Dijeron que Vd. no saldría.
   Vds. / tú / vosotros / yo / tú y yo / él
4. Creían que él lo tendría.
   tú / yo / nosotros / vosotros / ellos

C. More irregular futures and conditionals

INFINITIVE	FUTURE	CONDITIONAL	
querer	querré	querría	I would wish
saber	sabré	sabría	I would know
poder	podré	podría	I would be able
haber	habré	habría	I would have (gone, etc.)
poner	pondré	pondría	I would put, place
venir	vendré	vendría	I would come
valer	valdré	valdría	I would be worth

■ Práctica

a. *Cambie el singular por el plural, según el modelo.*

Yo querré hablar.
Nosotros querremos hablar.

1. Yo sabré estudiar.
2. Tú podrás hacerlo.
3. Él se pondrá el sombrero.
4. Yo vendré pronto.
5. La casa valdrá mucho.
6. Tú querrás salir.
7. Yo sabría estudiar.
8. Tú podrías hacerlo.
9. Él se pondría el sombrero.
10. Yo vendría pronto.
11. La casa valdría mucho.
12. Tú querrías salir.

b. *Cambie el plural por el singular, según el modelo.*

Vds. podrán volver pronto.
Vd. podrá volver pronto.

1. Ellos sabrán estudiar.
2. Ellas podrán hacerlo.
3. Nosotros nos pondremos el sombrero.
4. Vosotros vendréis pronto.
5. Los libros valdrán mucho.
6. Nosotros querremos salir.
7. Ellos sabrían estudiar.
8. Vosotros podríais hacerlo.

9. Nosotros nos pondríamos el sombrero.
10. Vosotros vendríais pronto.
11. Los libros valdrían mucho.
12. Nosotros querríamos salir.

D. Listening and speaking

aquel, aquella *demons. adj.* that
aquél, aquélla *demons. pron.*
 that (one)
el béisbol baseball
la cancha (tennis) court
demasiado too; too much
el deporte sport
desocupado unoccupied, free
ese, esa *demons. adj.* that
eso *n. demons. pron.* that
esperar to wait
este, esta *demons. adj.* this
éste, ésta *demons. pron.* this (one)
el gasto expense
generoso generous
el gimnasio gymnasium
interrumpir to interrupt
ligero light
más . . . que more . . . than
el minuto minute
observar to observe
pesar to weigh
prometer to promise

pues for, since
quedarse to remain, stay
la raqueta racket
regalar to give (*as a gift*)
el regalo gift
responder to answer
solo alone
el tenis tennis
el tío uncle

IDIOMS AND OTHER EXPRESSIONS

el año pasado last year
buen mozo good-looking
a estas horas at this time
de al lado next
me gusta más I like (it) better
(las tres) en punto (three
 o'clock) sharp
querer decir to mean
más tiempo longer
valer la pena to be worth while

Un partido de tenis

Una tarde Virginia le preguntó a María:—¿Dónde estará Juan?
—Estará jugando al tenis o estará en el gimnasio. Tú sabrás que le
gustan los deportes. Todos los días a estas horas va al gimnasio o juega[1]
al tenis o al béisbol.
—Eso querrá decir que no vendrá a buscarme. Son las tres y media, y
prometió anoche que vendría por mí a las tres y que jugaríamos un partido
de tenis. Me prometió que pasaría por aquí a las tres en punto. Ahora
tendré que quedarme en casa, pues no podría ir sola.
—No valdría la pena esperar más tiempo—contestó María. —Pero no
tendrás que quedarte en casa. Yo me pondré el traje de tenis, buscaré
mi raqueta, e[2] iré contigo.
Quince minutos después Virginia y María salieron de la casa para ir a la
cancha de tenis.

—Esa raqueta—observó Virginia—me gusta más que la mía. Parece más ligera que ésta. Ésta pesa demasiado.

—Esta raqueta—contestó María—es un regalo de un tío mío. Me la regaló cuando volví a la universidad esta semana. Me dio también cien dólares para los gastos de la universidad.

—Ese tío tuyo es más generoso que mi padre. ¡Él no me dio tanto!

—Pero hemos llegado—interrumpió María. —Hay dos canchas desocupadas. ¿Prefieres ésta o aquélla? Ésta está más cerca. Y es más interesante que aquélla. ¡Porque en la cancha de al lado están jugando aquellos dos jóvenes que son tan buenos mozos!

—¡Sí, claro! ¡Vamos a tomarla! Es la más interesante.

■ Preguntas

1. ¿Qué pregunta Virginia una tarde?
2. ¿Qué responde María?
3. ¿Qué le gusta a Juan?
4. ¿Adónde va Juan todos los días a estas horas?
5. ¿A qué juega?
6. ¿Qué hora es?
7. ¿Qué prometió Juan anoche?
8. ¿Qué tendría que hacer Virginia?
9. ¿Qué no podría hacer Virginia?
10. ¿Qué le dice María?
11. ¿Qué se pondrá María?
12. ¿Qué buscará?
13. ¿Cuál de las raquetas le gusta más a Virginia?
14. ¿Por qué?
15. ¿Quién le regaló la raqueta a María?
16. ¿Cómo es el tío de María?
17. ¿Cuál de las canchas prefieren las señoritas?
18. ¿Por qué?

NOTES

1. **Jugar,** *to play,* is conjugated like Class I stem-changing verbs with stem vowel **o.** It takes the preposition **a** before the name of a specific sport.

   Carlos juega al tenis. Charles plays tennis.
   Está jugando al fútbol ahora. He is playing football now.

2. **Y** becomes **e** before a word beginning with **i** or **hi.**

   e iré con usted and I shall go with you.
   padres e hijos parents and children

O becomes **u** before a word beginning with **o** or **ho.**

siete u ocho   seven or eight
pensiones u hoteles   boarding houses or hotels

E. Structure

1. *Special uses of the future and conditional.* The future tense has a special use: to express conjecture or probability in present time.

¿Dónde estará Juan?   Where can John be? I wonder where John is. Where do you suppose John is?
Estará en el gimnasio.   He is probably in the gymnasium. He must be in the gymnasium.
Tú lo sabrás.   You must know. You probably know.

The conditional tense expresses the same ideas in past time.

¿Dónde estaría Juan ayer?   Where could John have been yesterday? I wonder where John was yesterday. Where do you suppose John was yesterday?
Estaría en el gimnasio.   He probably was in the gymnasium. He must have been in the gymnasium.
Tú lo sabrías.   You must have known. You probably knew.

■ Práctica

a. *Diga en español.*
   1. María is probably at home.
   2. She is probably studying.
   3. She probably works a lot.
   4. She must like to play tennis.
   5. She must like horses.

b. *Diga en español.*
   1. Where do you suppose Juan and Carlos were?
   2. What do you suppose they were doing?
   3. Where do you suppose they went?
   4. They probably were in the gymnasium.
   5. They probably played tennis, too.
   6. They probably didn't study.

2. *Demonstrative adjectives.* Spanish has three demonstrative adjectives: **este,** *this*; **ese,** *that*; **aquel,** *that.*
Each has four forms: masculine singular and feminine singular, masculine plural and feminine plural.

SINGULAR		PLURAL	
Masculine	*Feminine*	*Masculine*	*Feminine*
este	esta	estos	estas
ese	esa	esos	esas
aquel	aquella	aquellos	aquellas

Ese means *that,* near or pertaining to the person spoken to; **aquel** means *that* remote from both the person speaking and the person spoken to,—*i.e., that over there, that yonder, etc.*

este libro y ese libro de Vd.   this book and that book of yours
esta cancha y aquella cancha   this court and that court (over there)

■ Práctica

a. *Conteste según el modelo.*

¿Prefieres esta raqueta?
No, prefiero esa raqueta.

1. ¿Prefieres este deporte?
2. ¿Prefieres estos zapatos?
3. ¿Prefieres estas blusas?
4. ¿Prefieres esta cancha?
5. ¿Prefieres este vapor?

b. *Conteste según el modelo.*

¿Quiere usted ese sombrero?
No, quiero este sombrero.

1. ¿Quiere usted esos libros?
2. ¿Quiere usted esa cancha?
3. ¿Quiere usted ese traje?
4. ¿Quiere usted esos regalos?
5. ¿Quiere usted esas flores?

c. *Conteste según el modelo.*

¿Necesitan ustedes esta casa?
No, necesitamos aquella casa.

1. ¿Necesitan ustedes estos calcetines?
2. ¿Necesitan ustedes estas raquetas?
3. ¿Necesitan ustedes este caballo?

4. ¿Necesitan ustedes esta cancha?
5. ¿Necesitan ustedes este rancho?

3. *Demonstrative pronouns.*

a. The demonstrative pronouns are the same in form as the demonstrative adjectives, except that they bear a written accent to distinguish them from the adjectives.

esta cancha y *aquélla*   this court and *that* (*one*)
esa raqueta y *ésas*   that racket and *those*
aquellos muchachos y *éste*   those boys and *this one*

b. Each demonstrative pronoun has a neuter form, which refers to a phrase, a clause, or an idea, not to a specific object of determined gender.

esto   this   **eso**   that   **aquello**   that

¿Qué es *esto*?   What is *this*?
Eso **querrá decir . . .**   *That* probably means . . .
Me gusta *aquello*.   I like *that*.

Note that these neuter pronouns have no written accent, since there is no corresponding adjective from which they must be distinguished.

■ Práctica

a. *Conteste según el modelo.*

¿Prefiere Vd. este sombrero?
No, prefiero ése.

1. ¿Prefiere Vd. esta camisa?
2. ¿Prefiere Vd. estas raquetas?
3. ¿Prefiere Vd. estos zapatos?
4. ¿Prefiere Vd. este regalo.

b. *Conteste según el modelo.*

¿Quiere Vd. esa corbata?
No, quiero ésta.

1. ¿Quiere Vd. esos calcetines?
2. ¿Quiere Vd. esa falda?
3. ¿Quiere Vd. esas medias?
4. ¿Quiere Vd. ese vestido?

c. *Conteste según el modelo.*

¿Prefieres este café?
No, prefiero aquél.

1. ¿Prefieres esta casa?
2. ¿Prefieres estos trajes?
3. ¿Prefieres estas flores?
4. ¿Prefieres este teatro?

d. *Diga en español.*

1. What is this?
2. What is that?
3. I don't like this.
4. I don't like that.

4. *The progressive tense:* **estar** *with the gerund.* **Estar** is used with the gerund to express an action *in progress at the moment,* when the fact of being in progress is to be stressed.

Están jugando al tenis.   They are playing tennis.
María está leyendo ahora.   Mary is reading now.

Otherwise the simple present tense translates English *to be* plus the present participle. Note that the gerund of **ir** is not used to form a progressive tense.

Estudiamos el español este año.   We are studying Spanish this year.
Aprende mucho en la universidad.   He is learning a lot at the university.
Vamos a comer ahora.   We are going to eat now.

■ Práctica

a. *Cambie según el modelo.*

Leo mucho.
No estoy leyendo ahora.

1. Trabajo mucho.
2. Como mucho.
3. Estudio mucho.
4. Escribo mucho.
5. Me divierto mucho.
6. Juego mucho.

b. *Cambie según el modelo.*

Hablan mucho.
No están hablando ahora.

1. Aprenden mucho.
2. Cantan mucho.
3. Juegan mucho.
4. Se pasean mucho.
5. Se divierten mucho.
6. Se bañan mucho.

5. *Comparison of adjectives and adverbs.* In Spanish the comparative of adjectives and adverbs is formed by placing **más** (*more*) before them. The superlative is the same in form, but its meaning is made clear by the context. The definite article is used or omitted as in English.

POSITIVE	COMPARATIVE AND SUPERLATIVE
alto tall	**(el) más alto** (the) taller, tallest
linda pretty	**(la) más linda** (the) prettier, prettiest
cerca near	**más cerca** nearer, nearest

María es inteligente, Juan es más inteligente, pero Carlos es el más inteligente.   Mary is intelligent, John is more intelligent, but Charles is the most intelligent.

Virginia es mi amiga más linda.   Virginia is my prettiest friend.

Carlos y María hablan despacio, pero Juan habla más despacio.   Charles and Mary speak slowly, but John speaks more (most) slowly.

After a comparative, **que** is used for English *than*.

Esa raqueta es más ligera que ésta.   That racket is lighter than this one.

Esta cancha está más cerca que aquélla.   This court is nearer than that one.

■ Práctica

a. *Cambie según el modelo.*

Juan es muy alto. (Carlos)
Es más alto que Carlos.

1. María es muy pequeña.   (Virginia)
2. Esta lección es muy fácil.   (la otra)
3. Estos calcetines son muy caros.   (ésos)
4. Ellos son muy inteligentes.   (yo)
5. Esa raqueta es muy ligera.   (la mía)
6. Su padre es muy rico.   (el mío)

7. Este libro es muy interesante.   (los otros)

8. Sevilla está muy cerca.   (Córdoba)

b. *Cambie según el modelo.*

Ése es muy inteligente.
Sí, es el más inteligente.

1. Ése es muy viejo.
2. Ésa es muy rica.
3. Ésos son muy interesantes.
4. Ésas son muy hermosas.
5. Ése es muy pobre.
6. Ésos son muy baratos.
7. Ésa es muy joven.
8. Ésas son muy pequeñas.

F.   Writing

Test yourself

1. "Where can Juan be?" Virginia asked María.
2. He must be playing tennis.
3. You probably know that he goes to the gymnasium at this time every day.
4. Then he won't come for me.
5. He promised her that he would come for her at three o'clock sharp and that they would play a game of tennis.
6. It wouldn't be worth while to wait for him, but you won't have to stay home.
7. I will put on my tennis dress and will go with you.
8. I like that racket of yours better than mine.
9. It is lighter than mine.
10. It is a gift of a very generous uncle of hers.
11. That uncle of yours is more generous than my father.
12. Which tennis court do you prefer: that one or this one?
13. That court is more interesting than this one, because those two good-looking young men are playing in the next court.
14. Let's take the more interesting court!

Composition

Suppose you could go on a boat trip up the river today. Write a composition telling what time you would leave, what friends would go with you, how you would spend the day (you would stroll around the deck, you would sing Spanish songs, you would have a picnic lunch, etc.), and what time you would return home.

LESSON 14

A. More irregular preterits

decir to say, tell	venir to come	querer to wish, want
dije	vine	quise
dijiste	viniste	quisiste
Vd. dijo	Vd. vino	Vd. quiso
dijo	vino	quiso
dijimos	vinimos	quisimos
dijisteis	vinisteis	quisisteis
Vds. dijeron	Vds. vinieron	Vds. quisieron
dijeron	vinieron	quisieron

Note that there is no **i** in the personal ending of **dijeron.**

■ Práctica

Cambie según se indica.

1. Vd. no dijo eso.
    tú / ellos / yo / vosotros / nosotros / Ramona
2. Mis amigos vinieron ayer.
    él / tú / vosotros / yo / Vd. y yo / ellas
3. Él quiso decírselo.
    nosotros / Vds. / yo / vosotros / tú / Inés

153

B. More irregular present indicatives

Several irregular verbs have only one irregularity in the present indicative, namely in the first person singular, which ends in **-go**. You have seen this irregularity in **decir (digo)** and **tener (tengo)**.

hacer to do, make	**salir** to go out, leave	**valer** to be worth	**poner** to put, place
hago	**salgo**	**valgo**	**pongo**
haces	**sales**	**vales**	**pones**
hace	**sale**	**vale**	**pone**
hacemos	**salimos**	**valemos**	**ponemos**
hacéis	**salís**	**valéis**	**ponéis**
hacen	**salen**	**valen**	**ponen**

Venir, *to come,* is like the four verbs above in the first person singular. In the other persons it follows the pattern of the stem-changing verbs of Class II. Compare with **tener.**

vengo	**venimos**
vienes	**venís**
viene	**vienen**

■ Práctica

Cambie según se indica.

1. Nosotros no hacemos eso.
   Vd. / vosotros / yo / tú / ellos
2. Él no vale nada.
   tú / nosotros / yo / ellos / vosotros
3. Ella sale temprano.
   ellas / vosotros / yo / tú / tú y yo
4. Vd. se pone el sombrero.
   Vd. y yo / tú / yo / vosotros / Vds.
5. Ellos vienen mañana.
   Vd. / vosotros / yo / nosotros / tú

C. Listening and speaking

el abrigo overcoat, coat
agosto *m.* August
allá there (*after verbs of motion*);
   back there
aunque although
cada *invariable adj.* each
caminar to walk
deber to owe; ought, should,
   must
diciembre *m.* December
durante during
enero *m.* January
esquiar to ski
la estación season
el estado state
febrero *m.* February
el hockey hockey
el invierno winter
julio *m.* July
junio *m.* June
mayor older, oldest
menos less, least; fewer, fewest
la montaña mountain
nada nothing

nevar (ie) to snow
la nieve snow
patinar to skate
peor worse, worst
predilecto favorite
propio own

IDIOMS AND OTHER EXPRESSIONS

hace buen tiempo the weather
   is good
hace calor it is warm (hot)
hace (mucho) frío it is (very)
   cold
la mayor parte most (*literally,*
   the greater part)
(montados) a caballo on horseback
no sirvo para nada I am of no
   use, I am good for nothing
¿qué tiempo hace? how is the
   weather?
no valgo nada I am not worth
   anything
el verano que viene next summer

En verano y el invierno

—El verano es mi estación predilecta—dijo María.

—¿Sí? Pues la mía es el invierno—dijo Carlos. —Por eso vine a esta universidad, porque aquí hace bastante frío en el invierno.

—No, hombre, el verano es la mejor estación del año. Hay menos deportes en el invierno. Durante los meses de junio, julio y agosto hace calor, y casi siempre hace buen tiempo. Juan—mi hermano mayor—y yo siempre pasamos el verano en Tejas. Visitamos el rancho de nuestro abuelo. Pasamos la mayor parte del día montados a caballo. Allá cada uno tiene su propio caballo. Yo tengo el mío y Juan tiene el suyo. Hacemos muchas excursiones a caballo. Siete u ocho amigos nuestros nos acompañan y nos divertimos muchísimo. También juego al tenis. Y a Juan le gusta jugar al béisbol.

—Para mí—dijo Carlos—el verano es la peor estación. Hace demasiado calor. En el verano no valgo nada.[1] No sirvo para nada. Prefiero el invierno, aunque hace mucho frío. Los deportes de diciembre, enero y febrero son para mí los mejores del año. Me gusta mucho patinar y jugar al hockey. A veces me pongo el abrigo y salgo para caminar en la nieve. Como nieva mucho en el estado de Nueva York, he aprendido a[2] esquiar.

—¿Pero no sabes que podrías esquiar en el verano?—dijo Juan.

—¿Qué quieres decir con eso?

—Cuando hace calor aquí, hace frío en la Argentina y en Chile. Debes[3] ir allá el verano que viene. En esos dos países hay montañas muy altas donde podrías esquiar. Además son países muy interesantes. Chile es más pequeño que la Argentina, pero los dos son países muy importantes e interesantes. Vale la pena de visitarlos.

—¿Quieres[4] acompañarme? Tendremos que hablar español, y tú lo hablas mejor que yo.

—¡Hombre, con mucho gusto! El año pasado invité a un amigo mío a ir allá, pero no quiso[5] acompañarme.

■ **Preguntas**

1. ¿Cuál es la estación predilecta de María?
2. ¿Cuál es la estación predilecta de Carlos?
3. ¿Por qué vino Carlos a esta universidad?
4. ¿Qué dice María del verano?
5. ¿Cuáles son los meses del verano?
6. ¿Qué tiempo hace en el verano?
7. ¿Dónde pasan el verano Juan y María?
8. ¿Qué tiene cada uno en el rancho?
9. ¿Qué hacen cuando visitan el rancho?
10. ¿Cuántos amigos los acompañan?
11. ¿Qué dice Carlos del verano?
12. ¿Cómo está Carlos en el verano?
13. ¿Cuáles son los meses del invierno?
14. ¿Qué le gusta a Carlos?
15. ¿Qué ha aprendido Carlos?
16. ¿Dónde podría esquiar Carlos en el verano?
17. ¿Qué tiempo hace en la Argentina y en Chile en agosto?
18. Si los jóvenes van a Chile, ¿qué tendrán que hablar?
19. ¿Qué hizo Juan el año pasado?
20. ¿Por qué no le acompañó su amigo?

NOTES

1. A double negative is often required in Spanish. You will learn more about it in Lesson 15.

   No valgo nada.   I am not worth anything.
   No sirvo para nada.   I am of no use. I am good for nothing.

2. **Aprender,** like verbs of motion (**ir,** *to go*) and verbs of beginning (**empezar** and **comenzar,** *to begin*), requires the preposition **a** before a following infinitive.

He aprendido a esquiar.   I have learned to ski.

3. When *should* means *ought to,* use **deber** plus an infinitive, instead of the conditional tense.

Debes ir allá.   You should (ought to) go there.
Debemos estudiar.   We ought to (should) study.

4. When *will* means *to be willing,* use **querer** plus an infinitive, instead of the future tense.

¿Quieres acompañarme?   Will you go with me?
¿Quiere usted sentarse?   Will you sit down?

5. **Querer** has special meanings in the preterit.

a. *Affirmative:*

Quisieron hacerlo.   They *tried* to do it.

b. *Negative:*

No quiso acompañarme.   He *would not* (*refused to*) go with me.

■ Práctica

1. Will you come in (enter)?
2. Will you sit down?
3. Will you have coffee?
4. Will you go with me?
5. Will you come back (return) tomorrow?

D. Structure

1. *The weather.* Some states of the weather are expressed by **hace** and a noun. The commonest ones are these:

Hace calor. It is warm (hot).	**Hace fresco.** It is cool.
Hace frío. It is cold.	**Hace sol.** It is sunny.

Hace viento.   It is windy.
Hace buen tiempo.   The weather is good.

Since **calor, frío,** etc., are nouns, the English adverb *very* ("*very* warm" etc.) must be translated by the Spanish adjective **mucho.**

Hace *mucho* frío.   It is *very* cold.

■ Práctica

Diga en español.

1. It is very cold.
2. It is very cool.
3. It is very windy.
4. It is very sunny.
5. It is very warm.
6. It is good weather.

2. More about the comparison of adjectives

a. After a superlative, **de** is used for English *in.*

Es la ciudad más interesante de América.   It is the most interesting city in America.

Carlos es el alumno más inteligente de la clase.   Charles is the most intelligent student in the class.

b. The following four adjectives have irregular comparisons:

POSITIVE	COMPARATIVE AND SUPERLATIVE
bueno good	**(el) mejor** (the) better, best
malo bad	**(el) peor** (the) worse, worst
grande large	**(el) mayor** (the) older, oldest
	(the) larger, largest
pequeño small	**(el) menor** (the) younger, youngest
	(the) smaller, smallest

Grande and **pequeño** have regular forms also **(más grande, más pequeño),** which refer strictly to size (larger, smaller). **Mayor** and **menor** usually, though not always, refer to age (older, younger), in which case they follow the noun. **Mejor** and **peor** regularly precede the noun.

Juan es el hermano mayor de María.   John is Mary's older brother.
María es la hija menor.   Mary is the youngest daughter.
Lima es la ciudad más grande del Perú.   Lima is the largest city in Peru.

■ Práctica

Conteste según el modelo.

¿Es ésta la mejor película?
No, es la peor.

1. ¿Es éste el peor sombrero?
2. ¿Es ésta la mejor camisa?
3. ¿Son éstos los peores alumnos?
4. ¿Son éstas las mejores medias?
5. ¿Es ésta la hermana mayor?
6. ¿Es éste el hermano menor?
7. ¿Es ésta la ciudad más grande?
8. ¿Es éste el país más pequeño?

3. *More about the comparison of adverbs.* Four adverbs have irregular comparisons.

POSITIVE	COMPARATIVE AND SUPERLATIVE
mucho much **poco** little **bien** well **mal** badly	**más** more, most **menos** less, least **mejor** better, best **peor** worse, worst

Just as **más . . . que** means *more than,* **menos . . . que** means *less* than.

El invierno es menos agradable que el verano.   Winter is less pleasant than summer.

■ Práctica

Conteste según el modelo.

¿Trabaja usted más?
No, trabajo menos.

1. ¿Estudia usted más?
2. ¿Hace usted menos?
3. ¿Aprende usted más?
4. ¿Dice usted menos?
5. ¿Canta usted mejor?
6. ¿Escribe usted peor?
7. ¿Juega usted mejor?
8. ¿Baila usted peor?

E. Writing

Test yourself

1. María said that summer is her favorite season, but Carlos said that his is winter.
2. It is quite cold here in winter.
3. It is hot in June, July, and August, but it's always good weather.
4. In summer Juan and María always visit their grandparents' ranch.
5. Each one has a horse, and they make many trips on horseback.
6. Seven or eight friends go with them.
7. They play baseball and tennis and have a good time.
8. Carlos says that summer is the worst season for him, because it is too hot.
9. The months that he likes best are December, January, and February.
10. He likes to skate, and he has learned to ski.
11. In August he could ski in Chile and Argentina, where it is cold.
12. Juan says that he ought to go there. A friend of his refused to go last year.

Composition

Write a composition telling why you like summer and why you like winter.

LESSON 15

A. Pluperfect indicative

The pluperfect indicative of a verb is formed by combining the past participle of the verb with the imperfect indicative of the auxiliary verb **haber.**

había hablado I had spoken	**habíamos hablado** we had spoken
habías hablado you had spoken	**habíais hablado** you had spoken
Vd. había hablado you had spoken	**Vds. habían hablado** you had spoken
había hablado he (she) had spoken	**habían hablado** they had spoken

■ Práctica

Cambie según se indica.

1. Vds. habían vuelto temprano.
    tú / vosotros / yo / nosotros / ellas / Vd.
2. Ella había salido a esa hora.
    yo / ellos / tú y yo / vosotros / tú / Vd.

B. More irregular preterits

poder to be able	poner to put, to place	saber to know	haber to have
pude	puse	supe	hube
pudiste	pusiste	supiste	hubiste
Vd. pudo	Vd. puso	Vd. supo	Vd. hubo
pudo	puso	supo	hubo
pudimos	pusimos	supimos	hubimos
pudisteis	pusisteis	supisteis	hubisteis
Vds. pudieron	Vds. pusieron	Vds. supieron	Vds. hubieron
pudieron	pusieron	supieron	hubieron

■ Práctica

Cambie según se indica.

1. Vd. no pudo hacerlo.
   Vds. / yo / tú / nosotros / vosotros
2. Nosotros nos pusimos el sombrero.
   ella / Vds. / vosotros / tú / yo / Vd. y yo
3. Él lo supo ayer.
   yo / tú / nosotros / vosotros / ellas / Vd.

C. Listening and speaking

abril *m.* April
la asignatura course
bien very
caliente hot
colorado red
completamente completely
enamorado in love
el enamorado sweetheart
francamente frankly
jamás never, not . . . ever
llover (ue) to rain
marzo *m.* March
las matemáticas mathematics
mayo *m.* May
nadie nobody, no one
naturalmente naturally
ni . . . ni neither . . . nor

ninguno none, not . . . any
noviembre *m.* November
nunca never
octubre *m.* October
el otoño autumn
ponerse to become, turn (*pale,
   red, etc.*)
la primavera spring
replicar to reply, answer back
resistir to stand; to resist
sentado seated, sitting
sentirse (ie) to feel
señalar to indicate; to point
   at
septiembre *m.* September
el sol sun
tranquilamente calmly

IDIOMS AND OTHER EXPRESSIONS

al entrar on entering
acabo (acababa) de + *infin.*
I have (had) just . . .
eso de that matter of
a mí no not me; not I (*with*
gustar)

prestar atención to pay attention
salir aprobado to pass (*a course*)
salir mal to fail, flunk
tomar el sol to take (sit in) the sun
me da vergüenza (it) makes me
ashamed

El otoño y la primavera

Habíamos ido al café a tomar un refresco. Al entrar[1] no habíamos visto a ninguno de nuestros amigos. Nos habíamos sentado y acabábamos de[2] pedir café cuando vimos al señor Martínez en otra mesa. Le invitamos a tomar café con nosotros.

—Gracias—nos dijo al sentarse con nosotros. —Voy a tomar una taza de café bien caliente. Hace mucho frío esta mañana.

—Éste—dijo María, señalando a Carlos,—dice que le gusta el invierno.

—A mí no—replicó el profesor Martínez. —Tampoco me gusta el verano. No puedo resistir ni el frío del invierno ni el calor del verano. Para mí, . . . el otoño. Como sabrán ustedes, escribo mucho. En septiembre, octubre y noviembre, cuando hace fresco, puedo trabajar tranquilamente. Entonces escribo más que nunca.[3]

—Pronto vendrá la primavera—observó Virginia. —¡Ésa es la estación que a mí me gusta!

—La primavera—dijo el señor Martínez—es para los jóvenes y para los enamorados. Y no siempre hace buen tiempo. En marzo hace viento y en abril llueve mucho.

—¡Pero el mes de mayo es el mejor del año!—exclamó Virginia.

—Es el peor para los profesores. Se lo digo francamente: los alumnos se sienten muy perezosos y no prestan atención. En la universidad nadie quiere hacer nada. Se toma el sol; se juega al tenis o al béisbol; pero no se trabaja. En la primavera no se estudia jamás.

—Eso de no estudiar—dijo María—me da vergüenza. Acabo de recordar que la primavera pasada no pude[4] trabajar. Sabía que tendría que estudiar mucho para salir aprobada en la asignatura de matemáticas. Quise estudiar y no pude. Al fin supe[4] que había salido mal.

—¡Naturalmente!—exclamó el señor Martínez. —Usted estaba com-pletamente enamorada, ¿verdad?

María se puso colorada, pero no dijo nada.

■ Preguntas

1. ¿Adónde habíamos ido?
2. ¿A quién habíamos visto en el café?

3. ¿Qué habíamos pedido?
4. Al fin, ¿a quién habíamos visto?
5. ¿Qué nos dijo el señor Martínez?
6. ¿Le gusta el invierno al señor Martínez?
7. ¿Le gusta el verano?
8. ¿Cuál es la estación predilecta del señor Martínez?
9. ¿Por qué?
10. ¿Cuáles son los meses del otoño?
11. ¿Qué dijo el señor Martínez de la primavera?
12. ¿Qué tiempo hace en marzo?
13. ¿En abril?
14. ¿Qué dijo Virginia del mes de mayo?
15. ¿Qué dijo el señor Martínez del mes de mayo?
16. ¿Cómo se sienten los alumnos en la primavera?
17. ¿Qué se hace en la primavera?
18. ¿Qué acaba de recordar María?
19. ¿Salió María aprobada en la asignatura de matemáticas?
20. ¿Qué dijo el señor Martínez y cómo respondió María?

NOTES

1. **Al** plus an infinitive means *on, upon* plus the English present participle. It often takes the place of an adverbial clause of time.

   al entrar   upon entering (when we entered)
   al sentarse   on sitting down (when he sat down)

2. The present and imperfect of **acabar de** plus an infinitive means *have just* and *had just* plus the English past participle.

   Acabo de recordar.   I have just remembered.
   Acabábamos de pedir café.   We had just ordered coffee.

3. After comparisons negative pronouns, adjectives, and adverbs **(nadie, nunca, etc.)** are used where English uses their affirmative counterparts (*anybody, ever, etc.*).

   Escribo más que nunca.   I write more than ever.
   Trabaja más que nadie.   He works more than anybody.

4. **Poder** and **saber** are other verbs that have special meanings in the preterit. **No pude** means *I could not* in the sense *I tried to but could not.* **Supe** means *I learned, I found out.*

No pude estudiar. I could not study.
Supe que había salido mal. I learned that I had failed.

These special meanings **(quise, pude, supe)** grow out of the basic use of the preterit to express a completed, instantaneous act.

■ Práctica

a. *Diga en español.*

   1. upon leaving   4. upon getting up
   2. upon returning   5. upon dressing
   3. upon reading   6. upon sitting down

b. *Diga en español.*

   1. We have just left.
   2. We have just returned.
   3. We have just read.
   4. We had just got up.
   5. We had just dressed.
   6. We had just sat down.

D. Structure

1. *Indefinite pronoun* **se.** The indefinite pronoun **se** is often used to express the English indefinite pronoun *one* (or indefinite *we, you, they*; or *people*).

Se puede trabajar. One can work.
Se juega al tenis. People play tennis.
Pero no se trabaja. But they don't work.
No se estudia jamás. You never study.

■ Práctica

Diga en español.

1. One doesn't know.
2. One doesn't listen.
3. One doesn't read.
4. One doesn't learn.
5. One doesn't explain.
6. One doesn't understand.

2. Negative words. Negative adverbs, pronouns, and adjectives may precede or follow the verb. When they precede, they tend to be more emphatic; more commonly they follow. When they follow, **no** is inserted before the verb, thus creating a double negative which is not tolerated in English.

ADVERBS

nunca ⎱
jamás ⎰ never, not ever

tampoco neither, not . . . either

ni . . . ni neither . . . nor

No soy ⎰ **nunca** ⎱ **perezoso.**   I am never lazy.
        ⎱ **jamás** ⎰

Nunca ⎱
Jamás ⎰ **soy perezoso.**   I am *never* lazy. *Never* am I lazy.

No estudio tampoco.   I do not study either.

Tampoco estudio.   Neither do I study.

No resisto ni el calor ni el frío.   I can stand neither the heat nor the cold. I can't stand either the heat or the cold.

PRONOUNS

nada nothing, not . . . anything

nadie nobody, no one, not . . . anybody, not . . . anyone

ninguno (-a) none, no one, not . . . any . . .

No comprendo nada.   I understand nothing. I do not understand anything.

Nada comprendo.   I understand *nothing*. I do not understand *anything*.

When **nadie** and **ninguno** referring to a person are direct objects of verbs, they must be preceded by personal **a.**

No veo a nadie.   I see nobody. I do not see anybody.

No conozco a ninguna de estas señoritas.   I know none of these young ladies. I do not know any of these young ladies.

ADJECTIVE

ningún, ninguna no, not . . . any

No he visto a ningún alumno.   I have seen no student. I have not seen any student.

Ninguna lección ha sido tan fácil.   No lesson has been so easy.

■ Práctica

Conteste según los modelos.

a. **¿Estudia usted mucho?**
    No estudio nunca.
    No estudio jamás.

    1. ¿Trabaja usted mucho?
    2. ¿Baila usted mucho?
    3. ¿Duerme usted mucho?
    4. ¿Se divierte usted mucho?

b. **¿Usted no estudia nunca?**
    Ella no estudia tampoco.

    1. ¿Usted no trabaja nunca?
    2. ¿Usted no baila nunca?
    3. ¿Usted no duerme nunca?
    4. ¿Usted no se divierte nunca?

c. **¿Qué ven ustedes?**
    No vemos nada.

    1. ¿Qué quieren ustedes?
    2. ¿Qué buscan ustedes?
    3. ¿Qué saben ustedes?
    4. ¿Qué dicen ustedes?

d. **¿A quién ven ustedes?**
    No vemos a nadie.

    1. ¿A quién buscan ustedes?
    2. ¿A quién necesitan ustedes?
    3. ¿A quién conocen ustedes?
    4. ¿A quién miran ustedes?

e. **Qué libro quiere usted?**
    Ninguno—no quiero ningún libro.

    1. ¿Qué sombrero quiere usted?
    2. ¿Qué corbata quiere usted?
    3. ¿Qué traje quiere usted?
    4. ¿Qué blusa quiere usted?

f. **¿Cuál prefieres: este reloj o ése?**
    Ni el uno ni el otro.

1. ¿Cuál prefieres: esta raqueta o ésa?
2. ¿Cuál prefieres: este sombrero o ése?
3. ¿Cuál prefieres: esta mesa o ésa?
4. ¿Cuál prefieres: este regalo o ése?

3. *Formation of adverbs.* Many adverbs are formed by adding the termination **-mente** to the feminine form of the adjective. If the adjective bears a written accent, the adverb retains it.

completo	complete	**completamente**	completely
constante	constant	**constantemente**	constantly
feliz	happy	**felizmente**	happily
fácil	easy	**fácilmente**	easily

■ Práctica

Cambie según el modelo.

fácil: fácilmente

1. difícil
2. típico
3. reciente
4. lento

5. sencillo
6. principal
7. nuevo
8. franco

E. Writing

Test yourself

1. The students had gone to the café.
2. They had not seen any of their friends.
3. They had just sat down when they saw Mr. Martínez.
4. They invited him to have coffee with them.
5. Mr. Martínez said that he needed a cup of hot coffee.
6. It was cold this morning.
7. Mr. Martínez doesn't like either winter or summer.
8. He prefers the autumn, when he can work calmly.
9. It is always cool in September, October, and November.
10. It is windy in March; it rains a lot in April; but in May the weather is good.
11. One doesn't study in spring, says the professor.
12. Nobody wants to do anything.

Composition

Write a composition telling why you like spring and why you like autumn.

CONVERSATIONAL INTERLUDE

La visita

Juan. Buenas tardes, señora.

La señora de González. Buenas tardes, Juan.

Juan. Permítame presentarle a usted mi amigo Carlos Brown. Ésta es la señora de González.

La señora de G. Tanto gusto, señor Brown.

Carlos. El gusto es mío, señora.

La señora de G. ¿De dónde es Vd., señor Brown?

Carlos. Soy de Nueva York, señora.

La señora de G. ¿Ha estado Vd. antes en mi país, o es ésta su primera visita?

Carlos. Acabo de llegar a su país. Es mi primer viaje a la América del Sur.

La señora de G. Y ¿le gusta mi país?

Carlos. ¡Cómo no, señora! Lo encuentro muy interesante, sobre todo el paisaje tan bello y los hermosos edificios de la capital.

The Puerta del Sol is the heart of Madrid (© Screen Traveler, from Gendreau)

With typical humor the people of Madrid call their Post Office "Nuestra Señora de los Correos." (Philip D. Gendreau)

Monument to Columbus in Madrid and Spain's tallest office building.
(© Screen Traveler, from Gendreau)

Monument to King Alfonso XII in the Parque del Retiro, Madrid.
(Philip D. Gendreau)

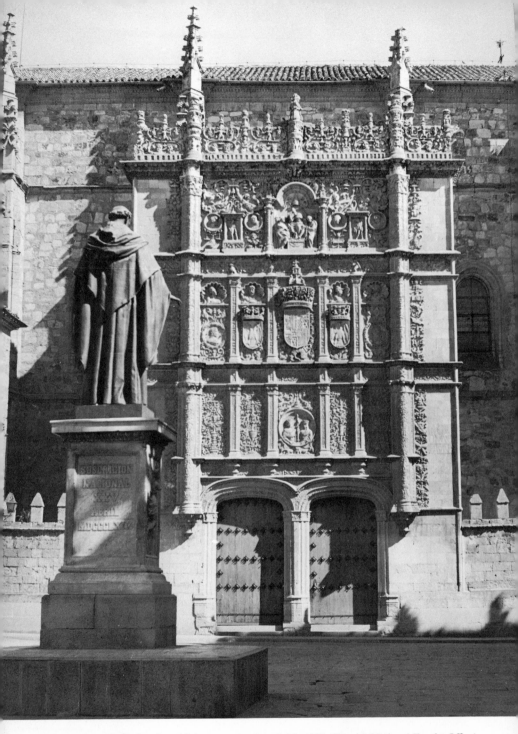

The University of Salamanca was founded in 1223. (Spanish National Tourist Office)

The house of El Greco (1548?–1625) in Toledo, now a museum. (Three Lions, Inc.)

Windmills in Ciudad Real remind us of Don Quixote de la Mancha.
(Spanish National Tourist Office)

LESSON 16

A. Present subjunctive of regular verbs

The present subjunctive of all regular and of most irregular verbs is formed on the stem of the first person singular, present indicative: the -o is removed and the following endings are added:

FIRST CONJUGATION		SECOND AND THIRD CONJUGATIONS	
-e	-emos	-a	-amos
-es	-éis	-as	-áis
-e	-en	-a	-an

hablar	aprender	vivir
hable	aprenda	viva
hables	aprendas	vivas
Vd. hable	Vd. aprenda	Vd. viva
hable	aprenda	viva
hablemos	aprendamos	vivamos
habléis	aprendáis	viváis
Vds. hablen	Vds. aprendan	Vds. vivan
hablen	aprendan	vivan

The subjunctive has various meanings, which will be explained as you study its uses.

■ Práctica

Substituya el singular por el plural, según el modelo.

que yo hable
que nosotros hablemos

a. 1. que yo baile
   2. que yo lea
   3. que yo escriba
   4. que yo compre

b. 1. que tú cantes
   2. que tú vivas
   3. que tú prepares
   4. que tú resistas

c. 1. que él mire
   2. que ella espere
   3. que Vd. suba
   4. que Vd. baje

Substituya el plural por el singular, según el modelo.

que nosotros estudiemos
que yo estudie

a. 1. que nosotros comamos
   2. que nosotros preguntemos
   3. que nosotros aprendamos
   4. que nosotros contestemos

b. 1. que vosotros estudiéis
   2. que vosotros escribáis
   3. que vosotros habléis
   4. que vosotros respondáis

c. 1. que ellas escriban
   2. que ellos descansen
   3. que Vds. aprendan
   4. que ellos canten

B.   Listening and speaking

el apartamento apartment
el ascensor elevator
así so, thus
el avión plane, airplane
bajar (de) to go down; to get
  out of, off (*a vehicle*)
el coche car
el convidado guest
cortés polite
corto short

la costumbre custom
la criada maid, servant
cuyo *rel. adj.* whose
delante de in front of
dirigirse a to address
enseñar to show
estacionar to park
funcionar to work, run
grande, gran great
el idioma language

la impresión impression
Jaime James
llamar to call; **llamarse** to be called
la mamá mother, mamma
el piso floor; **el piso bajo** ground floor; **el piso principal** main floor, second floor
presentar to introduce
primero first
la psicología psychology
la realidad reality
repetir (i) to repeat
Santo, San Saint
simpático nice, congenial
simplemente simply
sonriendo *gerund of* **sonreír** smiling
el té tea
tercero third
último last

las vacaciones vacation
el viaje trip

IDIOMS AND OTHER EXPRESSIONS

en avión by plane
bueno, pues all right then; well then
hacer un viaje to take (make) a trip
hay que + *infin.* one must, it is necessary to
se llama his name is
¿cómo se llama? what is his name?
de modo que so (that)
pase Vd. come in
tanto gusto (de conocerle, etc.) so pleased to meet you; how do you do? etc.
por primera vez for the first time

Entremos en la casa de Jaime

—Entremos en la casa para conocer[1] a mi familia—dice Jaime Montero.

Hemos hecho un viaje a España para ver el país cuyo idioma estudiamos. Es nuestro primer viaje, pero no será el último. Será un viaje muy corto, porque sólo tenemos dos semanas de vacaciones. Pero en avión se llega a Madrid en unas horas. En Madrid hemos conocido a un joven español muy simpático. Se llama Jaime Montero. Nos hemos visto casi todos los días y él nos ha mostrado casi toda la gran ciudad. Esta tarde nos ha invitado a ir a su casa para conocer a su familia.

Jaime ha estacionado el coche en la calle de San Ildefonso delante de una gran casa de apartamentos. —Ésta es su casa—nos dice al bajar. —Entremos.

—¿Nuestra casa?—le pregunto.

—Naturalmente quiero decir que es mía. Pero a nosotros no nos parece muy cortés decir simplemente que es nuestra. De modo que al mostrársela por primera vez a un amigo le decimos que es su casa. Es la costumbre española. Vivimos en el primer piso. Tomemos el ascensor, pues—dice sonriendo.

—¡Que tomen los otros el ascensor!—exclamo yo. —Si ustedes viven en el primer piso, yo me quedo aquí. No hay que subir.

—¡Que se quede aquí éste!—dice María. —Yo comprendo que hay que subir. Aquí estamos en el piso bajo. Luego viene el piso principal y luego

el primer piso. En realidad ustedes viven en el tercer piso, pero los españoles
lo llaman primer piso, ¿no es verdad?

—Así es—contesta Jaime—y es muy buena psicología cuando no
funciona el ascensor. ¡Bueno, pues, subamos!

Toda la familia Montero está en casa. Jaime nos presenta a su mamá,
doña[2] Matilde, y a su padre, don Roberto.

—Tanto gusto de conocerlos—nos dicen. —Pasen ustedes.

Jaime nos presenta también a sus dos hermanas menores y a su hermano
mayor.

—Siéntense ustedes—nos dice doña Matilde.

—Sentémonos—repite don Roberto—y hablemos de sus primeras
impresiones de España.

—¿Dónde está la criada?—dice doña Matilde, dirigiéndose a su hija
mayor. —Que prepare té para nuestros convidados.

■ Preguntas

1. ¿Qué hemos hecho?
2. ¿Por qué?
3. ¿Por qué será corto el viaje?
4. ¿Cómo hemos venido a Madrid?
5. ¿A quién hemos conocido en Madrid?
6. ¿Cómo se llama el joven español?
7. ¿Qué nos ha enseñado Jaime?
8. ¿Adónde nos ha invitado?
9. ¿Dónde ha estacionado el coche?
10. ¿Qué nos dice al bajar del coche?
11. ¿En qué piso vive su familia?
12. ¿Qué exclama Vd.?
13. ¿Por qué hay que tomar el ascensor?
14. ¿Qué explica María?
15. ¿Quiénes están en la casa de Jaime?
16. ¿Qué nos dicen los padres de Jaime?
17. ¿Qué nos dice doña Matilde?
18. ¿Qué nos dice don Roberto?
19. ¿Qué le dice doña Matilde a su hija mayor?

NOTES

1. **Conocer** often means *to meet*. This is especially true in the preterit.

   Los conocí ayer.   I met them yesterday.
   Hemos conocido a un joven español.   We have met a young Spaniard.

2. **Don** and **doña** are untranslatable titles used only before the given names of persons to whom, because of age or for other reasons, one wishes to express an attitude of respect. In American English the nearest equivalent for **doña** is the regional use of *Miss* with a woman's given name.

C. Structure

1. *Subjunctive mood in main clauses.*

a. You have already learned one of the main uses of the subjunctive, i.e., in the third person, singular or plural, with **Vd.** or **Vds.**, to express commands (see Lesson 5).

Aprenda Vd.   Learn.   **Siéntense Vds.**   Sit down.

■ Práctica

a. *Conteste según el modelo.*

Quiero cantar.
Cante usted, pues.

1. Quiero entrar.
2. Quiero volver.
3. Quiero pensar.
4. Quiero dormir.
5. Quiero leer.

b. *Conteste según el modelo.*

Queremos levantarnos.
Pues, levántense ustedes.

1. Queremos bañarnos.
2. Queremos vestirnos.
3. Queremos sentarnos.
4. Queremos lavarnos.
5. Queremos divertirnos.

b. The first person plural of the present subjunctive also expresses commands.

Entremos en la casa.   Let's go into the house.
Tomemos el ascensor.   Let's take the elevator.
Subamos.   Let's go up.

Object pronouns, including the reflexive pronoun **nos,** follow this form in the affirmative and are attached to it. Note that a written accent is then required. Note also that reflexive verbs drop the final **-s** before adding **nos.**

Tomémos*lo*.   Let's take *it*.   **Sentémo*nos*.**   Let's sit down.

But:

No *lo* tomemos.   Let's not take *it*.
No *nos* sentemos aquí.   Let's not sit down here.

■ Práctica

Conteste según los modelos.

a. **Preferimos entrar.**
   Entremos.

   1. Preferimos bajar.
   2. Preferimos escribir.
   3. Preferimos trabajar.
   4. Preferimos vivir.

b. **Preferimos sentarnos.**
   Sentémonos.

   1. Preferimos bañarnos.
   2. Preferimos levantarnos.
   3. Preferimos lavarnos.
   4. Preferimos acostarnos.

c. **Queremos tomarlo.**
   Tomémoslo.

   1. Queremos comerlo.
   2. Queremos escribirlos.
   3. Queremos aprenderla.
   4. Queremos leerlas.

d. **No queremos tomarlo.**
   No lo tomemos.

   1. No queremos comerlo.
   2. No queremos escribirlos.
   3. No queremos aprenderla.
   4. No queremos leerlas.

c. An indirect command is expressed by the third person, singular or plural, of the present subjunctive. It is often equivalent to English *let,* or *may,* plus a verb. In this construction the Spanish verb is usually preceded by **que** (*that*).

Que prepare **té.**   *Let her* (Have her) *prepare* tea.
Que se queden **aquí.**   *Let them stay* here.
¡*Viva* **el Presidente!**   *Long live* the President!
¡*No lo quiera* **Dios!**   (*May*) God *forbid* (it)!

When the subject is expressed in such sentences, it follows the verb.

Que lo escriba *Carlos.*   Let *Charles* write it.
Que tomen *los otros* **el ascensor.**   Let *the others* take the elevator.
Que se levanten *ellos.*   Let *them* get up.

■ Práctica

Conteste según el modelo.

Juan quiere trabajar.
Que trabaje, pues.

1. Dolores quiere cantar.
2. Ellos quieren leer.
3. Ramón quiere descansar.
4. Ellas quieren comer.
5. Don Ricardo quiere escuchar.
6. Ellos quieren aprender.

2. *Shortening (apocope) of adjectives*

a. In addition to **uno,** the following common adjectives drop the final **-o** before a masculine singular noun.

alguno some, any	**bueno** good	**primero** first
ninguno no, not . . . any	**malo** bad	**tercero** third

algún libro   some book
ningún hombre   no man
hace mal tiempo   it is bad weather
el tercer día   the third day

But:
alguna vez   some time
la primera lección   the first lesson
buenos días   good morning

b. **Grande** drops the final syllable before any singular noun, masculine or feminine. **Ciento,** as we have seen, drops its final syllable before any noun.

una gran ciudad   a great city
cien personas   a hundred people

But:

grandes ciudades   great cities

c. **Santo** (*Saint*) drops the final syllable before a masculine saint's name except those beginning with **Do-** and **To-.**

San Juan   **San Carlos**

But:

Santo Domingo   **Santa Ana**

■ Práctica

Diga en español.

1. no student
2. no farm
3. some café
4. some library
5. bad weather
6. a good book
7. the first day
8. the first lesson

9. the third man
10. a great country
11. a hundred days
12. a hundred girls
13. a hundred boys
14. Saint Mary
15. Saint Dominick
16. Saint John

3. *More about the reflexive pronoun.* The plural reflexive pronouns may be used to express reciprocal relationship.

Nos **hemos visto.**   We have seen *each other* (*one another*).
Se **verán mañana.**   They will see *each other* (*one another*) tomorrow.
Se **escribían con frecuencia.**   They wrote *to each other* frequently.

■ Práctica

Diga en español.

1. They see each other.
2. They know each other.
3. They write to each other.

4. We see each other.
5. We know each other.
6. We write to each other.

D. Writing

Test yourself

1. The students have taken a trip to Spain to see the country whose language they have studied.
2. They went by plane.
3. It is their first trip and it will be short.
4. They have met a very nice young Spaniard whose name is Jaime Montero.
5. They have seen each other every day.
6. Jaime invites them to go to his house to meet his family.
7. He parks the car and says, "Let's go in. This is your house."
8. They live on the third floor, but they call it (the) first floor.
9. "Let the others take the elevator," says Carlos. "I'm staying here."
10. He does not know that it is necessary to take the elevator.
11. "Let him stay here," says María. "This is only the ground floor."
12. Jaime introduces them to his family.
13. "Come in," they say. "We are pleased to meet you."
14. "Where is the maid?" asks doña Matilde. "Have her prepare tea."

Composition

You have taken a trip to Spain. Write a composition telling that you made the trip by plane. You went to Madrid. You met a nice Spanish family. They invited you to visit them. Tell where they live. Tell what you talked about when you visited them. Etc.

LESSON 17

A. Present subjunctive of stem-changing verbs

In the present subjunctive Class I has the same changes, in the same persons, as in the present indicative: final stem vowel e changes to ie and final stem vowel o changes to ue wherever the stress falls on the e or o, that is, throughout the singular and in the third person plural.

pensar		volver	
p*i*ense	pensemos	v*ue*lva	volvamos
p*i*enses	penséis	v*ue*lvas	volváis
Vd. p*i*ense	Vds. p*i*ensen	Vd. v*ue*lva	Vds. v*ue*lvan
p*i*ense	p*i*ensen	v*ue*lva	v*ue*lvan

Class II has the same changes as Class I and an additional change: in the first and second persons plural, stem vowel e changes to i and stem vowel o changes to u.

sentir		dormir	
s*i*enta	s*i*ntamos	d*ue*rma	d*u*rmamos
s*i*entas	s*i*ntáis	d*ue*rmas	d*u*rmáis
Vd. s*i*enta	Vds. s*i*entan	Vd. d*ue*rma	Vds. d*ue*rman
s*i*enta	s*i*entan	d*ue*rma	d*ue*rman

In Class III stem vowel e changes to i throughout.

pedir	
p*i*da	p*i*damos
p*i*das	p*i*dáis
Vd. p*i*da	Vds. p*i*dan
p*i*da	p*i*dan

■ **Práctica**

Cambie según el modelo.

Quieren que yo lo cuente.
Quieren que Vd. lo cuente.

1. Quieren que yo lo cuente.
   tú / él / Vd. y yo / vosotros / ellas
2. Quieren que Vd. se vista pronto.
   ellos / tú / yo / nosotros / vosotros
3. Quieren que nosotros nos sentemos aquí.
   yo / Vds. / tú y yo / vosotros / tú / Vd.
4. No quieren que él muera.
   yo / ellos / vosotros / tú / nosotros
5. No quieren que yo lo pierda.
   Vd. / Vds. / tú / tú y yo / vosotros

B. Listening and speaking

acá here
el arte art
célebre famous, celebrated
cerrar (ie) to close
la colección collection
contener to contain
el cuadro picture, painting
dormirse (ue) to go to sleep
especialmente especially
famoso famous
fastidiado annoyed
el fastidio boredom
el hotel hotel
impaciente impatient
impresionante impressive
insistir to insist
lentamente slowly
listo ready
llevar to take
maravilloso marvellous
morirse (ue) to die; to be dying
el museo museum

la obra work (*of art*)
el pintor painter
precisamente just at this moment
el punto de interés point of
   interest
sonar (ue) to sound, ring
la técnica technique
el timbre bell

IDIOMS AND OTHER EXPRESSIONS

¡Cuánto gusto de verlos! How
   pleased (I am) to see you!
dar con to meet, run into
dormir la siesta to take a siesta
se hace tarde it is becoming late
largo rato a long while
de pronto suddenly
pierda Vd. cuidado don't worry
volver a + *infin.* to (do something) again

En el Museo del Prado

Esta tarde quiero visitar un museo muy famoso. Es el famoso Museo del Prado. Este museo contiene colecciones impresionantes de cuadros españoles. Hay una colección especialmente impresionante de las obras de un gran pintor español, el célebre Velázquez.

Quiero que Juan me acompañe, porque a él le gusta el arte. Pero francamente, deseo que Carlos se quede en el hotel o que visite otro punto de interés. A él no le gusta el arte, y no quiero que se duerma en el museo ni que se muera de fastidio mirando los hermosos cuadros de los pintores españoles.

Hemos dormido la siesta. Se hace tarde, y quiero que Juan se vista pronto para no perder tiempo. Pero él se viste lentamente y yo me pongo impaciente. Al fin está listo y vamos al museo. Llegamos bastante tarde.

En el museo damos con Jaime Montero. Están con él Virginia y María.

—¡Cuánto gusto de verlos!—le digo. —Recuerdo que usted sabe mucho del arte español y deseo que me muestre la Sala de Velázquez.

—Precisamente íbamos allá—contesta Jaime. Nos lleva a esa sala, donde vemos cosas maravillosas. Jaime me explica la técnica del gran pintor español.

Virginia y María quieren que pasemos a otra sala para ver las obras de Murillo, de Zurbarán y de otros pintores. Así lo hacemos. Pero pronto dicen que están cansadas y quieren sentarse para descansar.

—Aunque las pobres muchachas están cansadas, no quiero que se sienten—le digo a Jaime, fastidiado. —Si se sientan, vamos a perder tiempo, y hay mucho que[1] ver. Se quedarán aquí largo rato y no volveremos a[2] ver los cuadros de Velázquez.

Pero las muchachas insisten y se sientan.

—Dejémoslas aquí con Juan—le digo a Jaime. —Yo quiero que Vd. vuelva conmigo a la Sala de Velázquez para volver a examinar esos maravillosos cuadros.

De pronto suena un timbre.

—No hay tiempo—dice Jaime. Van a cerrar.

—Pero no quiero que cierren el museo. Quiero ver más.

—Pierda Vd. cuidado—dice Jaime. —Mañana será otro día y volveremos acá.[3]

■ Preguntas

1. ¿Qué quiere Vd. visitar esta tarde?
2. ¿Cuál es el museo que quiere visitar?
3. ¿Qué contiene?
4. ¿Cuál es una colección especialmente impresionante que contiene?
5. ¿Por qué desea Vd. que Juan le acompañe?
6. ¿Quiere Vd. que Carlos visite el museo?
7. ¿Por qué quiere Vd. que Juan se vista pronto?
8. ¿A quiénes encuentran Vds. en el museo?
9. ¿Qué sabe Jaime?

10. ¿Qué quiere Vd. que le muestre Jaime?
11. ¿Qué le explica Jaime?
12. ¿Qué quieren Virginia y María?
13. ¿Qué quieren hacer ellas poco después?
14. ¿Adónde quiere Vd. que vuelva Jaime?
15. ¿Qué suena de pronto?
16. ¿Qué quiere decir eso?

NOTES

1. After negative and indefinite expressions and those containing a numeral English *to* is translated by Spanish **que.**

   No hay nada que hacer.   There is nothing to do.
   Hay mucho que ver.   There is much to see.
   ¿Tiene algo que comer?   Does he have anything to eat?
   Tengo tres cartas que escribir.   I have three letters to write.

2. **Volver** requires the preposition **a** before a following infinitive. In this construction **volver a** means *again.*

   Volveremos a ver los cuadros.   We shall see the paintings *again.*
   Volvió a leer ese libro.   He read that book *again.*

3. **Acá,** like **allá,** is frequently, though not always, used after verbs of motion.

   Volveremos acá.   We shall come back here.
   Vamos allá.   Let's go over there.

■ Práctica

a. *Conteste según el modelo.*

     ¿Hay algo que ver?
     No, no hay nada que ver.

1. ¿Hay algo que hacer?
2. ¿Hay mucho que estudiar?
3. ¿Hay algo que leer?
4. ¿Hay cartas que escribir?
5. ¿Hay lecciones que estudiar?

b. *Diga en español.*

1. We shall see it again.
2. We shall do it again.

3. I shall say it again.
4. I shall read it again.
5. They will lose it again.

C. Structure

1. *The noun clause.* Up to this point we have been using the infinitive as the object of the verb in Spanish, just as in English.

Yo quiero *estudiar.*   I want *to study.*

We use this same construction in English even when we introduce a separate subject for the infinitive: I want *you to study,* they want *us to work.*

But in Spanish, when a second subject is introduced into the sentence, we replace the infinitive by a noun clause. A noun clause is a clause used as a noun; in the following sentence, for example, it is the object of the verb **quiero.**

Yo quiero *que Vd. estudie.*   I want *you to study.* (I want *that you study.*)

2. *Subjunctive mood in the noun clause.* Some, not all, main verbs require the subjunctive in a noun clause which depends on them. Verbs of *wishing* and *desiring* require the subjunctive in a dependent noun clause.

Quiero que Juan me acompañe.   I want John to go with me.
Desean que Carlos se quede en el hotel.   They want Charles to stay at the hotel.
No queremos que cierren el museo.   We do not want them to close the museum.

■ Práctica

a. *Substituya siguiendo el modelo.*

Quieren que Vd. visite el museo.
Quieren que yo visite el museo.

1. Quieren que Vd. visite el museo.
   yo / tú / nosotros / vosotros / ellos
2. Quieren que Juan los acompañe.
   tú / vosotros / yo / Vd. y yo / Vds.
3. Quieren que Vds. vuelvan.
   él / tú / nosotros / yo / vosotros
4. Quieren que pasemos a otra sala.
   Vd. / tú / yo / vosotros / ellas / tú y yo

5. Quieren que nos vistamos inmediatamente.
   yo / Vd. / tú / nosotros / vosotros / ellos
6. No desean que Vd. les muestre los cuadros.
   tú / yo / Vd. y yo / ellas / vosotros
7. No desean que Paco se quede en el hotel.
   Vds. / tú / vosotros / yo / tú y yo / Vd.
8. No desean que yo me duerma.
   ella / tú / nosotros / Ana / vosotros
9. No desean que cierren el museo.
   Vd. / tú / yo / vosotros / nosotros
10. No desean que devolvamos el libro.
    yo / nosotros / vosotros / Vd. / tú / Vds.

b. *Diga en español.*

1. I want him to read.
2. I want them to speak.
3. I want you to return.
4. I want you all to count.
5. I want her to dance.
6. She wants them to eat.
7. She wants you all to understand.
8. She wants us to sit down.
9. She wants me to stay here.
10. She wants him to get dressed.

3. *Position of adjectives.* There are two kinds of adjectives, limiting adjectives (numerals, demonstratives, possessives, interrogatives, indefinites, negatives, etc.) and descriptive adjectives.

a. Limiting adjectives regularly precede the noun.

treinta muchachos	**sus camisas**
el primer viaje	**¿ qué lección?**
este museo	**ningún pintor**

b. Descriptive adjectives usually follow the noun. They regularly follow when they differentiate the noun from others of its class.

un pintor español a Spanish painter (not a French or an English painter)

una colección impresionante an impressive collection (not an ordinary collection)

un museo famoso a famous museum (not just any museum)

But when the descriptive adjective denotes an inherent or logical characteristic of the person or thing named by the noun, it precedes. An inherent characteristic is one which is normally associated with the person or thing. A logical characteristic is one which, in the light of our previous knowledge, is associated with the person or thing.

la blanca nieve   the white snow. (Snow is inherently white; normally, whiteness is a characteristic of snow.)

la hermosa naturaleza   beautiful nature. (Nature is inherently beautiful.)

el gran Simón Bolívar   the great Simón Bolívar. (In the light of what we know about Bolívar, greatness is a logical characteristic of his.)

el famoso Cervantes   the famous Cervantes. (In the light of our knowledge of Cervantes, fame is a logical characteristic of his.)

To illustrate further these two uses of the descriptive adjective:

We say **un museo famoso,** *a famous museum,* to distinguish a museum which is famous from just any museum. If we talk about *the famous Prado Museum,* we say **el famoso Museo del Prado,** since the Prado, being one of the great museums of the world, is logically famous.

Notice that differentiating adjectives are words that we stress. They follow the noun because this is the stressed position. Adjectives that normally precede their noun will follow the noun when stressed.

Es un buen libro.   It's a good book.

Es un libro muy bueno.   It's a very good book.

Éste es nuestro primer viaje.   This is our first trip.

Viven en la Avenida Primera.   They live on First Avenue (not Fifth Avenue, etc.).

Some adjectives vary in meaning, depending upon whether they follow or precede the noun. When they follow the noun, they are differentiating adjectives and usually have their basic meaning.

el muchacho pobre   the poor (not rich) boy
el pobre muchacho   the poor (pitiful) boy
un hombre grande   a big man
un gran hombre   a great man
un traje nuevo   a new suit
un nuevo traje   another suit

■ Práctica

Diga en español.

1. It's a famous museum.
   It's the famous Prado Museum.

2. It's an interesting city.
   It's the interesting city of Madrid.
3. It's a large university.
   It's the great University of Salamanca.
4. He's a Mexican actor.
   He's the well-known actor Cantinflas.
5. Murillo is a good painter.
   Goya is a very good painter.
6. Mr. González is a poor man.
   Poor Mr. González is very ill.

D. Writing

Test yourself

1. Today you want to visit a very famous museum, the famous Prado Museum.
2. It has some very impressive collections of Spanish paintings.
3. You want Juan to go with you, but you wish Carlos to stay in the hotel.
4. You don't want him to go to sleep or to die of boredom.
5. It is getting late and you want Juan to dress quickly.
6. In the museum you run into Jaime and the two girls.
7. You want Jaime to show you the Velázquez Room.
8. He takes you there and explains to you the great Spanish painter's technique.
9. Virginia and María want you to go into another room.
10. They are tired and want to sit down.
11. You want Jaime to return with you to the Velázquez Room to see those paintings again.
12. Suddenly a bell sounds.
13. You don't want them to close the museum.
14. "Don't worry," says Jaime. "We can come back here tomorrow."

Composition

You visit a famous museum near where you live. You want a friend to go with you, because he knows a lot about art. Write a composition telling whom you want to go with you, what collections the museum contains, what paintings you want him to show you, whom you run into in the museum, what they want you to see, etc.

AMAPOLA*

JOSEPH M. LACALLE

*Copyrighted by Edward B. Marks Music Corporation. Used by permission.

A - MA - PO - LA, ____ lin - dí - si - ma A-MA-

PO - LA, ____ se - rá siem - pre mi al - ma tu - ya so - la. ____ Yo te quie - ro, ____ a - ma-da ni - ña mí - a, ____ i - gual que a-ma la flor la luz del

dí - a._____ A - MA - PO - LA,_____ lin - dí - si - ma A - MA -

PO - LA,_____ no se - as tan in - gra - ta y á - ma -

me._____ A - MA - PO - LA, _____ A - MA - PO - LA,_____

poco rall.

_____ ¿có - mo pue - des tú vi - vir tan so - la?_____

LESSON 18

A. Regular present subjunctive of some irregular verbs

Among the irregular verbs which form their present subjunctive regularly (that is, on the stem of the first person singular, present indicative) are the following ten:

decir: diga	**salir: salga**
hacer: haga	**tener: tenga**
poder: pueda	**valer: valga**
poner: ponga	**venir: venga**
querer: quiera	**conocer: conozca**

■ Práctica

Cambie según se indica, siguiendo el modelo.

Quieren que yo se lo diga.
Quieren que Vd. se lo diga.

1. Quieren que yo se lo diga.
   Vd. / tú / nosotros / ellas / vosotros

2. Quieren que Vd. lo haga pronto.
   tú / vosotros / yo / nosotros / Vds.

3. Quieren que tú lo pongas aquí.
   vosotros / yo / Vd. y yo / él / ellos

4. Quieren que él lo tenga para mañana.
   yo / nosotros / ellas / tú / vosotros

5. Desean que Vds. salgan ahora.
   nosotros / tú / vosotros / él / yo

6. Desean que nosotros también vengamos.
   Vd. / Vds. / yo / tú y yo / vosotros / tú

7. Desean que yo los conozca bien.
   tú / Vd. / vosotros / Vd. y yo / ella

B.　Irregular present subjunctive of some irregular verbs

A few irregular verbs are irregular in the present subjunctive. Among them are **dar, estar,** and **ir.** Others will be introduced in Lesson 19.

dar		estar		ir	
dé	demos	esté	estemos	vaya	vayamos
des	deis	estés	estéis	vayas	vayáis
Vd. dé	Vds. den	Vd. esté	Vds. estén	Vd. vaya	Vds. vayan
dé	den	esté	estén	vaya	vayan

■ Práctica

Cambie según se indica, siguiendo el modelo.

Quieren que yo se lo dé mañana.
Quieren que Vd. se lo dé mañana.

1. Quieren que yo se lo dé mañana.
   Vd. / vosotros / ellos / Vd. y yo / tú
2. Quieren que ella vaya allá.
   yo / tú / vosotros / nosotros / ellas
3. Desean que ustedes estén aquí.
   tú / yo / él / tú y yo / vosotros

C.　Listening and speaking

aconsejar to advise
Andalucía Andalusia (*region in southern Spain*)
andaluz, andaluza Andalusian
antes de before
el asunto matter
avisar to inform, let know
el consejo (piece of) advice
el contacto contact
Córdoba Cordova
decidirse a to decide to
desde from
El Escorial palace, church, and monastery 27 miles northwest of Madrid, built (1563–1584) by Philip II
la estación station

Horacio Horace
inmediatamente immediately
el negocio business
la oportunidad opportunity
el par pair, couple
partir to start, leave
permitir to permit, allow
rogar (ue) to beg
Sevilla Seville
sugerir (ie) to suggest
el sur south
el taxi taxi
el teléfono telephone
terminar to finish
el tren train
urgente urgent
urgir to be urgent

IDIOMS AND OTHER EXPRESSIONS

¡cómo no! of course!
cuanto antes as soon as possible
estar de vuelta to be back
haga Vd. el favor (de + *infin.***)** please
¡mire Vd.! look!

¿qué hacer? what to do? what shall I do? etc.
quiera Dios (may) God grant
en seguida at once
a tiempo in time
¡vaya con Dios! off with you! good-by!

Hagamos un viaje a Andalucía

Eran las nueve y media de la mañana cuando sonó el teléfono.
—¡Diga![1]
—¡Oiga![1] Habla Jaime Montero.[1] ¿Con quién hablo yo?
—Con Horacio Jones.
—Mire Vd., mi padre acaba de decirme que vaya a Córdoba en nuestro coche. Es un asunto de negocios y es muy urgente. Sugiere que los lleve a Vds. si quieren acompañarme. Queremos que Vds. tengan la oportunidad de conocer el sur de España. ¿Podrían estar listos a las tres de la tarde?
—Muchas gracias. Nos gustaría mucho acompañarle. Pero mire, mis amigos están hoy en El Escorial. Tomaron el tren de las ocho[2] y no volverán hasta las siete. No podría ponerme en contacto con ellos. ¿Qué hacer?
—¿Me permite que le dé un consejo?
—¡Cómo no! ¿Qué me aconseja?
—Que tome el tren de las diez y que vaya a buscarlos. Salga inmediatamente a la calle y tome un taxi. Llegará a tiempo a la estación y será muy fácil encontrarlos en El Escorial. Pueden estar de vuelta antes de las tres. Dígales que vengan, porque será un viaje muy agradable. Al terminar mis negocios en Córdoba, iremos a Sevilla, porque quiero que conozcan Vds. esa maravillosa ciudad andaluza. Pasaremos un par de días allí y luego iremos a Granada para ver la Alhambra. Mire, al volver a Madrid haga el favor de llamarme por teléfono desde la estación para avisarme.
—Bueno, voy en seguida.
—Muy bien, vaya con Dios. Pero les ruego que estén listos a las tres. Urge el negocio y debemos partir cuanto antes. Quiera Dios que encuentre a sus amigos y que se decidan a hacer el viaje.
Eran las diez menos veinte cuando salí del hotel. Pero llegué a tiempo a la estación, tomé el tren de las diez, y encontré fácilmente a mis amigos en El Escorial.

■ Preguntas

1. ¿A qué hora suena el teléfono?
2. ¿Quién llama?
3. ¿Qué dice?
4. ¿Qué le acaba de decir su padre?
5. ¿Qué sugiere su padre?
6. ¿Por qué quieren que Vds. acompañen a Jaime?
7. ¿Adónde han ido los amigos de Vd.?
8. ¿Qué tren tomaron?
9. ¿A qué hora volverán?
10. ¿Qué le aconseja Jaime?
11. ¿A qué hora podrían Vds. estar de vuelta?
12. ¿Qué ciudades visitarán Vds.?
13. ¿Qué quiere Jaime que haga Vd. al llegar a la estación?
14. ¿A qué hora desea Jaime que Vds. estén listos?
15. ¿Qué hora era cuando Vd. salió del hotel?
16. ¿Llegó Vd. tarde a la estación?

NOTES

1. In Spain the person who answers the telephone says, **"Diga."** The person calling replies, **"Oiga"** ("Listen") and may ask, **"¿Con quién hablo?"** ("With whom am I speaking?" "Who is this?"). In other countries other expressions are used for **"Diga,"**—for example, **"Bueno"** in Mexico, **"Aló"** in Chile, **"Hola"** in Argentina, **"A ver"** in Colombia.
2. Expressions like "the eight-o'clock train," "the twelve-o'clock bus" are in Spanish, **"el tren de las ocho," "el autobús de las doce."**

D. Structure

1. *Subjunctive mood in the noun clause.* Another group of verbs which require the subjunctive in a noun clause depending on them are verbs of *commanding* and *requesting.*

Mi padre me dice que vaya.   My father tells me to go. (My father tells me that I go.)

Les ruego que estén listos a las tres.   I beg you to be ready at three o'clock. (I beg you that you be ready . . .)

Le pido a Carlos que me acompañe.   I ask Charles to go with me. (I ask Charles that he go with me.)

Note that, unlike **querer** and **desear,** these verbs of commanding and requesting may take an indirect object in the main clause.

Le **ruegan a** *Vd.* **que venga.** They beg *you* to come. (They beg *you* that you come.)

Díga*les* que vuelvan. Tell *them* to come back. (Tell *them* that they come back.)

Some common verbs of commanding and requesting are

pedir (i) to ask, request	**mandar** to command
rogar (ue) to beg, request	**decir** to tell

Do not confuse the two meanings of **decir**. **Decir** means (1) *to tell* in the sense of *to inform* and (2) *to tell* in the sense of *to order*. The second meaning takes the subjunctive in a dependent noun clause, as you have just seen. The first you have been using since early in the book, with the indicative:

Haga Vd. el favor de *decir***le** *que ha llamado* **el señor Núñez.** Please *tell* him *that* Mr. Núñez *has called.*

Many verbs similar in idea to verbs of commanding and requesting also require the subjunctive in a dependent noun clause.

preferir (ie) to prefer	**dejar** to let, allow
sugerir (ie) to suggest	**impedir (i)** to prevent
aconsejar to advise	**proponer** to propose, suggest
permitir to permit	**insistir en** to insist on

Me aconseja que tome el tren. He advises me to take the train.

Les propongo que salgamos temprano. I suggest to them that we leave early.

■ Práctica

a. *Cambie según se indica, siguiendo el modelo.*

Tomo un taxi.
Sugieren que tome un taxi.

1. Voy a la estación en seguida.
   aconsejan que / insisten en que / prefieren que
2. Me avisan a tiempo.
   les ruego que / les digo que / les propongo que
3. Se lo damos mañana.
   Vd. sugiere que / Vd. permite que / Vd. aconseja que
4. Ella sale hoy.
   no impiden que / insisten en que / prefieren que
5. Lo ponen aquí.
   les sugiero que / les propongo que / les permito que

b. *Cambie según se indica, siguiendo el modelo.*

Les ruego a Vds. que estén de vuelta temprano.
Le ruego a él que esté de vuelta temprano.

1. Les ruego a Vds. que estén de vuelta temprano.
   a Vd. / a ellas / a Pepe / a ellos
2. Le permito a María que lo devuelva.
   a ellas / a ella / a Vds. / a la muchacha
3. Les dice a Vds. que lo hagan cuanto antes.
   a ellas / a Vd. / a los alumnos / a Dolores
4. Le propongo a él que lo termine mañana.
   a Vds. / al abogado / a los alumnos / a Marta
5. Les sugiero a ellos que vayan en avión.
   a Vd. / a mis amigos / a él / a mis hermanas

c. *Diga en español y cambie según se indica.*

1. I tell you to leave as soon as possible.
   to go / to come
2. They ask me to return tomorrow.
   to finish / to be back
3. We beg him to remain.
   to sit down / to get up
4. He orders them to do it at once.
   to say it / to buy it
5. You tell us to be here in time.
   to order it / to read it

   2. *Imperfect tense of* ser *in expressions of time.* The imperfect of **ser** is used in expressing time in the past. As in expressions of time in the present, the plural is used from *two o'clock* on.

   Era la una y media de la tarde. It was one-thirty in the afternoon.
   Eran las diez de la mañana. It was ten o'clock in the morning.

■ Práctica

Diga en español.

1. It was nine o'clock.
2. It was twelve-thirty.
3. It was quarter after one.

4. It was seven o'clock in the morning.
5. It was four o'clock in the afternoon.
6. It was ten o'clock at night.

E. Writing

Test yourself

1. Jaime Montero has just called her.
2. His father has told him to go to Córdoba in his car.
3. He suggests that she and her friends accompany him.
4. He wants them to have the opportunity of seeing the south of Spain—Andalusia.
5. They would like to go, but they could not be ready at three o'clock.
6. Her friends are at El Escorial and will not be back until seven o'clock.
7. He advises her to take the ten o'clock train and go to look for them.
8. He suggests that she go out and take a taxi to the station.
9. Tell your friends to come, because we shall go to that marvellous Andalusian city, Seville.
10. Please telephone me from the station upon returning to Madrid.
11. He begs her to be ready at three, because they ought to start as soon as possible.
12. It was twenty minutes to ten when she left.

Composition

Write a composition in which you give María some advice. Her father has just telephoned from Texas. He wants her and her brother to come home at once, because their grandfather is ill. But Juan has gone off on a field trip, and María cannot reach him by phone. Advise her what to do in order to find him.

Street scenes: The Calle de Alcalá in the business center of Madrid. (© Screen Traveler, from Gendreau)

(Left) City streets:
Subway entrance,
Calle de Alcalá, Madrid.
(Philip D. Gendreau)

(Below) Sidewalk
café on the
Avenida de Jose
Antonio, Madrid.
(Philip D. Gendreau)

Seville: A residential street. (Philip D. Gendreau)

(Top and center) Along the Rambla in Barcelona. (Top: © Screen Traveler, from Gendreau; Center: Three Lions, Inc.)

Seville: The Calle de las Sierpes. Notice the sun screen stretched between the buildings. (Philip D. Gendreau)

LESSON 19

A. Present subjunctive of *ser, ver, saber*

ser		ver		saber	
sea	seamos	vea	veamos	sepa	sepamos
seas	seáis	veas	veáis	sepas	sepáis
Vd. sea	Vds. sean	Vd. vea	Vds. vean	Vd. sepa	Vds. sepan
sea	sean	vea	vean	sepa	sepan

■ Práctica

Cambie según se indica, siguiendo el modelo.

Prefieren que yo lo sepa.
Prefieren que nosotros lo sepamos.

1. Prefieren que yo lo sepa.
   Vds. / tú / vosotros / tú y yo / él
2. Quieren que Vd. vea la ciudad.
   tú / ellos / vosotros / nosotros / yo
3. Deseo que tú seas honrado.
   él / nosotros / ellos / vosotros / Vd.

B. Present perfect subjunctive

The present perfect subjunctive of a verb is formed by combining the present subjunctive of **haber,** which is formed irregularly, with the past participle of the verb.

hablar	vivir
haya hablado	haya vivido
hayas hablado	hayas vivido
Vd. haya hablado	Vd. haya vivido
haya hablado	haya vivido
hayamos hablado	hayamos vivido
hayáis hablado	hayáis vivido
Vds. hayan hablado	Vds. hayan vivido
hayan hablado	hayan vivido

■ Práctica

Cambie según se indica.

1. Esperan que él haya llegado temprano.
   ellas / yo / tú / vosotros / nosotros / Paco
2. Esperan que Vds. hayan vuelto a la universidad.
   yo / nosotros / él / vosotros / tú / ellos
3. Esperan que ella lo haya escrito.
   nosotros / yo / tú / vosotros / los alumnos / él

C. Listening and speaking

alegrarse (de) to be glad
el azulejo colored tile
el camarero waiter
el canto flamenco flamenco
  (*Andalusian gypsy singing*)
la catedral cathedral
la comedia comedy
la copa (wine) glass
creer to believe, think
el dramaturgo playwright
dudar to doubt
entender (ie) to understand
esperar to hope

estrecho narrow
extrañar to surprise
el flan custard
la función performance, show
la Giralda cathedral tower in
  Seville
el inconveniente objection
la mezquita mosque
el monumento monument
negar (ie) to deny
la pared wall
posible possible
el postre dessert

sabroso delicious
la sopa soup
temer to fear
todo every
el vino wine

IDIOMS AND OTHER EXPRESSIONS

el arroz (rice) con pollo
(chicken) chicken with rice
comerse las eses to eat up
(swallow) the (letter) *s*

darse prisa to hurry
estar bien de salud to be in
good health
estar para (+ *infin.*) to be
about to
(le extraña) que haya . . . (she
is surprised) that there is, that
there are . . .
es lástima it's too bad
por aquí this way
de postre as (for) dessert
quedar agradecido to be grateful

En un café de Sevilla

—Por aquí—dijo Jaime Montero. Pasamos por una de esas calles estrechas de Sevilla y entramos en un café muy interesante. Por las paredes había azulejos muy hermosos. Había un guitarrista y una muchacha que cantaba canto flamenco.

Nos sentamos a una mesa y Jaime pidió una comida muy sabrosa: una buena sopa, arroz con pollo y, de postre, flan. En la mesa había copas para vino, pero no tomamos vino, porque no nos gusta. Nos sirvió un camarero andaluz, naturalmente, y por ser andaluz no pudimos entenderle.

—Cuando salimos para España—dijo Carlos—yo no entendía muy bien el español. Aquí he aprendido mucho, pero no puedo entender a este camarero.

—Sepa Vd.—contestó Jaime—que habla y entiende muy bien. Vd. no entiende al camerero porque, como todo andaluz, se come las eses.

—Me alegro de que Vd. nos haya invitado a hacer este viaje—dijo Virginia. Vd. ha hecho mucho por nosotros y le quedamos muy agradecidos. Sólo siento que mi padre no haya venido con nosotros. Siempre ha querido ver esos monumentos que acabamos de visitar: la Mezquita de Córdoba, la Catedral de Sevilla con su Giralda, y sobre todo la Alhambra, que veremos mañana.

—Es lástima que no la haya acompañado. Pero algún día vendrá a España, ¿verdad?

—No creo que sea posible. Es muy viejo y no está muy bien de salud. Por eso dudo que haga el viaje.

—Si Vds. no tienen inconveniente, vamos ahora al teatro. Quiero que vean una comedia de dos dramaturgos andaluces, los hermanos Álvarez Quintero. Espero que sea divertida. Pero temo que sea un poco tarde. Por eso tenemos que darnos prisa. Debemos estar en el teatro a las diez y media. La función está para empezar.

—Me extraña que haya funciones a esa hora—exclamó María.
—Para nosotros no es tarde—explicó Jaime. —En España las funciones siempre empiezan a esa hora.

■ Preguntas

1. ¿Dónde estaba el café?
2. ¿Cómo era el café?
3. ¿Quién tocaba y quién cantaba?
4. ¿Qué cantaba?
5. ¿Qué comieron Vds.?
6. ¿Qué copas había en la mesa?
7. ¿Qué era el camarero?
8. ¿Qué dijo Carlos?
9. ¿Qué le responde Jaime?
10. ¿Cómo hablan muchos andaluces?
11. ¿De qué se alegra Virginia?
12. ¿Qué siente ella?
13. ¿Qué ha querido siempre su padre?
14. ¿Cómo está el padre de Virginia?
15. ¿Qué duda Virginia?
16. ¿Adónde propone Jaime que vayan?
17. ¿Qué van a ver?
18. ¿Qué espera Jaime?
19. ¿Qué teme?
20. ¿Qué le extraña a María?

D. Structure

1. *Subjunctive mood in the noun clause*
a. Verbs of *emotion* require the subjunctive in a dependent noun clause.

Me alegro de que Vd. nos haya invitado.   *I am glad (that) you have invited us.*
Temo que sea un poco tarde.   *I am afraid (that) it is* a little late.

Note that the present subjunctive expresses future as well as present time.

Espero que la comedia *sea* divertida.   I hope (that) the comedy *will be* amusing.

Some common expressions of emotion are

sentir (ie)　to regret, feel sorry	**alegrarse (de)**　to be glad
esperar　to hope	**es lástima**　it's too bad
temer　to fear	**extrañar**　to surprise

b. Verbs of *doubt, denial,* and *uncertainty* require the subjunctive in a dependent noun clause. Included in this group are *verbs of belief used negatively.*

Dudo que haga el viaje.　*I doubt that he will take* the trip.
Carlos niega que lo hayan hecho.　Charles *denies that they have done* it.
No creo que sea posible.　*I do not think it is* possible.

But verbs of doubt and denial, when used negatively, are followed by the indicative.

No dudo que está en la ciudad.　I do not doubt that he is in the city.
No niega que lo han hecho.　He does not deny that they have done it.

And verbs of belief, when used affirmatively, are followed by the indicative.

Creo que estarán aquí mañana.　I think they will be here tomorrow.

a. *Cambie según el modelo.*

No están aquí.
Siento que no estén aquí.

1. No toman sopa.
    me extraña que / me alegro de que
2. Don Roberto lo hará mañana.
    espero que / temo que
3. Mi amiga no lo sabe.
    siento que / es lástima que
4. Isabel se va ahora.
    no creo que / me alegro de que
5. Ellos vendrán hoy.
    dudo que / niego que

b. *Diga en español, cambiando según se indica.*

1. He is glad that we are here.
    that you are here / that I am here

2. She hopes that you will give it to them soon.
    that they will give it to them / that we will give it to them
3. It surprises her that we know it.
    that you know it / that they know it
4. We doubt that he is Spanish.
    that they are Spanish / that you are Spanish
5. I don't believe they will leave today.
    that he will leave / that we shall leave

2. *Use of the present perfect subjunctive.* The present perfect subjunctive
is used wherever we use a present perfect tense in English, but where a
subjunctive is required in Spanish.

Siento que mi parde *no haya venido.*   I am sorry that my father *has not
come.*
No creemos que *hayan visto* **la Alhambra.**   We don't think *they have seen*
the Alhambra.

■ Práctica

Diga en español, cambiando según se indica.

1. They are sorry she has left.
    we have left / I have left
2. He denies that we have done it.
    that I have done it / that you have done it
3. It is too bad that she has returned.
    that they have returned / that we have returned
4. I am afraid he is ill.
    we are ill / they are ill
5. She is glad that I have arrived.
    that he has arrived / that they have arrived.

3. *Uses of* **para** *and* **por.** **Para** means *in order to.*

Estudiamos *para* **aprender.**   We study *to* (*in order to*) learn.

Por means *by, through, along, around.*

Me llamaron *por* **teléfono.**   They called me *by* telephone.
Es un libro escrito *por* **Cervantes.**   It is a book written *by* Cervantes.
Vamos *por* **aquí.**   Let's go this way (*through* here).

Viajamos *por* España.   We traveled *through* Spain.
Pasamos *por* una calle estrecha.   We went *through* (*along*) a narrow
street.
***Por* las paredes había azulejos.**   *Around* the walls there were colored tiles.
Estará de vuelta *por* Navidad.   He'll be back *around* Christmas.

But both **para** and **por** have several uses in which they are translated
generally by English *for*. Here the meanings of English *for* must be carefully distinguished.

para

1. *for* (destination)

Salimos *para* España.   We left *for* Spain.
Este libro es *para* Vd.   This book is *for* you.
Ésta es la lección *para* mañana.   This is the lesson *for* tomorrow.

2. *for* (purpose)

Había copas *para* el vino.   There were glasses *for* the wine.

3. *for* (comparison)

***Para* nosotros no es tarde.**   *For* us it isn't late.

por

1. *for* (*because of, on account of, out of*)

***por* eso**   *for* that reason, *because of* that, *therefore*
***Por* ser andaluz no le entendimos.**   *Because of* (*On account of*) his being
an Andalusian we did not understand him.
Lo hizo *por* caridad.   He did it *for* (*out of*) charity.

2. *for* (*on behalf of, for the sake of*)

Vd. ha hecho mucho *por* nosotros.   You have done a lot *for* us.

3. *for* (*in exchange for*)

Pagué dos pesetas *por* las flores.   I paid two pesetas *for* the flowers.

4. *for* (duration of time)

Estaremos en Sevilla *por* ocho días.   We shall be in Seville *for* a week.

5. *for* (in exclamations)

¡*por* Dios!   *for* heaven's sake!

■ Práctica

Diga en español, cambiando según se indica.

1. We read in order to understand.
   in order to learn / in order to know
2. He has left for Spain.
   for Argentina / for Brazil
3. The flowers are for me.
   for her / for them / for you all
4. This lesson is for Thursday.
   for tomorrow / for Friday
5. They did it out of charity.
   out of kindness
6. They will do it for me.
   for her / for us / for them
7. I don't understand him on account of his being a Frenchman.
   on account of his being an Englishman / on account of his being
   Italian
8. There were glasses for wine.
   for sherry (jerez) / for champagne (champaña)
9. They have paid ten pesos for the book.
   for the hat / for the tie
10. She will be here for a month.
    for a year / for a week
11. It is very early for them.
    for us / for me / for him
12. They will be here around February.
    around Christmas / around August
13. We're about to leave.
    about to return / about to enter
14. He is traveling through France.
    through England / through Spain

E.   Writing

Test yourself

1. "This way," Jaime said to us, and we went into a very interesting
   café.
2. In the café there was a guitarist, and a girl was singing flamenco.
3. We ordered a delicious dinner of soup, chicken with rice, and custard.

4. Because the waiter was Andalusian, Carlos could not understand him.
5. Like many Andalusians, he swallowed his *s*'s.
6. Virginia is glad that Jaime has invited us, but she is sorry that her father has not come with us.
7. She doesn't think that he will make the trip to Spain, because he is old and is not in good health.
8. Jaime wants us to see a comedy of two Andalusian dramatists.
9. He hopes that it will be amusing.
10 We have to hurry, because the performance is about to begin.
11. María is surprised that there are performances at ten-thirty.

Composition

Write a composition telling how you feel about things today. Tell what you are glad about, what you regret, and what you hope will happen. Use as many verbs of emotion as you can. Tell what you don't think or you doubt has happened and what you think will take place.

CONVERSATIONAL INTERLUDE

En la casa de correos

Carlos. Tenga Vd. la bondad de decirme dónde se puede comprar sellos.

Primer Empleado. Pase Vd. a la ventanilla número trece.

Carlos. ¿Me hace Vd. el favor de un sello para el correo aéreo?

Segundo Empleado. ¿Para el interior?

Carlos. Para los Estados Unidos.

Segundo Empleado. Aquí lo tiene Vd. Son seis pesetas y veinticinco centavos.

Carlos. Muchas gracias. ¿Se puede certificar la carta aquí?

Segundo Empleado. No, señor. En la ventanilla de al lado se certifican cartas.

Carlos. Muchas gracias. Dígame Vd., ¿cuánto tarda en llegar a Nueva York el correo aéreo?

Segundo Empleado. Tarda dos días, señor.

LESSON 20

A. Present subjunctive of orthographic-changing verbs in *-car, -gar, -zar*

You have already seen (Lesson 9) that in the first person singular of the preterit, verbs ending in **-car** and **-gar** change **c** to **qu (busqué)** and **g** to **gu (pagué)**. These changes are made so that the sound of **c** and **g** in the infinitive may be preserved throughout the conjugation. An **e** in the personal ending, if added directly to **c** or **g** would change the pronunciation of these letters. The same change in spelling (**c** to **qu** and **g** to **gu**) is made throughout the present subjunctive. You have also learned that verbs in **-zar** change **z** to **c** in the first person singular of the preterit **(empecé)**. While this change is not necessary to preserve the sound of **z,** it is conventional. It occurs also throughout the present subjunctive.

buscar to look for	**pagar** to pay	**empezar** to begin
bus*que*	pa*gue*	empie*ce*
bus*que*s	pa*gue*s	empie*ce*s
Vd. bus*que*	Vd. pa*gue*	Vd. empie*ce*
bus*que*	pa*gue*	empie*ce*
bus*que*mos	pa*gue*mos	empe*ce*mos
bus*qué*is	pa*gué*is	empe*cé*is
Vds. bus*que*n	Vds. pa*gue*n	Vds. empie*ce*n
bus*que*n	pa*gue*n	empie*ce*n

■ Práctica

Cambie según se indica.

1. Prefieren que Vd. llegue pronto.
   tú / ellos / vosotros / yo / nosotros
2. Ruegan que lo busquemos hoy.
   yo / vosotros / Vd. / ellas / tú / tú y yo
3. Sugieren que yo lo comience.
   Vd. / nosotros / tú / Vds. / vosotros

B. Present indicative and present subjunctive of orthographic-changing verbs in -*guir*

Verbs ending in **-guir** change **gu** to **g** in the first person singular of the present indicative and throughout the present subjunctive.

seguir (i)   to follow; to continue

PRESENT INDICATIVE		PRESENT SUBJUNCTIVE	
si*g*o	seguimos	si*g*a	si*g*amos
sigues	seguís	si*g*as	si*g*áis
Vd. sigue	Vds. siguen	Vd. si*g*a	Vds. si*g*an
sigue	siguen	si*g*a	si*g*an

■ Práctica

Cambie según se indica.

1. Los alumnos siguen conversando.
   Vd. / vosotros / tú / nosotros / yo
2. Esperan que tú sigas bien.
   Vds. / él / yo / Vd. / tú y yo / vosotros

C. Listening and speaking

almorzar (ue) to lunch
la animación bustle, movement
el árbol tree
la cantidad quantity
el catalán Catalan
conviene it is advisable
la derecha right (hand)
derecho straight (ahead)
el edificio building
enseñar to teach

la esquina corner
fabricar to manufacture
el ferrocarril railroad
fundar to found
el habitante inhabitant
industrial industrial
la izquierda left (hand)
lejos far
lo the
lo que *rel. pron.* that which, what

la **Lonja** Exchange
el **material rodante** rolling stock
moderno modern
necesario necessary
ofrecerse a to offer to
la **palabra** word
preciso necessary
probable probable
producir to produce
puntual punctual
la **rambla** boulevard (*in Barcelona*)
saludar to greet
tacaño stingy
el **tejido** textile
Tomás Thomas

varios several
el **yanqui** Yankee

IDIOMS AND OTHER EXPRESSIONS

estar citado to have an appointment, date
unos cuantos a few
parece mentira it seems incredible
en todas partes everywhere
a pie on foot
la **Plaza** (Square) **de Cataluña** (Catalonia) central square in Barcelona
lo de siempre the same old thing

En Barcelona

—Es preciso que estemos en la Plaza de Cataluña a las nueve y media— le dije a Carlos mientras tomábamos el desayuno en el hotel en Barcelona. —Estamos citados con don Tomás Milá.

—¿Dónde queda[1] la Plaza de Cataluña?—le pregunté al camarero que nos servía.

—Está bastante lejos, señor. Si Vd. va a pie, vaya a la izquierda al salir del hotel. Al llegar a la esquina hay que ir a la derecha hasta la Rambla. Luego vaya otra vez a la izquierda y siga derecho.

—¡Son las nueve y veinte!—exclamé al salir del hotel. —Conviene que busquemos un taxi. Es necesario llegar a tiempo, porque estos catalanes son muy puntuales. ¡Son los yanquis de España!

Don Tomás era un viejo amigo del profesor Martínez. —¿Cómo sigue[2] mi buen amigo allá en América?—fue lo primero que nos dijo don Tomás después de saludarnos.[3] —Veo que les ha enseñado muy bien el español. Pero es probable que no les haya enseñado nada de catalán. ¡Lástima! Como aquí se habla catalán, conviene saber unas cuantas palabras.

Don Tomás iba a mostrarnos algunos de los puntos de interés de Barcelona. —Empecemos con la Catedral—nos dijo. —No está muy lejos.

Vimos también la Lonja, fundada en 1383, la Universidad, fundada en 1450—pero cuyos edificios son modernos—y otras cosas muy interesantes. Barcelona es una ciudad impresionante. Tiene más de[4] un millón de habitantes. (Madrid tiene más de dos millones, pero Sevilla es más pequeña: tiene menos de 500.000.) Es una ciudad industrial. Aquí se fabrican tejidos en grandes cantidades y se produce mucho material rodante para los ferrocarriles.

Después de visitar varios puntos de interés, Carlos exclamó de pronto:
—Propongo que almorcemos. ¡Tengo mucha hambre!

Almorzamos en un buen café que había en una de las Ramblas. —Lo mejor de Barcelona—dijo Carlos—es esta Rambla con sus flores y sus árboles.

—Para mí—dije—lo más interesante es la animación que se ve en todas partes. Estos catalanes se dan mucha prisa, como los norteamericanos. Parece mentira que sean españoles.

Después de hablar un rato de lo que habíamos visto, don Tomás se despidió. Al quedarme solo con Carlos, no me ofrecí a pagar la cuenta. Carlos no había pagado nada hasta entonces. Es un poco tacaño.

—¡Caramba!—exclamó de pronto. —¿Es posible que haya dejado mi dinero en el hotel? No lo encuentro.

—¡Lo de siempre!—pensé. —¡Ahora es necesario que yo pague otra vez!

■ Preguntas

1. ¿Dónde es preciso que estemos a las nueve y media?
2. ¿Con quién estamos citados?
3. ¿Qué le pregunta Vd. al camarero?
4. Al salir del hotel ¿cómo se llega a la Plaza de Cataluña?
5. ¿Qué conviene que busquemos?
6. ¿Quién es don Tomás?
7. ¿Qué nos pregunta?
8. ¿Qué lengua se habla en Barcelona?
9. ¿Qué nos sugiere don Tomás?
10. ¿Qué vemos también?
11. ¿Cuántos habitantes tiene Barcelona?
12. ¿Cuántos tiene Madrid?
13. ¿Cuántos tiene Sevilla?
14. ¿Qué se fabrica en Barcelona?
15. ¿Qué más se produce?
16. ¿Qué propone Carlos?
17. Para Vd. ¿qué es lo más interesante de Barcelona?
18. ¿Cómo es Carlos?
19. ¿Qué exclama él?
20. ¿Qué es necesario que haga Vd.?

NOTES

1. **Quedar** sometimes means *to be.*

   Quedamos muy agradecidos.   We are very greatful.
   ¿Dónde queda la Plaza?   Where is the Square?

2. **Seguir** sometimes means *to be now, to still be.*

   ¿Cómo sigue el señor Martínez?   How is Mr. Martínez now?
   Sigue muy bien.   He is still very well.

3. You have been using **al** plus an infinitive to mean *upon* (*doing something*). This is a pattern in Spanish. After a preposition the infinitive must be used to translate the English verbal noun in *-ing.*

   Al entrar en el café . . .   On entering the café . . .
   Después de hablar un rato . . .   After talking a while . . .
   Antes de comer . . .   Before eating . . .

4. **Más que** (*more than*) becomes **más de** before a numeral. Likewise **menos que** (*less than*) becomes **menos de** (*fewer than*).

   Barcelona tiene más de un millón de habitantes.   Barcelona has more than one million inhabitants.
   Sevilla tiene menos de 500.000.   Seville has fewer than 500,000.

■ Práctica

Diga en español, cambiando según se indica.

a. 1. before leaving
      lunching / sitting down / reading
   2. after returning
      answering / writing / studying
   3. upon getting up
      going to bed / waking up / getting dressed

b. 1. I have more than ten.
      more than fifty / more than seventy
   2. He needs more than I.
      more than you / more than they
   3. We want more than a hundred.
      more than ninety / more than sixty

D. Structure

1. *Subjunctive mood in the noun clause.* Impersonal expressions *not stressing a fact,* i.e. those of *necessity, possibility, probability, advisability, etc.,* require the subjunctive in a noun clause depending on them.

Ahora es necesario que yo pague.   Now it is necessary that I pay (for me to pay).
Es preciso que estemos allí.   It is necessary that we be there.
Es probable que no les haya enseñado el catalán.   It is probable that he has not taught you Catalan.
Conviene que busquemos un taxi.   It is advisable that we look for a taxi.

Some common impersonal expressions of this type are

es necesario   it is necessary
es preciso   it is necessary
es posible   it is possible
es probable   it is probable
conviene   it is advisable
basta   it is sufficient
parece mentira   it seems incredible

When the dependent verb has no subject, the infinitive is used.

Es necesario llegar a tiempo.   It is necessary to arrive on time.
Conviene saber unas cuantas palabras.   It is advisable to know a few words.

Impersonal expressions that *stress a fact* take the indicative in a dependent noun clause.

Es verdad que están aquí.   It is true that they are here.
Es cierto que lo han hecho.   It is certain that they have done it.

■ Práctica

a. *Cambie según se indica.*

1. Es posible que ellos no vengan.
   yo / Vd. / nosotros / vosotros / tú
2. Es probable que él lo haga mañana.
   tú / vosotros / ellos / yo / vosotros
3. Conviene que yo lo pague.
   Vds. / ella / tú / tú y yo / vosotros

4. Basta que Vd. lo diga.
   Vd. y yo / vosotros / tú / yo / Vds.
5. Parece mentira que hayan vuelto.
   nosotros / Vd. / yo / tú / vosotros
6. Es verdad que lo han visto.
   vosotros / tú / ella / yo / Vd. y yo

b. *Diga en español, cambiando según se indica.*

1. It is advisable that we see it.
   that you see it / that they see it / that I see it
2. It is sufficient for him to know it.
   for me to know it / for them to know it
3. It seems incredible that she has left.
   that you have left / that they have left
4. It is necessary that we read a lot.
   that I read / that you read / that she read
5. It is possible that they have seen it.
   that you have seen it / that he has seen it

2. *Reflexive verb for the passive voice.* In Spanish a reflexive construction is commonly used instead of the passive voice when no agent is expressed. Note that the subject regularly follows the verb.

Aquí *se habla* catalán.   Catalan *is spoken* here.
***Se ve* mucha animación en todas partes.**   A great deal of movement *is seen* everywhere.
***Se fabrican* tejidos.**   Textiles *are manufactured.*

■ Práctica

Conteste según el modelo.

¿Qué se habla aquí?
español / francés
Aquí se habla español.
Aquí se habla francés.

1. ¿Qué se habla aquí?
   inglés / italiano / portugués
2. ¿Qué se estudia aquí?
   historia / francés / español
3. ¿Qué se fabrica aquí?
   zapatos / sombreros / tejidos / material rodante

4. ¿Qué se ve aquí?
   muchas fincas / edificios interesantes / ranchos enormes
5. ¿Qué se produce aquí?
   muchos caballos / muchos automóviles / muchas vacas
6. ¿Qué se lee aquí?
   muchos libros / muchos periódicos
7. ¿Qué se escribe aquí?
   muchas composiciones / muchos ejercicios

3. *Neuter article* **lo.** The neuter article **lo** is used with the masculine singular of an adjective as the equivalent of an abstract noun. **Lo** in such expressions is often the equivalent of English *that which is,* or *what is.*

lo bueno ~~the good, that which is good~~
lo malo the bad, what is bad
lo bello the beautiful, that which is beautiful

Sometimes these expressions are equivalent to the corresponding English expression plus the word *thing* or *part* (*of*).

lo primero que nos dijo the first *thing* (that) he said to us
lo mejor de Barcelona the best *thing about* Barcelona
lo más interesante de la lección the most interesting *part of* the lesson

■ Práctica

Diga en español.

1. that which is good
2. that which is easy
3. that which is best
4. the difficult thing
5. the interesting thing
6. the worst part

4. *Cardinal numerals above 100*

101 ciento uno, -a	**600 seiscientos, -as**
102 ciento dos	**700 setecientos, -as**
199 ciento noventa y nueve	**800 ochocientos, -as**
200 doscientos, -as	**900 novecientos, -as**
208 doscientos ocho	**1000 mil**
300 trescientos, -as	**1008 mil ocho**
400 cuatrocientos, -as	**1200 mil doscientos, -as**
500 quinientos, -as	**1970 mil novecientos setenta**

2000 dos mil	**100.000 cien mil**
2010 dos mil diez	**500.000 quinientos mil**
3593 tres mil quinientos noventa	**1.000.000 un millón**
y tres	

a. From **doscientos** up, the hundreds have a feminine form.

doscientas mujeres   **trescientas cinco alumnas**

b. *A* or *one* before *hundred* and *thousand* is not translated, but before **millón** it is. **Millón** is followed by **de** before a noun. Like any other noun it has a plural: **millones.**

ciento uno   one hundred one
mil casas   a thousand houses
un millón de libros   a million books
dos millones de habitantes   two million inhabitants

c. **Y** is found only between tens and units.

cuarenta y nueve   *But:* **doscientos dos**
sesenta y cinco   **nueve mil siete**

d. Spanish-speaking people do not count, or express dates, by hundreds after 1000 (*eleven hundred, nineteen hundred (and) sixty,* etc.). Instead they express such numbers in terms of a thousand.

1492 mil cuatrocientos noventa y dos
1969 mil novecientos sesenta y nueve

■ Práctica

Lea en español.

a. 1. $100 + 70 = 170$
    2. $100 + 85 = 185$
    3. $200 + 100 = 300$
    4. $300 + 100 = 400$
    5. $400 + 100 = 500$
    6. $500 + 100 = 600$
    7. $600 + 100 = 700$
    8. $700 + 100 = 800$
    9. $800 + 100 = 900$
   10. $900 + 100 = 1000$

b. 1. 1500
    2. 1669
    3. 1970
    4. 3400

   5. 4700
   6. 600.000
   7. 100.000
   8. 400 casas
   9. 1000 edificios
  10. 1.000.00

E. Writing

Test yourself

   1. It is necessary for us to be in the Plaza de Cataluña at nine-thirty.
   2. On leaving the hotel, we go to the left, and at the corner we go to the right.
   3. It is advisable for us to look for a taxi.
   4. We tell Don Tomás that Mr. Martínez is still well.
   5. He says it is probable that Mr. Martínez has not taught us Catalan.
   6. It is too bad, because Catalan is spoken here.
   7. Let's begin with the Cathedral, which is not far away.
   8. We also visit the Exchange, founded in 1383, and the University, founded in 1450.
   9. Barcelona has more than a million inhabitants, but Seville has fewer than 500,000.
  10. In Barcelona textiles are manufactured.
  11. "Let's have lunch in a café," says Carlos.
  12. For him the best part of Barcelona is the *Rambla*.
  13. It seems incredible that the Catalans are not Yankees.
  14. It is probable that Carlos has left his money in the hotel.

Composition

Write a composition about your activities today and in the near future. Tell what it is necessary and advisable for you to do, what it is possible for you to do, what it is probable that you will do. Use as many impersonal expressions as you can.

LESSON 21

A. Imperfect subjunctive

The imperfect subjunctive in Spanish has two forms. Both forms, in all verbs, derive from the third person plural of the preterit. The **-ron** is removed and the following two sets of endings are added:

1. **-ra** -ras -ra -ramos -rais -ran

hablar	aprender, vivir

THIRD PERSON PLURAL PRETERIT	
hablaron	aprendieron, vivieron

hablara	habláramos	aprendiera	aprendiéramos
hablaras	hablarais	aprendieras	aprendierais
Vd. hablara	Vds. hablaran	Vd. aprendiera	Vds. aprendieran
hablara	hablaran	aprendiera	aprendieran

2. **-se** -ses -se -semos -seis -sen

hablase	hablásemos	viviese	viviésemos
hablases	hablaseis	vivieses	vivieseis
Vd. hablase	Vds. hablasen	Vd. viviese	Vds. viviesen
hablase	hablasen	viviese	viviesen

Note that the same two sets of endings are used for all three conjugations. Note also that the stress always falls on the syllable before the ending, making necessary an accent on the first person plural.

In most circumstances these two forms may be used interchangeably.

■ Práctica

Cambie según se indica.

1. Convenía que tú contestaras.
   nosotros / ellos / vosotros / yo / Vd.
2. Esperaban que Vd. aprendiese.
   yo / nosotros / Vds. / tú / vosotros
3. Querían que yo escribiera.
   tú / vosotros / Vd. / Vd. y yo / ellas

B. Imperfect subjunctive of stem-changing verbs

Since the imperfect subjunctive of all verbs is formed on the third person plural of the preterit, the only stem changes in this tense in stem-changing verbs occur in Classes II and III: e changes to **i**, and o changes to **u**. (See Lesson 8, B.)

Class I

INFINITIVE	THIRD PERSON PLURAL PRETERIT	IMPERFECT SUBJUNCTIVE	
pensar	**pensaron**	**pensara**	**pensase**
volver	**volvieron**	**volviera**	**volviese**

Class II

sentir	**sintieron**	**sintiera**	**sintiese**
dormir	**durmieron**	**durmiera**	**durmiese**

Class III

pedir	**pidieron**	**pidiera**	**pidiese**

■ Práctica

Cambie según se indica.

1. Sentían que Vd. lo perdiera.
   yo / nosotros / ellos / tú / vosotros
2. Permitieron que él lo devolviese.
   tú / yo / Vds. / vosotros / Vd. y yo
3. Era lástima que Vd. no se sintiera bien.
   Vds. / tú / vosotros / yo / nosotros
4. Rogaron que nos vistiéramos pronto.
   él / yo / tú / vosotros / Vds.
5. Esperaban que yo durmiera bien.
   nosotros / ella / vosotros / Vds. / tú

C. Listening and speaking

algo something, anything
alguien anybody, someone, somebody
el Cabildo Town Hall
la carta letter
la clase kind
colonial colonial
la comisión commission
la compañía company
el contrato contract
el destierro exile
el dictador dictator
el que *rel. pron.* who, the one who
el entusiasmo enthusiasm
el estudiante student
el estudio study
extraño strange
fascinar to fascinate
fuera *imperf. subj. of* **ir** that he go
fuésemos *imperf. subj. of* **ir** that we go
ganar to earn
histórico historical
huir to flee
impresionar to impress

interesar to interest
lleno full
la maquinaria agrícola agricultural (farm) machinery
negociar to negotiate
el oeste west
la oficina office
la ópera opera
el período period
precioso pretty, beautiful
quien *rel. pron.* who
recibir to receive
rosado pink
sorprender to surprise
los tíos uncle and aunt
vender to sell

IDIOMS AND OTHER EXPRESSIONS

de aquí en (cuatro días) (four days) from now
como de costumbre as usual
haber de + *infin.* to be to; to be supposed to; must
sin más ni más just like that; without more ado

Buenos Aires

Esta mañana hablábamos de la América del Sur. El señor Martínez preguntó: —¿Hay alguien[1] en la clase que haya estado en la Argentina?

Dos estudiantes levantaron la mano. Uno de ellos era Juan. El profesor le pidió que nos hablara un poco de su viaje.

—Bueno, —dijo Juan, —han de[2] saber Vds. que un tío mío vende maquinaria agrícola. Esta clase de maquinaria se vende mucho en la Argentina. Un día mi tío recibió una carta de la oficina de su compañía en Chicago. Le pedían que fuera a Buenos Aires para negociar un contrato muy importante, porque no había nadie en la compañía que hablara español tan bien como él.

—Le sorprendió a mi tío que le pidiesen eso sin más ni más. « ¡Dios mío! » exclamó. « De aquí en cuatro días he de estar en Buenos Aires! » Le propuso a mi tía que le acompañase. Mis padres les rogaron a mis tíos que me llevaran a mí también.

—Hicimos el viaje en avión. Buenos Aires nos impresionó mucho. Es una ciudad tan grande como Chicago y con tantos habitantes como Chicago: más de tres millones. Mi tía y yo vimos más de la ciudad que mi tío. Él no tenía tanto tiempo como nosotros para visitar museos y monumentos históricos. Fuimos a ver el Cabildo, un precioso edificio colonial, y la Casa Rosada, que se encuentra en la Plaza de Mayo y que es la Casa Blanca de la Argentina. Una noche mi tía quería que fuésemos al famoso Teatro Colón. Esa noche se dio la ópera *Carmen*.

—Lo que me gustó más fue la excursión que hicimos a Luján, una pequeña ciudad al oeste de Buenos Aires, para ver la catedral y el maravilloso museo histórico. Nunca he visto ningún museo que me haya interesado más. Me fascina la historia argentina. Hice un estudio especial del período de Rosas, quien fue dictador de 1829 a 1852. Como muchos dictadores, tuvo que huir, y no es extraño que muriera en el destierro.

—Mientras nosotros nos divertíamos, mi pobre tío trabajaba tanto como de costumbre. Pero al fin le dieron el contrato. Naturalmente estaba lleno de entusiasmo. «¡Qué ciudad ésta para los negocios!» exclamó. «¡He de ganar más de diez mil dólares en comisiones! ¿Conocen Vds. una ciudad que sea tan interesante?»

■ Preguntas

1. ¿Qué preguntó el señor Martínez?
2. ¿Qué hicieron dos estudiantes?
3. ¿Qué le pidió a Juan el señor Martínez?
4. ¿Qué vende un tío de Juan?
5. ¿Dónde se venden muchas de las máquinas?
6. ¿Qué recibió su tío?
7. ¿Qué le pedían en la carta?
8. ¿Por qué?
9. ¿Qué propuso el tío de Juan?
10. ¿Qué le rogaron al tío los padres de Juan?
11. ¿Cómo hicieron el viaje?
12. ¿Es grande Buenos Aires?
13. ¿Cuántos habitantes tiene?
14. ¿Por qué no visitó el tío tantos museos como Juan?
15. ¿Qué puntos de interés vieron Juan y su tía?
16. ¿Qué le gustó más a Juan?
17. ¿Cuándo fue Rosas dictador de la Argentina?
18. ¿Qué exclamó el tío de Juan?
19. ¿Cuánto dinero había de ganar en comisiones?

NOTES

1. Although **alguien** (*anybody, somebody*) is here the subject, note that when it is the object of a verb, it is preceded by the personal **a.** So is **alguno** (*some, any, someone, anyone*) when it is the object of a verb and refers to a person.

   ¿Conoce Vd. a alguien que haya estado en Méjico? Do you know anybody who has been in Mexico?
   ¿Conoce Vd. a alguna española? Do you know any Spanish girl?

2. **Haber de** followed by the infinitive expresses future time, sometimes with a slight degree of obligation. It means *to be to* or *to be supposed to.* It may translate English *must,* but without the degree of compulsion expressed by **tener que.**

   De aquí en cuatro días *he de estar* **en Buenos Aires.** Four days from now *I am to be* (*am supposed to be*) in Buenos Aires.
   Ha de ganar **diez mil dólares.** *He is to earn* ten thousand dollars.
   Han de saber Vds. . . . *You must know . . .*

But:
   Tengo que **estudiar.** *I must* (*have to*) study.

■ Práctica

Diga en español.

1. They are to be here.
2. They are to sing.
3. They are to speak.
4. I am supposed to study.
5. I am supposed to work.
6. I am supposed to go.

D. Structure

1. *Use of the imperfect subjunctive.* Up to this point our subordinate noun clauses have depended upon a main verb in the present tense. When the subjunctive was required in the dependent clause, we used the present or the present perfect subjunctive.

   Quiero que Vd. me pague. I want you to pay me.
   Dudo que hayan llegado. I doubt that they have arrived.

When, however, the main verb is in the imperfect, preterit, or conditional and a subjunctive is required in the subordinate clause, the verb of the dependent clause is normally in the imperfect subjunctive.

Quería que fuésemos al teatro.   She wanted us to go to the theater.
Le pidieron que fuera a Buenos Aires.   They asked him to go to Buenos Aires.
Preferiría que Vd. hablara español.   I should prefer that you speak Spanish.

But the imperfect subjunctive may follow any verb which logically calls for a simple past tense in the dependent clause.

Dudo que llegaran.   I doubt that they arrived.
No es extraño que Rosas muriera en el destierro.   It is not strange that Rosas died in exile.

■ Práctica

a. *Cambie según el modelo.*

Carlos salió.
Querían que Carlos saliera.

1. Vd. llegó temprano.
    esperaban / se alegraban
2. Yo volví.
    sentían / temían
3. Él dormía.
    convendría / preferían
4. Ellos lo pidieron.
    negaron / mandaron
5. Ella me buscó.
    fue preciso / parecía mentira

b. *Diga en español, cambiando según se indica.*

1. I am glad they saw it.
    they wrote it / they prepared it
2. They asked me to sing.
    to dance / to speak
3. She told us to study.
    to eat / to work

4. You didn't think we would return.
   we would leave / we would enter
5. It was advisable for me to learn.
   to pay / to answer

2. Subjunctive mood in the adjective clause. An adjective clause is a subordinate clause used like an adjective,—that is, it modifies a noun or pronoun. It is regularly introduced by a relative pronoun. The noun or pronoun which the adjective clause modifies is called the antecedent of the relative pronoun. When that antecedent is either indefinite or negative, the verb of the adjective clause must be in the subjunctive. But when the antecedent is definite, the verb is in the indicative.

¿**Conoce Vd. una ciudad que sea tan interesante?** Do you know a city (any city) that is as interesting?

But:

Conozco una ciudad que es más interesante. I know a city (a definite city) which is more interesting.

¿**Hay alguien que haya estado en la Argentina?** Is there anybody who has been in Argentina?

But:

Tengo un amigo que ha estado en Buenos Aires. I have a friend (a definite person) who has been in Buenos Aires.

No había nadie que hablara español tan bien como él. There was nobody who spoke Spanish as well as he.

But:

Ayer conocí a una persona que hablaba español. Yesterday I met a person (a definite person) who spoke Spanish.

■ Práctica

Diga en español.

1. Do you know anybody who speaks Spanish?
   Did you know anybody who spoke Spanish?
2. There is nobody who works so much.
   There was nobody who worked so much.
3. I have a book that is easy.
   I need a book that is easy.
4. Is there anything you like better?
   Was there anything you liked better?

5. We know a man who has traveled in South America.
   We are looking for a man who has traveled in South America.
6. I saw a movie that was interesting.
   I wanted to see a movie that was interesting.

3. *Comparative of equality.*

a. With an adjective or adverb, the comparative of equality is expressed
by **tan . . . como,** *as . . . as.*

Buenos Aires es tan grande como Chicago.   Buenos Aires is as large as
   Chicago.
Este museo es tan interesante como aquél.   This museum is as interesting
   as that one.
Vd. habla tan bien como ella.   You speak as well as she.

b. With a verb, by **tanto . . . como,** *as much . . . as.*

Mi tío trabajaba tanto como de costumbre.   My uncle worked as much
   as usual.
Vd. no estudia tanto como yo.   You don't study as much as I.

c. With a noun, by **tanto (-a, -os, -as) . . . como,** *as much (many) . . . as.*

No tenía tanto tiempo como nosotros.   He did not have as much time
   as we.
Buenos Aires tiene casi tantos habitantes como Chicago.   Buenos Aires
   has almost as many inhabitants as Chicago.
Ella lee tantas novelas como él.   She reads as many novels as he.

■ Práctica

Cambie según los modelos.

a. **Esto es muy interesante.**
   Esto es tan interesante como aquello.

   1. Esto es muy fácil.
   2. Esto es muy difícil.
   3. Esto es muy importante.
   4. Esto es muy agradable.

b. **Él llega muy temprano.**
   Llega tan temprano como yo.

   1. Él llega muy tarde.
   2. Él llega muy pronto.

3. Él llega muy puntualmente.
4. Él llega muy cansado.
5. Él llega muy enojado.

c. **Trabajan mucho.**
   Trabajan tanto como yo.

1. Estudian mucho.
2. Juegan mucho.
3. Se divierten mucho.
4. Bailan mucho.
5. Comen mucho.

d. **No tengo muchos libros.**
   No tengo tantos libros como usted.

1. No tengo muchas flores.
2. No tengo mucho dinero.
3. No tengo muchas corbatas.
4. No tengo mucho tiempo.
5. No tengo muchos vestidos.

4. Distributive singular and distributive plural.

a. Where English uses the plural, Spanish uses the singular in referring to parts of the body, articles of clothing, etc., of which only *one per person* is referred to.

Dos estudiantes levantaron *la mano*.　　Two students raised *their hands*.
Se pusieron *el sombrero*.　　They put on *their hats*.

b. Spanish uses the masculine plural to designate groups of people containing individuals of both sexes.

mis padres y mis abuelos　my parents and grandparents
sus hermanos　his brother and sister (brothers and sisters)
mis tíos　my uncle and aunt
los reyes　the king and queen

■ Práctica

Diga en español.

a. 1. They washed their faces.
   2. They raised their hands.
   3. They put on their shirts.
   4. They put on their hats.

b. 1. his father and mother
   2. his grandfather and grandmother
   3. his uncle and aunt
   4. his brother and sister

E. Writing

Test yourself

1. Is there any student in this class who has been in Argentina?
2. Juan was one of the students who raised their hands.
3. Mr. Martínez asked him to speak about his trip.
4. You must know that his uncle sells agricultural machinery.
5. His uncle's company asked him to go to Argentina.
6. It surprised him that they should ask him to go just like that.
7. There was no one in the company who spoke Spanish as well as he.
8. His parents asked his uncle to take him too.
9. He made the trip by plane with his uncle and aunt.
10. Buenos Aires is as large as Chicago and has nearly as many inhabitants.
11. One night his aunt wanted him to accompany her to the Teatro Colón.
12. He has never seen a museum that interested him as much as the historical museum of Luján.
13. It is not strange that the dictator Rosas died in exile.
14. They don't know any other city that is as interesting as Buenos Aires.

Composition

Write a composition about your activities yesterday. Tell what it was necessary and advisable for you to do, what it was not possible for you to do, what you asked your friends to do and hoped they would do, etc. (It was necessary for you to study; it was not possible for you to play tennis; you hoped your friends would accompany you to the movies, etc.)

Village in Mexico with Popocatepetl Volcano (17,800 ft.) in the background.
(Philip D. Gendreau)

The new University library, Mexico City, is decorated with lavish mosaics by Juan O'Gorman. (Philip D. Gendreau)

Two Mexican churches:
The Church of Santa
Prisca, Taxco, and the
Convent of San Francisco
in Tlascala, the oldest
church in Mexico.
(Philip D. Gendreau)

LESSON 22

A. Irregular imperfect subjunctive

Here are the imperfect subjunctives of some common irregular verbs. You remember that the imperfect subjunctive is formed on the third person plural of the preterit.

INFINITIVE	THIRD PLURAL PRETERIT	IMPERFECT SUBJUNCTIVE -ra	-se
dar	dieron	diera	diese
decir	dijeron	dijera	dijese
estar	estuvieron	estuviera	estuviese
hacer	hicieron	hiciera	hiciese
ir	fueron	fuera	fuese
ser	fueron	fuera	fuese
poder	pudieron	pudiera	pudiese
poner	pusieron	pusiera	pusiese
querer	quisieron	quisiera	quisiese
saber	supieron	supiera	supiese
tener	tuvieron	tuviera	tuviese
venir	vinieron	viniera	viniese

Verbs like **leer** (whose stem ends in a strong vowel) change the unstressed **i** of the personal endings to **y.**

leer	leyeron	leyera	leyese
creer	creyeron	creyera	creyese

■ Práctica

Cambie según se indica, siguiendo el modelo.

Convenía que yo estuviera aquí.
Convenía que Vd. estuviera aquí.

1. Convenía que yo estuviera aquí.
   tú / él / vosotros / ellos / nosotros
2. No querían que Vd. fuese al café.
   Vd. y yo / vosotros / ellas / tú / yo
3. Sentían que él no pudiera hacerlo.
   tú / yo / vosotros / Vds. / nosotros
4. Parecía mentira que Vd. no quisiera hacerlo.
   Vds. / nosotros / yo / tú / vosotros
5. No creían que él fuera español.
   yo / tú / nosotros / ellos / vosotros
6. Rogaron que yo les diera el dinero.
   tú / ellas / vosotros / nosotros / ella
7. Es probable que ella dijera la verdad.
   Vds. / vosotros / Vd. y yo / tú / Paco
8. Le pedí a él que lo hiciera.
   a ti / a ellos / a vosotros / a Vds. / a ella
9. Les dijo a ellos que se pusieran el sombrero.
   a mí / a tí / a Vd. / a Vds. / a ella
10. Dudaban que yo lo supiera.
    Vd. / vosotros / nosotros / tú / Vds.
11. Esperaban que Vd. no tuviera miedo.
    yo / Vd. y yo / vosotros / ellas / tú
12. Es posible que ellos vinieran ayer.
    tú / nosotros / Vd. / vosotros / yo
13. Era preciso que yo lo leyera.
    Vd. / Vd. y yo / ellas / tú / vosotros
14. Bastaba que él lo creyera.
    yo / vosotros / ellas / tú y yo / tú

B. Listening and speaking

anunciar to announce
cierto (a) certain
el cliente cliente
confidencial confidential

debieras you (really) ought to
decidir to decide
dentro de within
discutir to discuss

el **documento** document
entregar to hand over
imposible impossible
la línea aérea airline
la llegada arrival
de manera que so that
a menos que unless
para que in order that
¿para qué? for what reason?
el parecer opinion
el pasaje passage
quisiera I should like to
reservar to reserve

sino but
sumamente extremely, exceedingly
con tal que provided that
telefonear to telephone

IDIOMS AND OTHER EXPRESSIONS

hacer la maleta to pack one's
suitcase
poner un telegrama to send a
telegram
al principio at first
sin embargo nevertheless

Otro asunto urgente

—Como el tío de Juan,—dijo Carlos—mi padre tuvo que hacer un viaje
urgente el año pasado. ¿Saben Vds. que mi padre es abogado? Pues lo es.
Un cliente suyo le telefoneó desde San Francisco rogándole que fuera allá.
Le pidió que hiciera el viaje para que hablara con él de un asunto urgente
y confidencial. Quería que mi padre leyese ciertos documentos y que le
dijese ciertas cosas que no podían discutir por teléfono. Esperaba también
que mi padre le diera su parecer sobre ciertos asuntos. Era necesario que
estuviera en San Francisco dentro de veinticuatro horas. Al principio mi
padre no creía que fuera posible. Le dijo al cliente que sería imposible.

—« Quisiera ir » nos dijo después. Pero se sentía un poco enfermo y
además no creía tener tiempo. Sobre todo no quería ir a menos que mi
mamá le acompañara.

—« Debieras ir » le dijo mamá. « Ya sabes que es sumamente
importante. »

—« Lo sé » contestó mi padre. « Pero sólo iré con tal que vayas tú. »

—Pero fue imposible que mamá le acompañase. Iba a visitarnos una
tía suya. Sin embargo mi padre decidió hacer el viaje.

—« ¿Quieres hacerme la maleta? » le preguntó a mamá. Y buscó unas
camisas y unas corbatas que le entregó a mamá de manera que ella le
hiciera la maleta.

—Mi padre siempre viaja en tren. Pero esta vez, naturalmente, no tomó
el tren, sino el avión. Yo llamé a la línea aérea para que le reservasen el
pasaje. Fue preciso también que yo pusiese un telegrama anunciando su
llegada.

—« ¿No te lo dije? » me preguntó mamá después. « Es lo de siempre.
Tu padre nunca quiere hacer un viaje a menos que yo vaya también.
Pero al fin se va. »

■ Preguntas

1. ¿Qué tuvo que hacer el padre de Carlos?
2. ¿Quién le telefoneó?
3. ¿Qué le rogó?
4. ¿Para qué le pidió que hiciera el viaje?
5. ¿Qué quería que leyese?
6. ¿Qué quería que le dijera?
7. ¿Qué esperaba que su padre le diera?
8. ¿Cuándo era necesario que su padre estuviera en California?
9. ¿Creía su padre que sería posible ir a San Francisco?
10. ¿Qué le dijo el cliente?
11. ¿Qué dijo después a la familia?
12. ¿Por qué no quería ir?
13. ¿Por qué fue imposible que la madre de Carlos le acompañara?
14. ¿Qué buscó su padre?
15. ¿Para qué se las entregó a la madre de Carlos?
16. ¿Tomó el tren?
17. ¿Para qué telefoneó Carlos a la línea aérea?
18. ¿Qué fue preciso que hiciera Carlos?
19. ¿Qué dijo después la madre de Carlos?

C. Structure

1. *Subjunctive mood in the adverb clause.* An adverb clause is a subordinate clause with the function of an adverb. It modifies a verb, telling why, when, under what circumstances, the action of the main verb is accomplished. Use of the subjunctive or indicative in an adverb clause depends upon the meaning of the clause itself.

a. When an adverb clause expresses *purpose,* its verb must be in the subjunctive.

Iremos al museo *para que* Vd. *vea* los cuadros. We shall go to the museum *in order that* you *may see* the pictures.

Hizo el viaje *para que pudieran* hablar de cosas confidenciales. He made the trip *in order that* they *might be able* to talk of confidential things.

Se las entregó *de modo que* ella *hiciera* la maleta. He handed them over to her *so that* she *might pack* the suitcase.

Adverb clauses of purpose are introduced by the following conjunctions:

para que	in order that	**de modo que**	so, so that
a fin de que	in order that	**de manera que**	so, so that

b. An adverb clause of *proviso* must also be in the subjunctive.

Mi padre irá *con tal que* mi madre *vaya* también.   My father will go
provided my mother *goes* too.

***A menos que estudien* no aprenderán.**   *Unless they study* they will not
learn.

Él no quería ir *a menos que* mi madre *fuera* también.   He did not want to
go *unless* my mother *went* too.

Proviso clauses are introduced by the following conjunctions:

con tal que   provided (that)
a menos que   unless
en caso de que   in case

■ Práctica

Cambie según los modelos.

a. **Les daré el dinero.**
   Comprarán el coche.
   Les daré el dinero para que compren el coche.

   1. Les daré el dinero.
      Irán a España.
   2. Les daré el dinero.
      Verán la película.
   3. Les daré el dinero.
      Saldrán.
   4. Les daré el dinero.
      Tomarán un taxi.
   5. Les daré el dinero.
      Harán el viaje.

b. **Les di el dinero.**
   Compraron el coche.
   Les di el dinero para que compraran el coche.

   1. Les di el dinero.
      Fueron a España.
   2. Les di el dinero.
      Vieron la película.

3. Les di el dinero.
   Salieron.
4. Les di el dinero.
   Tomaron un taxi.
5. Les di el dinero.
   Hicieron el viaje.

c. **Ella no irá al teatro.**
   Usted insiste.
   Ella no irá al teatro a menos que usted insista.

1 Ella no irá al teatro.
   Usted va.
2 Ella no irá al teatro.
   Usted quiere.
3. Ella no irá al teatro.
   Usted vuelve.
4. Ella no irá al teatro.
   Usted paga.

d. **Dijeron que irían.**
   Usted insistiría.
   Dijeron que irían, con tal que usted insistiera.

1. Dijeron que irían.
   Usted iría.
2. Dijeron que irían.
   Usted querría.
3. Dijeron que irían.
   Usted volvería.
4. Dijeron que irían.
   Usted pagaría.

2. *Imperfect subjunctive in softened statements.* The **-ra** form of the imperfect subjunctive of **querer, deber,** and **poder** is used to soften a statement, that is, to make it less brusque and more courteous than the present indicative.

Quisiera ir a San Francisco.   I should like to go to San Francisco.
Vd. debiera estudiar más.   You (really) should (*or* ought to) study more.
¿No pudieran Vds. hacerlo ahora?   Couldn't you do it now?

■ Práctica

Diga en español.

1. I should like to know it.
2. I should like to see it.
3. You should work more.
4. You should play more.
5. Couldn't you tell me?
6. Couldn't you return now?

3. *Dative of interest.* The indirect object pronoun is often used to indicate the person in whose interest, or to whose advantage or disadvantage, an act is done.

¿Quieres hacer*me* la maleta?   Will you pack the suitcase *for me?*
Le **reservaron el pasaje.**   They reserved the passage *for him.*
Nos **resultó muy fácil.**   It turned out to be very easy *for us.*

Sometimes this indirect object is untranslatable except by English colloquial expressions.

Se *me* murió el caballo.   The horse died (*"on me"*).

■ Práctica

Diga en español.

1. They paid the passage for me.
2. They reserved the table for me.
3. They packed the suitcase for me.
4. They paid the passage for him.
5. They reserved the table for him.
6. They packed the suitcase for him.

4. *Neuter pronoun* **lo.** The neuter pronoun **lo,** *it* or *so,* is regularly used as the object or predicate of a verb, even where its English counterparts are omitted.

¿No *lo* sabes? Sí *lo* sé.   Don't you know (it)? Yes, I know (it).
Se *lo* dije.   I told you (so).
¿Es abogado? *Lo* **es.**   Is he a lawyer? He is.
¿Es rica la muchacha? *Lo es.*   Is the girl rich? She is.

■ Práctica

Diga en español.

1. We know.
2. We told you.
3. We asked you.
4. Are they doctors? They are.
5. Are they students? They are.
6. Are they intelligent? They are.

5. Sino *and* sino que. Sino means *but* in the sense of *but on the contrary.* It replaces **pero** after a negative statement when the following statement contradicts the preceding negative one.

No tomó el tren, sino el avión.   He did not take the train but the plane.
No es español, sino catalán.   He is not a Spaniard but a Catalan.

Before a clause **sino** becomes **sino que.**

No fui al museo, sino que me quedé en el hotel.   I did not go to the museum, but (I) stayed in the hotel.

■ Práctica

Cambie según los modelos.

a. **No es español.**
   francés
   No es español, sino francés.

   1. No es norteamericano.
      cubano
   2. No es alta.
      baja
   3. No es viejo.
      joven
   4. No es rubia.
      morena
   5. No es rico.
      pobre

b. **No es español.**
   Es francés.
   No es español, sino que es francés.

   1. No es norteamericano.
      Es cubano.

2. No es alta.
    Es baja.
3. No es viejo.
    Es joven.
4. No es rubia.
    Es morena.
5. No es rico.
    Es pobre.

D. Writing

Test yourself

1. Some clients of Carlos' father telephoned him from California.
2. They wanted him to go (out) there.
3. They asked him to make the trip in order that they might discuss a certain urgent matter.
4. They wanted him to read some documents and to tell them his opinion.
5. They hoped he would give them some advice.
6. It was necessary for him to be in San Francisco within twenty-four hours.
7. His father didn't think it was possible and told them so.
8. "I should like to go," he said later.
9. But he didn't want to go unless Carlos' mother would go too.
10. It was impossible for her to accompany him.
11. He looked for some ties, so that she could pack the suitcase for him.
12. He didn't go by train but by plane.
13. Carlos phoned the airline in order that they might reserve a passage for him.
14. It was also necessary for him to send a telegram.

Composition

You invite some friends to go on a boat trip. Tell why you invite them (so that they may have a good time, in order that they may see the river, etc.) Tell under what conditions you will go (in case the weather is good, unless it is cold, provided they don't have to study, etc.).

CONVERSATIONAL INTERLUDE

La aduana del aeropuerto

Agente de Inmigración. ¿Me hace Vd. el favor
de mostrarme su pasaporte, señor?

Juan. Aquí lo tiene Vd.

Agente. ¿Es Vd. norteamericano?

Juan. Sí, señor, soy de Tejas.

Agente. Veo que tiene pasaporte de turista.
Puede permanecer tres meses en la capital.

Juan. ¿Puedo viajar libremente por el país?

Agente. No, señor. Primero será preciso
solicitar una tarjeta de identidad.

Juan. ¿Dónde la solicito?

Agente. En la Secretaría de Policía. Entre las
diez de la mañana y las dos de la tarde.
¿Cuál es su equipaje?

Juan. Estas dos maletas.

Agente. Haga Vd. el favor de abrirlas, pues
tendré que revisarlas.

Juan. Con mucho gusto.

Agente. Muy bien. Todo está en orden.
Aquí tiene Vd. su pasaporte.

Juan. Muchas gracias.

Agente. No hay de qué.

LESSON 23

A. Pluperfect subjunctive

The pluperfect subjunctive of a verb is formed by combining the imperfect subjunctive of **haber** with the past participle of the verb.

hubiera			hubiese	
hubieras			hubieses	
Vd. hubiera			Vd. hubiese	
hubiera	hablado		hubiese	hablado
	aprendido			aprendido
hubiéramos	vivido		hubiésemos	vivido
hubierais			hubieseis	
Vds. hubieran			Vds. hubiesen	
hubieran			hubiesen	

■ Práctica

Cambie según se indica, siguiendo el modelo.

Dudaban que lo hubiéramos visto.
Dudaban que él lo hubiera visto.

1. Dudaban que lo hubiéramos visto.
   tú / él / Vds. / vosotros / yo
2. Negaron que Vd. lo hubiera dicho.
   yo / vosotros / Vds. / tú / tú y yo
3. No creían que él hubiese vuelto.
   ellos / yo / Vd. / tú / Vd. y yo

B. Orthographic-changing verbs in *-uir*

Verbs whose infinitive ends in **-uir** (except **-guir** and **-quir**) insert **y** before the ending (except before **i**) in the present tenses.

construir to build, construct

PRESENT INDICATIVE		PRESENT SUBJUNCTIVE	
construyo	construimos	construya	construyamos
construyes	construís	construyas	construyáis
construye	construyen	construya	construyan

As in verbs like **leer,** unstressed **i** of the personal endings changes to **y.** This change occurs in the third person, singular and plural, of the preterit, throughout the imperfect subjunctive, and in the gerund.

construyó **construyeron** **construyera, etc.** **construyese, etc.**

Gerund: **construyendo** *Past Participle:* **construido**

■ Práctica

Cambie según se indica.

1. Su cliente construye edificios.
   tú / nosotros / Vds. / vosotros / yo
2. Él no construyó ese edificio.
   yo / vosotros / Vds. / tú / nosotros
3. Desean que Vd. construya la casa.
   ellos / yo / nosotros / tú / vosotros
4. Dudan que ellos la construyeran.
   Vd. / tú / vosotros / nosotros / yo

C. Listening and speaking

antes (de) que before
aun cuando even though
la cabeza head
la clínica hospital
construir to build, construct
el consultorio doctor's office
cuarto fourth
después (de) que after
el doctor doctor
doler (ue) to ache, pain, hurt
enfermar to become ill, get sick
estúpido stupid

la fiebre fever
la garganta throat
grave serious
hasta que until
mejorarse to get better, recover
a pesar de in spite of; **a pesar de que** in spite of the fact that
público public
la pulmonía pneumonia
recomendar (ie) to recommend
la regla rule; order
resultar to turn out; to result

la suerte luck
varios several
la visita visit

IDIOMS AND OTHER EXPRESSIONS

darse cuenta de to realize

guardar cama to stay in bed
¡qué lástima! what a pity!
estar en regla to be in order
(dijo) para sí (he said) to himself
¿qué tengo? what is the matter
with me?

El padre de Carlos y el médico

¿Hay alguien que tenga tan mala suerte como mi padre? (Carlos hablaba del viaje de su padre a San Francisco.)

Después de hablar con su cliente, se dio cuenta de que su viaje no había sido necesario. Sentía mucho haberlo hecho. Su cliente es un ingeniero famoso que construye obras públicas. Estaba construyendo un edificio público en California. Temía que su contrato no estuviera en regla. En efecto parecía mentira que no hubiera comprendido el documento, pero así era.

—A pesar de todo—dijo mi padre para sí—este cliente mío es poco inteligente.

Ésa fue la primera visita de mi padre a San Francisco. —Antes que se vaya—le dijo el cliente—quiero que vea la ciudad.

Y en efecto, antes que mi padre volviera a Nueva York le mostró los puntos de interés. Después del tercer día no había nada que mi padre no hubiera visto y se sentía muy cansado.

Como dije, mi padre había estado un poco enfermo antes de hacer el viaje. El cuarto día de su visita se sentía peor. Fue al consultorio de un médico que le había recomendado su cliente.

—No sé qué tengo—le dijo al médico—pero me duelen la cabeza y la garganta.

—Vd. tiene fiebre—le dijo el médico. —Tendrá que volver a casa y guardar cama por varios días. Debe guardar cama mañana y pasado mañana, aun cuando no tenga fiebre.

—No puedo, doctor—contestó mi padre. —Soy de Nueva York y es preciso que vuelva allá esta tarde.

—Imposible—dijo el médico. —Aunque no le guste, tendrá que quedarse aquí hasta que se mejore. Le aconsejo que vaya a la clínca. Esto puede ser grave. Vaya a la clínica antes que enferme gravemente.

A pesar de que mi padre no quería hacerlo, fue a la clínica. Resultó que tenía pulmonía. Tuvo que estar en la clínica quince días, hasta que se mejoró.

¡Qué lástima que hubiera ido a California!

■ Preguntas

1. ¿De qué se dio cuenta el padre de Carlos?
2. ¿Qué sentía?
3. ¿Qué es su cliente y qué construye?
4. ¿Qué estaba construyendo en California?
5. ¿Qué temía?
6. ¿Qué dijo para sí el padre de Carlos?
7. ¿Qué le dijo el cliente?
8. Antes que volviera a Nueva York el padre de Carlos, ¿qué le mostró el cliente?
9. ¿Había algún punto de interés de San Francisco que no hubiera visto su padre?
10. ¿Por qué fue su padre al consultorio del médico?
11. ¿Qué le dijo al médico?
12. ¿Qué le aconsejó el médico que hiciera?
13. ¿Qué le explicó el padre de Carlos?
14. ¿Qué le dijo luego el médico?
15. ¿Qué hizo luego el padre de Carlos?
16. ¿Hasta cuándo se quedó en California?

D. Structure

1. *Use of the pluperfect subjunctive.* The pluperfect subjunctive is used in Spanish wherever we use the pluperfect tense in English, but where Spanish requires the subjunctive.

Mi padre sentía que yo hubiera hecho el viaje.   My father was sorry that I had made the trip.
No había nada que no hubiéramos visto.   There was nothing that we had not seen.
¡Qué lástima que hubieran vendido la casa!   What a pity that they had sold the house!

■ Práctica

Cambie según los modelos.

a. **Usted había llegado.**
   Se alegraban.
   Se alegraban de que usted hubiera llegado.

1. Usted había vuelto.
2. Usted había salido.

3. Usted había ido.
4. Usted había venido.
5. Usted había terminado.

b. **Ustedes lo habían comprado.**
Yo lo sentía.
Yo sentía que ustedes lo hubieran comprado.

1. Ustedes lo habían hecho.
2. Ustedes lo habían dicho.
3. Ustedes lo habían vendido.
4. Ustedes lo habían visto.
5. Ustedes lo habían preguntado.

2. *Subjunctive mood in the adverb clause* (continued).

a. An adverb clause of *time* must be in the subjunctive when the time of the clause is *future.*

Antes que se vaya **Vd., quiero que vea la ciudad.**   *Before* you *leave,* I want you to see the city.

Quédese Vd. aquí *hasta que se mejore.*   Stay here *until you recover.*

Se lo diré *cuando venga.*   I shall tell him *when he comes.*

Tan pronto como hayan leído **el libro, me lo prestarán.**   *As soon as they have read* the book, they will lend it to me.

Dijo que volvería *después que Vd. hubiera terminado* **su trabajo.**   He said he would return *after you had finished* your work.

But when the clause expresses present or past time, the verb is in the indicative.

Cuando estudio, **aprendo.**   *When(ever) I study,* I learn.

Se quedó aquí *hasta que se mejoró.*   He stayed here *until he recovered.*

Mientras ellas jugaban **al tenis, él volvió a casa.**   *While they were playing* tennis, he returned home.

The conjunction **antes (de) que** is always followed by the subjunctive, because the *idea* of the clause which it introduces is always *future* in relation to the main verb, even though the *tenses* used be past.

Antes que volviera **a Nueva York, le mostró la ciudad.**   *Before he returned* to New York, he showed him the city.

Time clauses are introduced by the following conjunctions:

cuando when	**después (de) que** after
tan pronto como as soon as	**hasta que** until
antes (de) que before	**mientras (que)** while

■ Práctica

Cambie según los modelos.

a. **Los veo cuando vienen.**
   Los veré cuando vengan.

   1. Lo hago cuando puedo.
      Lo haré cuando _____.

   2. Los compro cuando tengo dinero.
      Los compraré cuando _____.

   3. Tomo el desayuno tan pronto como me visto.
      Tomaré el desayuno tan pronto como _____.

   4. Estudio tan pronto como vuelvo a casa.
      Estudiaré tan pronto como _____.

   5. Hablo con ellos mientras están en el café.
      Hablaré con ellos mientras _____.

   6. Se lo expliqué después de que llegaron.
      Se lo explicaré después de que _____.

   7. Yo salí después de que salieron.
      Yo saldré después de que _____.

   8. Leo hasta que me duermo.
      Leeré hasta que _____.

b. **¿Saldrán tus amigos?**
   Sí, pero los veremos antes de que salgan.

   1. ¿Volverán tus amigos?
      Sí, pero los veremos antes de que _____.

   2. ¿Comerán tus amigos?
      Sí, pero los veremos antes de que _____.

   3. ¿Irán al cine?
      Sí, pero los veremos antes de que _____.

   4. ¿Se acostarán temprano?
      Sí, pero los veremos antes de que _____.

c. **¿Salieron tus amigos?**
   Sí, los vimos antes de que salieran.

   1. ¿Volvieron tus amigos?
      Sí, los vimos antes de que _____.

   2. ¿Comieron tus amigos?
      Sí, los vimos antes de que _____.

3. ¿Fueron al cine?
   Sí, los vimos antes de que ____.
4. ¿Se acostaron?
   Sí, los vimos antes de que ____.

d. **Lo haré cuando sea posible.**
   Dije que lo haría cuando fuera posible.

1. Volveré tan pronto como pueda.
   Dije que volvería tan pronto como ____.
2. Iremos al café cuando ella llegue.
   Dije que iríamos al café cuando ella ____.
3. Estaremos aquí hasta que ustedes terminen.
   Dije que estaríamos aquí hasta que ustedes ____.
4. Estaré con usted tan pronto como escriba la composición.
   Dije que estaría con usted tan pronto como ____.
5. Esperaremos hasta que vuelvan.
   Dije que esperaríamos hasta que ____.

e. **Lo haremos cuando usted haya comido.**
   Dije que lo haríamos cuando usted hubiera comido.

1. Lo haremos después de que usted lo haya terminado.
   Dije que lo haríamos después de que usted lo ____.
2. Lo haremos tan pronto como usted haya escrito la composición.
   Dije que lo haríamos tan pronto como usted ____.
3. Lo haremos después de que él haya llegado.
   Dije que lo haríamos después de que él ____.
4. No lo haremos hasta que él se haya mejorado.
   Dije que no lo haríamos hasta que él ____.

b. An adverb clause of *concession* is in the subjunctive when it expresses a mere possibility.

Hay que guardar cama, *aun cuando no tenga* fiebre.   It is necessary to stay in bed, *even though you may not have* a fever.
***Aunque no le guste*, tendrá que quedarse aquí.**   *Although you may not like to,* you will have to stay here.

But when the clause expresses a fact, it is in the indicative.

***Aunque está aquí,* no le veo.**   *Although he is here,* I don't see him.
***A pesar de que no quería* hacerlo, fue a la clínica.**   *In spite of the fact that he didn't want* to do it, he went to the hospital.

Concessive clauses are introduced by the following conjunctions:

aunque although
aun cuando even though
a pesar de que in spite of the fact that

■ Práctica

Diga en español.

a. **Harán el viaje:**

1. although they are ill
   although they may be ill
2. although I am not going
   although I may not go
3. even though they do not have the money
   even though they may not have the money
4. in spite of the fact that you do not recommend it
   in spite of the fact that you may not recommend it

b. **Dijeron que harían el viaje:**

1. although they might be ill
2. although I might not go
3. even though they might not have the money
4. in spite of the fact that you might not recommend it

3. *Prepositional forms of the reflexive pronouns.* All the forms of the reflexive pronouns used as the object of a preposition are the same as the other prepositional pronouns, except the third person, **sí.**

mí myself	**nosotros (-as)** ourselves
ti yourself	**vosotros (-as)** yourselves
sí himself, herself, yourself, itself	**sí** themselves, yourselves

We have already learned the forms **conmigo** and **contigo,** which are also reflexive. There is a corresponding reflexive form for the third person when the preposition is **con: consigo.**

Hablaba para mí. I was talking to myself.
Me llevaron consigo. They took me with them.

■ Práctica

Cambie según el modelo.

Ellos hablaban para sí.
Yo hablaba para mí.

1. Ellos hablaban para sí.
   Vd. / tú / ella / yo / él / Vds.
2. Vd. los llevó consigo.
   yo / ella / tú / ellos / Vds.

4. *Ordinal numerals*

primer(o)	first	**sexto**	sixth
segundo	second	**séptimo**	seventh
tercer(o)	third	**octavo**	eighth
cuarto	fourth	**noveno**	ninth
quinto	fifth	**décimo**	tenth

The ordinal numerals agree in gender and number with the nouns they modify. Beyond **décimo** they are commonly replaced by the cardinal numerals. The article *the* in titles in English is not translated.

The ordinal numerals may precede or follow their nouns. They follow when they denote a member of a recognized series.

las primeras flores   the first flowers
la Avenida Primera   First Avenue
la cuarta lección   the fourth lesson
la lección cuarta   Lesson Four
Carlos Quinto   Charles the Fifth
Alfonso Trece   Alphonse the Thirteenth

■ Práctica

Diga en español.

1. the first day
2. the first class
3. the second lesson
4. the third man
5. Charles the Fourth
6. the fifth week
7. the sixth street
8. the seventh time

9. the eighth day
10. the ninth person
11. Alfonso the Tenth
12. Alfonso the Twelfth

E. Writing

Test yourself

1. Carlos' father realized that his trip had not been necessary.
2. He was sorry that he had gone to California.
3. His client, who builds public works, was constructing a building in San Francisco.
4. He had feared that his contract was not in order.
5. We doubted that he had understood the document.
6. Before my father returned to New York, the client showed him that city.
7. After the third day there was nothing my father had not seen.
8. He had been sick before he made the trip.
9. His head ached and his throat hurt.
10. You will have to stay in bed, even though you may not have a fever.
11. Although you may not like it, you will have to go to the hospital.
12. He would have to stay there until he recovered.
13. In spite of the fact that he wanted to go home, he stayed in the hospital.
14. What a pity he had taken the trip!

Composition

Write a composition telling how you felt about things yesterday. Tell what you were glad or sorry you had done. Tell some things you doubted or didn't believe your friends had done. Tell when and under what circumstances you will do things differently. (You were glad you had studied for an exam; when you returned from class, you were sorry you had not studied more; it was too bad you had not read all the lessons; you didn't think anybody had worked more; when we have another exam, you will begin to study earlier; you will prepare the lesson tomorrow, even though you may not like to, etc.)

LESSON 24

A. Irregular verbs *oír, caer,* and *traer*

1. *Present indicative*

oír to hear	caer to fall	traer to bring
oigo	caigo	traigo
oyes	caes	traes
oye	cae	trae
oímos	caemos	traemos
oís	caéis	traéis
oyen	caen	traen

In **caer** and **traer** the only irregularity in the present indicative is the first person singular: **caigo, traigo.**

2. *Present subjunctive.*

As in most verbs, the present subjunctive is formed on the first person singular of the present indicative.

**oiga, oigas, oiga, oigamos, oigáis, oigan
caiga, caigas, caiga, caigamos, caigáis, caigan
traiga, traigas, traiga, traigamos, traigáis, traigan**

3. *Preterit, imperfect subjunctive, and gerund.*

The preterit of **oír** and **caer** is like that of **leer** (see Lesson 9). The unaccented **i** of the personal ending in the third person, singular and plural, changes to **y**. In the other forms the **i** bears a written accent. The preterit of **traer** is completely irregular.

Preterit	oí	caí	traje
	oíste	caíste	trajiste
	oyó	cayó	trajo
	oímos	caímos	trajimos
	oísteis	caísteis	trajisteis
	oyeron	cayeron	trajeron
Imperfect	oyera	cayera	trajera
Subjunctive	oyese	cayese	trajese
Gerund	oyendo	cayendo	trayendo

■ Práctica

Cambie según se indica.

a. 1. Vd. lo oye.
   nosotros / tú / yo / vosotros / Vds.
2. Vd. lo oyó.
   ellos / nosotros / yo / tú / vosotros
3. Desean que Vd. lo oiga.
   tú / yo / tú y yo / vosotros / Vds.
4. Deseaban que Vd. lo oyera.
   vosotros / ellas / yo / tú / Vd. y yo

b. 1. No caen nunca.
   tú / nosotros / yo / vosotros / Vd.
2. No cayeron nunca.
   yo / tú / nosotros / él / vosotros
3. Parece mentira que no caigan.
   nosotros / ellas / yo / vosotros / tú
4. Parecía mentira que no cayesen.
   ella / vosotros / yo / tú / Vd. y yo

c. 1. Él no lo trae.
   yo / tú / nosotros / vosotros / Vds.
2. Él no lo trajo.
   nosotros / tú / yo / ellos / vosotros
3. Conviene que él lo traiga.
   yo / Vds. / tú / nosotros / Vd.
4. Convenía que él lo trajera.
   vosotros / ellas / tú / yo / nosotros

B. Listening and speaking

acercarse (a) to approach
el automóvil automobile
¡ay! oh!
caerse de to fall out of
la capital capital
cómodo comfortable
completamente completely
contar (ue) to tell
Cortés Hernán Cortés, con-
    queror of Mexico (1485–1547)
la cuna cradle
el chiste joke
hermosísimo most (very,
    exceedingly) beautiful
el individuo individual, person
limpio clean
llevar to wear
magnífico magnificent
muchísimo very much, a very
    great deal
nada *adv.* (not) at all
el Pacífico Pacific
el palacio palace
pintoresco picturesque

la pirámide pyramid
la playa beach
la prima cousin
progresista progressive
recobrar to recover
sin que without
el traje de baño bathing suit
el único the only one
viajar to travel
ya que since

IDIOMS AND OTHER EXPRESSIONS

al aire libre in the open air
ya caigo now I get it
concentrar la atención en to
    concentrate on
¡ahora lo oigo! this is the first
    time I've heard about it!
oír decir to hear that, to hear it
    said that
a orillas de beside
yo sí I was (did, have, had, etc.)

Virginia en la playa de Acapulco

Hacía una hora que los estudiantes estaban en la biblioteca.

—Traigan sus libros y salgamos a la playa a[1] estudiar—les dijo Juan.

—Hace una hora que trabajamos y aquí hace demasiado calor.

Pero nadie dijo nada. El pobre Juan hablaba sin que nadie le oyera. Los estudiantes concentraban la atención en los libros.

—¿No me oyen? Les dije que trajeran los libros. Será más cómodo estudiar al aire libre.

Al salir de la biblioteca Virginia empezó a contarles una cosa. —En la playa de Acapulco, cuando estuve en Méjico hace dos años . . . —empezó.

—¿Tú has estado en Méjico?—interrumpió Juan. —¡Ahora lo oigo!

—Tú y tus tíos no son los únicos que han estado en Hispanoamérica— contestó ella. —Hace dos años que fui a Méjico con mi madre. Hacía tiempo que ella quería ver ese país tan pintoresco. Como saben Vds., hace varios años que mi padre está enfermo. Cayó enfermo y no recobró completamente la salud. Pero ese verano se sentía mejor, de modo que fuimos a Méjico. Hicimos el viaje en automóvil. De Nuevo Laredo fuimos a Monterrey . . .

—¿Por qué pasaron por Nuevo Laredo?—volvió a interrumpir Juan.

—Ya que Vds. viven en California, debieron[2] ir a El Paso.

—Es que[3] tenemos una prima en San Antonio.

—Ya caigo—dijo Juan. —Vds. fueron a visitarla.

—Pues, como decía, pasamos por Monterrey, esa ciudad industrial, tan progresista y tan limpia. Estuvimos quince días en la capital. Es hermosísima la capital. Vimos los magníficos edificios de la nueva universidad. Fuimos a ver las pirámides de San Juan Teotihuacán. Visitamos el palacio de Cortés en Cuernavaca y pasamos un par de días en Taxco. Habíamos oído decir que Acapulco tiene una playa muy buena. De manera que pasamos una semana en esa ciudad a orillas del Pacífico. Nos divertimos muchísimo.

—Una tarde estábamos en la playa. Mi madre no llevaba traje de baño, pero yo sí.[4] Se acercó un individuo a quien habíamos conocido en el hotel. « Señora, » dijo, dirigiéndose a mamá, « veo que no lleva Vd. traje de baño. ¿No nada nada? » « No, señor, » contestó ella. « Es que no traje traje. »

—¡Ay, Virginia!—exclamó Juan. Ese chiste es muy viejo. ¡La primera vez que lo oí me caí de la cuna!

■ Preguntas

1. ¿Cuánto tiempo hacía que los estudiantes estaban en la biblioteca?
2. ¿Qué les dijo Juan?
3. ¿Qué dijeron los amigos de Juan?
4. ¿Por qué no dijeron nada?
5. ¿Qué quería Juan que hicieran los otros al salir de la biblioteca?
6. ¿Cuándo estuvo Virginia en Méjico?
7. ¿Qué exclamó Juan?
8. ¿Cuándo fue Virginia a Méjico con su madre?
9. ¿Qué quería su madre?
10. ¿Cuánto tiempo hace que el padre de Virginia está enfermo?
11. ¿Por qué pasaron por Nuevo Laredo Virginia y su madre?
12. ¿Cómo es Monterrey?
13. ¿Cómo es la capital de Méjico?
14. ¿Qué habían oído decir de Acapulco Virginia y su madre?
15. ¿Quién se acercó a la madre de Virginia en la playa de Acapulco?
16. ¿Qué le dijo?
17. ¿Cómo contestó su madre?
18. ¿Qué le dijo Juan del chiste?

NOTES

1. You have learned that verbs of motion require the preposition **a** before a following infinitive. With such verbs **a** may be used instead of **para** to express purpose.

   Salgamos a la playa a estudiar.   Let's go out to the beach to study.
   Fuimos a Tejas a verla.   We went to Texas to see her.

2. The preterit of **deber** plus an infinitive may be used in Spanish where English uses *ought* or *should* plus a perfect infinitive.

   Vds. debieron ir a El Paso.   You ought to have gone to El Paso.
   Debí hacerlo antes.   I should have done it before.

3. **Es que . . .** , or **ello es que . . .** (*the fact is that*) may be used in beginning an explanation.

   Es que no he estudiado hoy.   The fact is that I haven't studied today.

4. An emphatic **sí** or **no** may be used with a verb, or in place of a verb, where English uses an emphatic auxiliary verb. (We *did* go, but he *didn't,* etc.)

   El niño no sabe escribir, pero *sí* sabe leer.   The child doesn't know how to write, but he *does* know how to read.
   Ellos fueron, pero yo *no*.   They went, but I *didn't*.

■ Práctica

Diga en español.

a. 1. He should have said so.
    2. I should have done it.
    3. They should have seen it.
    4. We should have read it.

b. 1. The fact is I didn't hear.
    2. The fact is he didn't fall.
    3. The fact is she didn't wear it.
    4. The fact is you didn't bring it.

c. 1. He doesn't hear, but I do.
    2. He doesn't know, but I do.
    3. She approached, but you didn't.
    4. She traveled, but you didn't.

C. Structure

1. *Expressions of time with* hacer.

a. The third person singular present of **hacer, hace,** followed by **que** and a *present tense* means *I (you, he, etc.) have (has) been doing something for* a certain length of time.

Hace una hora que trabajamos. We have been working for an hour.
Hace varios años que mi padre está enfermo. My father has been ill for several years.

b. The imperfect, **hacía que,** followed by the *imperfect tense,* means *I (you, he, etc.) had been doing something for* a certain length of time.

Hacía una hora que estaban en la biblioteca. They had been in the library for an hour.
Hacía tiempo que ella quería ver ese país. She had wanted to see that country for some time.

c. With a verb in the preterit tense **hace (que)** means *ago*.

Hace dos meses que leyó ese libro. He read that book two months ago.

When the verb precedes, **hace** is used without **que**.

Estuve en Méjico hace dos años. I was in Mexico two years ago.

■ Práctica

Cambie según los modelos.

a. **¿Cuánto tiempo hace que lee usted?**
media hora
Hace media hora que leo.

1. ¿Cuánto tiempo hace que estudia usted?
   quince minutos
2. ¿Cuánto tiempo hace que trabaja usted?
   dos horas
3. ¿Cuánto tiempo hace que escribe usted?
   veinte minutos
4. ¿Cuánto tiempo hace que vive usted aquí?
   diez años

b. **¿Hace mucho tiempo que la conoces?**
siete años
Hace siete años que la conozco.

1. ¿Hace mucho tiempo que estudian el español?
   más de un año
2. ¿Hace mucho tiempo que viajan?
   cuatro meses
3. ¿Hace mucho tiempo que esperas?
   cuarenta minutos
4. ¿Hace mucho tiempo que se pasean ustedes?
   más de una hora

c. **¿Cuánto tiempo hacía que esperaban?**
   una hora
   Hacía una hora que esperaban.

1. ¿Cuánto tiempo hacía que trabajaba Roberto?
   seis semanas
2. ¿Cuánto tiempo hacía que leían?
   media hora
3. ¿Cuánto tiempo hacía que lo buscaba usted?
   varios meses
4. ¿Cuánto tiempo hacía que los conocían ustedes?
   once meses
5. ¿Cuánto tiempo hacía que dormían?
   ocho horas

d. **¿Cuándo empezó la película?**
   cinco minutos
   Hace cinco minutos que empezó.
   Empezó hace cinco minutos.

1. ¿Cuándo estuvo usted en Méjico?
   un año
2. ¿Cuándo fuiste a Panamá?
   seis meses
3. ¿Cuándo trajeron la carta?
   quince minutos
4. ¿Cuándo leyó usted ese libro?
   unas semanas
5. ¿Cuándo llegaron a Puerto Rico?
   varios días
6. ¿Cuándo salió ella de Cuba?
   nueve semanas

2. *Subjunctive mood in the adverb clause* (continued). **De modo que** and **de manera que** (*so that*) express *result* as well as purpose. When they introduce an adverb clause expressing *result,* the verb of the clause is always in the indicative.

Se sentía mejor, de modo que fuimos a Méjico.   He felt better, so (that) we went to Mexico.

Me dio el dinero, de manera que compré los libros.   He gave me the money, so I bought the books.

Sin que (*without*), however, introduces a clause of negative result and always requires the subjunctive.

Juan hablaba sin que nadie le oyera.   Juan was speaking without anyone's hearing him.

¿Podremos salir sin que nos vean?   Shall we be able to leave without their seeing us?

■ Práctica

Cambie según los modelos.

a. **Nos invitaron.**
   Los acompañamos.
   Nos invitaron, de modo que los acompañamos.

   1. Nos invitaron.
      Nos quedamos.
   2. Nos invitaron.
      Fuimos al cine.
   3. Nos invitaron.
      Tomamos un refresco.
   4. Nos invitaron.
      Bailamos.

b. **Insistieron mucho.**
   Lo compré.
   Insistieron mucho, de manera que lo compré.

   1. Insistieron mucho.
      Se lo dije.
   2. Insistieron mucho.
      Se lo expliqué.

3. Insistieron mucho.
   Volví temprano.
4. Insistieron mucho.
   Les prometí hacerlo.

c. **Siempre salen del hotel.**
   No los oigo.
   Siempre salen del hotel sin que los oiga.

1. Siempre salen del hotel.
   No los oímos.
2. Siempre salen del hotel.
   No los veo.
3. Siempre salen del hotel.
   No los percibimos.
4. Siempre salen del hotel.
   No lo sé.

3. *Definite article with geographical names.* You have learned certain geographical names with which the definite article is used: **la Argentina, el Brasil, la América del Sur,** etc. The following are some of the commonest names with which the definite article is regularly used:

la Argentina	Argentina	**el Uruguay**	Uruguay
el Brasil	Brazil	**el Paraguay**	Paraguay
el Perú	Peru	**el Canadá**	Canada
el Ecuador	Ecuador	**el Japón**	Japan

Geographical names of which adjectives or phrases are a part, or which happen to be modified by adjectives or phrases, almost always take the definite article. For example:

los Estados Unidos The United States
la Gran Bretaña Great Britain
la América del Sur South America
la España pintoresca picturesque Spain

But:
Sudamérica   Costa Rica

■ Práctica

Diga en español.

a. 1. Let's go to Peru!
   2. Let's go to Spain!

   3. Let's go to Brazil!
   4. Let's go to Paraguay!
   5. Let's go to England!

b. 1. They like Uruguay.
   2. They like picturesque Spain.
   3. They like Ecuador.
   4. They like Costa Rica.
   5. They like Great Britain.

    4. Absolute superlative. To express a high degree of quality—for example, *exceedingly beautiful, very easy indeed*—Spanish frequently uses the "absolute superlative." This superlative contains no idea of comparison. It is formed by adding **-ísimo (-ísima)** to an adjective or adverb after dropping a final vowel.

hermoso	beautiful	**hermosísimo**	most (very, exceedingly) beautiful
fácil	easy	**facilísimo**	very easy
mucho	much	**muchísimo**	very much (indeed)

Occasionally a spelling change must also be made (as in orthographic-changing verbs) to preserve the original sound of the final consonant.

rico	rich	**riquísimo**	extremely rich
largo	long	**larguísimo**	exceedingly long

Adverbs in **-mente** add **-ísima** to the adjective stem before adding **-mente.**

correctamente	correctly	**correctísimamente**	most (extremely) correctly

■ Práctica

Dé el superlativo de los siguientes adjetivos.

1. contento	6. poco
2. difícil	7. amargo
3. barato	8. grande
4. interesante	9. tanto
5. mucho	10. rico

D. Writing

Test yourself

1. The students have been in the library for a long while.
2. "Bring your books," said Juan. "We have been working too long."

3. But he said it without anybody's hearing him.
4. I told you to bring your books.
5. Virginia was in Mexico two years ago.
6. This is the first time I've heard it!
7. She went with her mother two years ago.
8. Her mother had been wanting to see the country for some time.
9. Her father has been ill for several years.
10. He was feeling better, so they took the trip.
11. They should not have gone to Nuevo Laredo, should they?
12. The fact is that they have cousins in San Antonio.
13. They had heard that Acapulco is a most interesting city.
14. So they spent a week there.
15. On the beach Virginia was wearing a bathing suit.
16. Don't you swim at all?
17. I didn't bring a suit.

Composition

Write a composition telling how long you have (or had) been doing certain things. (Tell how long you have been a student, how long you have lived where you do and have known some of your friends, how long you had studied English before you came to the university, etc.)

LESSON 25

A. Orthographic-changing verbs in -ger, -gir

In order to preserve the sound of the final consonant of the infinitive stem throughout the conjugation, verbs whose infinitive ends in **-ger** and **-gir** change **g** to **j** before the letters **o** or **a**. The forms affected are the first person singular of the present indicative and the entire present subjunctive which, you remember, is derived from the first person singular of the present indicative.

PRESENT INDICATIVE		PRESENT SUBJUNCTIVE	
coger to pick up; to catch			
co*j*o	cogemos	co*j*a	co*j*amos
coges	cogéis	co*j*as	co*j*áis
coge	cogen	co*j*a	co*j*an
dirigir to direct			
diri*j*o	dirigimos	diri*j*a	diri*j*amos
diriges	dirigís	diri*j*as	diri*j*áis
dirige	dirigen	diri*j*a	diri*j*an

■ Práctica

Cambie según se indica.

1. Ellos siempre cogen al criminal.
   él / tú / vosotros / yo / Vd. y yo
2. Esperan que Vd. no coja una pulmonía.
   Vds. / nosotros / tú / yo / vosotros

3. Ahora se dirigen a la plaza.
   ella / vosotros / yo / Vd. y yo / tú
4. Conviene que se dirijan a la plaza.
   tú / nosotros / vosotros / yo / él

B. Conditional perfect tense

The conditional perfect is formed by combining the conditional of **haber**
and a past participle.

habría hablado   I should have spoken
habrías hablado   you would have spoken
Vd. habría hablado   you would have spoken
habría hablado   he (she) would have spoken

habríamos hablado   we should have spoken
habríais hablado   you would have spoken
Vds. habrían hablado   you would have spoken
habrían hablado   they would have spoken

■ Práctica

Cambie según se indica.

1. Vd. lo habría dicho.
   yo / nosotros / tú / vosotros / Vds.
2. Tú lo habrías hecho.
   ellos / vosotros / yo / Vd. y yo / él
3. Ellos lo habrían devuelto antes.
   tú / nosotros / yo / vosotros / Vds.

C. Listening and speaking

bello beautiful
el bridge bridge (*card game*)
el cielo sky
como si as if
el ejemplo example
ello it
la estrella star
la filosofía philosophy
lo que *rel. pron.* that which,
   what

la lluvia rain
el millonario millionaire
el mundo world
la necesidad necessity
nublado cloudy
el ocio idleness
¡ojalá (que) . . .! oh, that; if
   only; I wish; would that!
el producto product
el resfriado cold

rico rich
soñar (ue) to dream
el sueño dream

IDIOMS AND OTHER EXPRESSIONS
llegar a ser to become

pensar en to think of
poner por ejemplo to take for
    example
soñar (ue) con to dream of

La vida es sueño

Todos soñamos en este mundo. Si somos pobres, soñamos con ser ricos.
Si estamos enfermos, soñamos con estar bien de salud. Casi siempre
deseamos lo que no tenemos y soñamos con ello.[1]

Conviene que haya en el mundo los que sueñan. La filosofía y el arte
son productos de los sueños. El hombre no podría vivir sin soñar.

Pongamos por ejemplo un día típico. Es una tarde de primavera, pero
el cielo está nublado y está lloviendo. Juan y las dos muchachas están
hablando de lo que harían si pudieran.

—¡Ojalá[2] pudiéramos ir al partido de béisbol!—dice Juan. —Si no
hubiera llovido, yo habría ido.

—Si Carlos estuviera aquí,—dice María—podríamos jugar al bridge.
Ojalá que no hubiera cogido ese resfriado.

—Con esta lluvia—dice Virginia—no hay nada que hacer. ¡Tendremos
que estudiar!

—Pensemos en lo que haremos mañana—propone Juan. —Si no llueve
mañana, ¿quieres jugar un partido de tenis conmigo?—pregunta,
dirigiéndose a Virginia.

—Con mucho gusto. Pero si lloviese otra vez, no sería posible jugar.

—¡Cuántas cosas no son posibles!—exclama María. —Si fuera posible,
me gustaría ser actriz. ¡Ojalá fuera tan bella como las estrellas de Holly-
wood!

—¡Ojalá fuera millonario!—dice Juan. —Si fuera rico, no haría nada
más que viajar y divertirme.

—Pero Juan,—le dice María—si algún día llegases a ser rico, no te
gustaría pasar la vida sin trabajar. Los sueños y el ocio son agradables,
pero el trabajo es una necesidad. Los hombres necesitan trabajar.

—¡Ay, María,—responde Juan—tú hablas como si fueras mi abuela!
¡Con tus buenos consejos hablas como si tuvieras ochenta años!

■ Preguntas

1. ¿Qué hacemos todos en este mundo?
2. ¿Con qué soñamos?
3. ¿Qué son la filosofía y el arte?

4. ¿Qué tiempo hace esta tarde de primavera?
5. ¿De qué hablan Juan y las dos muchachas?
6. ¿Qué exclama Juan?
7. ¿Qué harían los estudiantes si Carlos estuviera con ellos?
8. ¿Qué le pregunta Juan a Virginia?
9. ¿Es cierto que jugarán al tenis mañana?
10. ¿Qué quisiera ser María?
11. ¿Qué exclama ella?
12. ¿Qué haría Juan si fuera rico?
13. ¿Qué le dice María?
14. ¿Cómo habla María?
15. ¿Habla como una señorita de dieciocho años?

NOTES

1. **Ello** (*it*) is a neuter personal pronoun. It is used chiefly as object of a preposition, less commonly as subject of a verb. When used as object of a preposition it refers to a previously expressed idea, never to a specific object of determined gender. Its use as subject of a verb is practically limited to the expression **ello es que** (*the fact is that*).

   Deseamos lo que no tenemos y soñamos con ello.   We want what we do not have, and we dream of it.
   No tengo tiempo para ello.   I have no time for it.
   Ello es que no puedo ir.   The fact is that I can't go.

2. **¡Ojalá (que) . . . !** (*oh, that; if only; I wish; would that*) is used with the imperfect subjunctive when referring to present time and with the pluperfect subjunctive when referring to past time.

   ¡Ojalá fuera rico!   Oh, that (if only) I were rich!
   ¡Ojalá que hubieran venido!   If only (I wish that) they had come!

■ Práctica

Diga en español.

a. 1. I dream of it.
   2. I am glad of it.
   3. We haven't the time for it.
   4. We haven't the money for it.

b. 1. Oh that I were tall!
   2. Oh that I were intelligent!
   3. If only she were here!

4. If only she were in Spain!
5. I wish they had come!
6. I wish they had left!
7. Would that I had seen it!
8. Would that I had done it!

D. Structure

1. *Conditional clauses* (**if** *clauses*). There are three main types of conditional clause:

a. *Neutral conditional clauses.* A neutral conditional clause merely states a condition without implying either that it is or is not fact or likely to become so. The same tenses are used in Spanish as in English except that **si,** *if,* may not be followed by the future or the subjunctive.

Si están en casa, están estudiando. If they are at home, they are studying.
Si estaban en casa, estaban estudiando. If they were at home, they were studying.
Si Vd. ahorra dinero, podrá ir a Sudamérica. If you save (will save) money, you will be able to go to South America.
Si Carlos estudia, aprenderá. If Charles studies, he will learn.

b. *Conditions contrary to fact.* A conditional clause contrary to fact expresses a condition that is (or was) untrue or impossible. It is in the imperfect (or pluperfect) subjunctive, and the main clause is usually in the conditional tense (or in the conditional perfect).

Si Carlos estuviera aquí, jugaríamos al bridge. If Carlos were here (but he isn't), we should play bridge.
Si fuera rico, no haría nada. If I were rich (but I am not), I would do nothing.
Si no hubiera llovido, yo habría ido al partido. If it had not rained (but it did), I would have gone to the game.

c. *Conditions expressing uncertainty.* A conditional clause that expresses uncertainty implies that the condition either may or may not become fact. It is in the imperfect subjunctive, and the main clause is in the conditional.

Si Vd. llegase a ser rico, no le gustaría pasar la vida sin trabajar. If you became (should become, were to become) rich, you would not like to pass your life without working.
Si lloviese mañana, no sería posible jugar. If it should rain (were to rain) tomorrow, it would not be possible to play.

Si, *if,* is never followed by the conditional.

■ Práctica

Cambie según los modelos.

a. **Tienen hambre.**
   Comerán.
   Si tienen hambre, comerán.

   1. Llueve mucho.
       No saldremos.
   2. Hace frío.
       Nos quedaremos en casa.
   3. Tenemos tiempo.
       Jugaremos al bridge.
   4. Ella llega temprano.
       La veremos.
   5. Usted estudia mucho.
       Aprenderá mucho.

b. **Si tienen hambre, comerán.**
   Si tuvieran hambre, comerían.

   1. Si llueve mucho, no saldremos.
   2. Si hace frío, nos quedaremos en casa.
   3. Si tenemos tiempo, jugaremos al bridge.
   4. Si ella llega a tiempo, la veremos.
   5. Si usted estudia mucho, aprenderá mucho.

c. **Si ha cogido un resfriado, irá a la clínica.**
   Si hubiera cogido un resfriado, habría ido a la clínica.

   1. Si ha llamado, me lo dirán.
   2. Si ha estado aquí, lo sabremos.
   3. Si ha comprado el coche, lo pagará.
   4. Si llegamos temprano, asistimos a la clase.
   5. Si vendió la casa, ganó mucho dinero.
   6. Si se levantaron tarde, no tomaron el desayuno.

2. *Clauses introduced by* **como si.** **Como si** (*as if*) introduces a clause which is essentially a contrary-to-fact condition. It is followed by the imperfect subjunctive to express present time and by the pluperfect subjunctive to express past time.

Hablas como si fueras mi abuela.   You talk as if you were my grandmother.

Hablaba como si lo hubiera visto.   He spoke as if he had seen it.

■ Práctica

Diga en español.

1. You describe it as if you were there.
2. You described it as if you had been there.
3. He speaks as if he understood it.
4. He spoke as if he had understood it.

3. *Definite article with general and abstract nouns.*

a. The definite article is required before general nouns,—that is, nouns that stand for *all* of whatever they name.

Los hombres necesitan trabajar.   Men (all men) need to work.
Me gusta la música.   I like music (all music in general).

b. It is required before abstract nouns.

La vida es sueño.   Life is a dream.
El trabajo es una necesidad.   Work is a necessity.

■ Práctica

Diga en español.

1. I like horses.
2. I like soup.
3. I like flowers.
4. Life is interesting.
5. Philosophy is interesting.
6. Art is interesting.

E.   Writing

Test yourself

1. We all dream.
2. If we are poor, we dream of being rich.
3. They always want what they don't have and they dream of it.
4. Philosophy and art are the products of dreams.
5. This spring afternoon the sky is cloudy, and it is raining.
6. The students are talking of what they would do, if they could.
7. I wish I could go to the baseball game!
8. If it had not rained, I would have been able to go.
9. If our friend were here, we would play bridge.

10. If only he had not caught a cold!
11. There was nothing to do that afternoon.
12. Will you play a game of tennis tomorrow, if it doesn't rain?
13. If it should rain tomorrow, we would not be able to play.
14. If it were possible, María would like to be an actress.
15. If Juan were rich, he would do nothing but have a good time.
16. If he should become rich, he would want to work.
17. María talks as if she were eighty years old and as if she were Juan's grandmother.

Composition

Write a composition telling what you would do today, if you could, and what you would have done yesterday, if you had been able to. (You would go to the movies this evening, if you didn't have to study; you would have played tennis yesterday, if it hadn't rained, etc.)

Mayan stele in the jungle in Guatemala. (Philip D. Gendreau)

(Below) Chichén Itzá, Yucatán: Temple of Kukulcán, built by the Mayas. (Philip D. Gendreau)

The Cabildo (old City Hall) of Buenos Aires was built in 1771 and reconstructed in 1941. (Three Lions, Inc.)

El Castillo del Morro, San Juan, Puerto Rico. (Philip D. Gendreau)

Peru: Street market in a small town in the Andes. (Philip D. Gendreau)

Street scene in
Guanajuato, Mexico.
(Philip D. Gendreau)

(Right) The Chilean *huaso* is the counterpart of the Argentine *gaucho*. Notice the typical, large spurs. (Philip D. Gendreau)

(Below) These huasos are about to participate in a rodeo near Santiago de Chile. (Philip D. Gendreau)

LESSON 26

A. Verbs in -*eír*

Verbs like **reír,** *to laugh,* whose infinitive ends in **-eír,** follow the pattern of the **pedir** type of stem-changing verb (that is, Class III), with the following exceptions:

1. Wherever the **i** is stressed, it bears a written accent.

PRESENT INDICATIVE		PRESENT SUBJUNCTIVE	
río	reímos	ría	riamos
ríes	reís	rías	riáis
ríe	ríen	ría	rían

PAST PARTICIPLE **reído**

2. Two contiguous **i**'s are reduced to one. Among the forms affected are the third person singular and plural of the preterit, the entire imperfect subjunctive, and the gerund.

PRETERIT		IMPERFECT SUBJUNCTIVE
reí	reímos	r*i*era, r*i*eras, etc.
reíste	reísteis	
r*i*ó	r*i*eron	r*i*ese, r*i*eses, etc.

GERUND **r*i*endo**

Notice that the first and second persons, singular and plural, of the preterit follow the rule stated in 1 above.

Another common **-eír** verb is **sonreír** (*to smile*).

■ Práctica

Cambie según se indica.

1. Ellos ríen siempre.
   Vd. / tú / nosotros / yo / vosotros
2. Vd. no se rió de eso.
   yo / Vd. y yo / vosotros / ellas / tú
3. Conviene que no se rían tanto.
   nosotros / tú / yo / vosotros / él
4. Convenía que no se rieran tanto.
   Vds. / vosotros / yo / tú / Vd. y yo

B. Verbs in -*iar*

Some verbs whose infinitive ends in **-iar** accent the **i** throughout the singular and in the third person plural of both the present indicative and the present subjunctive.

---

enviar   to send

PRESENT INDICATIVE		PRESENT SUBJUNCTIVE	
envío	**enviamos**	**envíe**	**enviemos**
envías	**enviáis**	**envíes**	**enviéis**
envía	**envían**	**envíe**	**envíen**

But compare **estudiar: estudio, estudias, estudia, etc.**

■ Práctica

Cambie según se indica.

1. Él les envía el dinero.
   yo / nosotros / vosotros / tú / Vds.
2. Quieren que Vd. se lo envíe.
   tú / yo / nosotros / él / Vds.

C. Listening and speaking

el acero steel
alrededor de about, around
añadir to add
la clase kind

conseguir (i) to get, obtain
el cual, la cual who, whom, that, which
lo cual which

cualquier(a) whichever, whatever
cursar to take, study (*a course*)
el detalle detail
el dineral large amount of money
dondequiera wherever
la economía economics
el empleo job, employment
el esposo husband
la exportación export
exportar to export
la fábrica factory
interesarse en (*or* **por**) to be interested in
la inversión investment
el mercado market
notar to notice
particular private

la pintura paint
el porvenir future
el presidente president
el progreso progress
el que, la que he who, the one who, the one which
los que those who, those which
reírse (de) to laugh (at)
el representante representative
le república republic
sonreír to smile
el total total

IDIOMS AND OTHER EXPRESSIONS

con todo empeño with great determination
al menos at least
de todos modos at any rate

Carlos quiere ser millonario

—¡No se rían Vds.!—dijo Carlos. —He dicho que voy a ser millonario y lo seré. Hay muchas compañías que envían representantes a Hispanoamérica. Voy a cursar al menos otros dos años de español. Estaré bien preparado para ir allá. Luego, después de terminar mis estudios, voy a conseguir un empleo en una compañía que tenga intereses en los países hispanoamericanos. Me enseñarán lo que deba saber. Iré allá y dondequiera que me envíen trabajaré con todo empeño. Tal vez llegue[1] a ser presidente de la compañía. De todos modos voy a ser muy rico.

—No nos reímos de eso—respondió Juan. —Es muy posible que resulte así. El esposo de mi tía, el cual me llevó a la Argentina, empezó así. Ahora gana un dineral.

—Es verdad—dijo Carlos—que hay grandes oportunidades en Hispanoamérica. El que se prepara aprendiendo primero el español y luego aprendiendo todos los detalles de los negocios de la compañía en que trabaja hallará muchas oportunidades. Acabo de saber que el total de las inversiones particulares norteamericanas en la república más pequeña de Sudamérica, el Uruguay, es alrededor de 80.000.000 de dólares, lo cual no me sorprende. El total de nuestras inversiones particulares en Méjico es alrededor de 600.000.000, lo cual sí me sorprende.

—En todos los países por los cuales viajamos mi tío y yo—añadió Juan —en cualquier ciudad que visitáramos, noté que se están haciendo grandes progresos. En Caracas, donde pasamos un par de días, se están construyendo magníficos edificios y grandes obras públicas. En Chile se están construyendo nuevas fábricas de todas clases. Para estas cosas los hispanoamericanos necesitan la maquinaria, el acero, las pinturas y otras cosas que exportamos nosotros.

—Mi padre,—dijo Virginia—quien se interesa también en la economía, dice que Hispanoamérica es el mejor mercado para nuestras exportaciones. Los que quieren que el porvenir les sonría deben pensar en Hispanoamérica.

■ Preguntas

1. ¿Qué les dijo Carlos a sus amigos?
2. ¿Qué quiere ser Carlos?
3. ¿Qué va a cursar?
4. Después de terminar sus estudios, ¿qué va a hacer?
5. ¿Qué hará Carlos en Hispanoamérica?
6. ¿Qué será Carlos tal vez?
7. ¿Cuánto gana ahora el tío de Juan?
8. ¿Qué hallará en Hispanoamérica el que se prepara bien para ir allá?
9. ¿Cuál es el total de las inversiones norteamericanas en el Uruguay?
10. ¿Cuál es el total de nuestras inversiones en Méjico?
11. ¿Qué notó Juan en cualquier ciudad que visitara?
12. ¿Qué se están construyendo en Caracas?
13. ¿Qué necesitan los hispanoamericanos?
14. ¿Qué dice el padre de Virginia?
15. ¿Quiénes deben pensar en ir a Hispanoamérica?

NOTES

1. **Tal vez, quizá(s),** and **acaso** (*perhaps*) may take the subjunctive when the verb follows and uncertainty is stressed.

   Tal vez llegue a ser presidente de la compañía. Perhaps I may (shall) become president of the company.

But:

   Llegará a ser presidente, tal vez. He will become president, perhaps.

■ Práctica

Diga en español.

a. **Tal vez:**

   1. they may arrive late.
   2. they may leave early.
   3. they may return soon.

b. **Quizás:**

1. he has done it.
2. he has seen it.
3. he has said so.

D. Structure

1. *Simple relative pronouns after a preposition.*

a. *Whom,* as the object of a preposition, is **quien (quienes).**

el tío *con quien* **fui a Sudamérica**   the uncle *with whom* I went to South
   America
las personas *a quienes* **me dirijo**   the people *to whom* I speak

b. *Which* is **que** after the prepositions, **a, de, en,** and **con.**

la compañía *con que* **trabaja**   the company *with which* he works
la ciudad *a que* **vamos**   the city *to which* we are going

c. *Which* is **el cual (la cual, los cuales, las cuales)** after other prepositions.

la mesa *sobre la cual* **puso los libros**   the table *on which* he put the books
los países *por los cuales* **viajamos**   the countries *through which* we
   traveled

■ Práctica

Diga en español.

a. **la amiga:**

1. for whom he bought it
2. to whom I sent it
3. with whom I went out

b. **los alumnos:**

1. for whom you bought it
2. to whom you sent it
3. with whom you went out

c. **el país:**

1. to which he is going
2. from which he has come
3. through which he traveled
4. about (*acerca de*) which he spoke to us

d. la casa:

1. in which they live
2. to which they are going
3. near which they live
4. in front of which they parked the car

2. *Simple relative pronouns as subject or object of a verb.*

a. As subject or object of a verb, *who, whom, that,* or *which* is usually **que,** the commonest relative pronoun.

> **Hay muchas compañías *que* envían representantes a Sudamérica.** There are many companies *that* send representatives to South America.
> **las personas *que* vemos en la calle** the people *whom* we see in the street

b. *Who* or *whom,* introducing a *nonrestrictive* or *nonessential* clause— that is, one set off by commas—may be **quien (quienes)** as well as **que.**

> **Mi padre, *quien* vive en Nueva York, está aquí ahora.** My father, *who* lives in New York, is here now.
> **Su hermana, *a quien* acabo de conocer, es muy linda.** His sister, *whom* I have just met, is very pretty. (Note the personal **a** when **quien** is the object, *whom.*)

c. *Who, whom, that,* or *which* is **el cual (la cual, los cuales, las cuales)** when referring to the *first* of two possible antecedents of a *nonrestrictive* clause.

> *el esposo* **de mi tía, *el cual* me llevó a la Argentina ...** my aunt's *husband, who* took me to Argentina ...
> *la hermana* **de mi amigo, *la cual* es muy linda ...** my friend's *sister, who* is very pretty ...

d. *Which* introducing a *nonrestrictive* clause and referring to a previously expressed idea or statement (not to a concrete object) is the neuter **lo cual.**

> **Nuestras inversiones en Méjico son alrededor de seiscientos millones de dólares, *lo cual* me sorprende.** Our investments in Mexico are around six hundred million dollars, *which* surprises me.
> **Se levantó temprano esta mañana, *lo cual* es extraordinario.** He got up early this morning, *which* is unusual.

■ Práctica

Cambie según los modelos.

a. **Ésta es la señora.**
   Vive aquí.
   Ésta es la señora que vive aquí.

   1. Ésta es la muchacha.
      Habla español.
   2 Éste es el muchacho.
      La conoce.
   3. Éstos son los hombres.
      Lo trajeron.
   4. Éstos son los individuos.
      Me lo enviaron.

b. **Esta es la cinta.**
   La escuchamos.
   Ésta es la cinta que escuchamos.

   1. Éste es el libro.
      Lo leemos.
   2. Éstas son las lecciones.
      Las estudiamos.
   3. Éste es el ejercicio.
      Lo escribimos.
   4. Éstas son las canciones.
      Las cantamos.

c. **Su padre vive en Chile.**
   Está aquí.
   Su padre, quien vive en Chile, está aquí.

   1. Su madre es española.
      Está aquí.
   2. Su tía es muy joven.
      Está aquí.
   3. Sus primas son muy ricas.
      Están aquí.
   4. Sus amigas son venezolanas.
      Están aquí.

d. **Conozco a sus padres.**
   No han llegado.
   Sus padres, a quienes conozco, no han llegado.

   1. Conozco a su hermano.
      No ha llegado.
   2. Busco a su hermana.
      No ha llegado.
   3. He conocido a sus abuelos.
      No han llegado.
   4. No veo a sus primos.
      No habrán llegado.

e. **La hermana de mi amigo es actriz.**
   Acaba de entrar.
   La hermana de mi amigo, la cual es actriz, acaba de entrar.

   1. La hermana del profesor es muy rica.
      Acaba de entrar.
   2. El tío de Juan es ingeniero.
      Acaba de entrar.
   3. Los abuelos de los alumnos son de Quito.
      Acaban de entrar.
   4. Las tías de mis amigas son muy viejas.
      Acaban de entrar.

f. **Dicen que tiene cinco automóviles.**
   Me sorprende.
   Dicen que tiene cinco automóviles, lo cual me sorprende.

   1. Dicen que ha comprado el edificio.
      Es muy posible.
   2. Dicen que ganaremos el campeonato.
      Es imposible.
   3. Dicen que será presidente.
      No es probable.
   4. Dicen que tiene noventa años.
      Parece mentira.

3. *Compound relative pronouns.* A compound relative pronoun is one which contains its own antecedent, for example, *he who, those who, that which.*

a. *He who (the one who, those who, the one which, those which, etc.)* is **el que (la que, los que, las que).**

El que se prepara hallará grandes oportunidades. *He who* prepares himself will find great opportunities.
De estas corbatas prefiero las que son de seda. Of these ties I prefer *the ones which* are of silk.

b. *That which* (often contracted to *what*) is the neuter **lo que.**

Me enseñarán lo que hay que saber. They will teach me *what* it is necessary to know.
Haré lo que Vd. quiera. I shall do *what(ever)* you wish.

Note that the neuter **lo cual** (*which*) is a simple relative pronoun and never has this function

■ Práctica

Diga en español.

a. 1. Juan is the one who is laughing.
   2. Teresa is the one who is laughing.
   3. The students are the ones who are laughing.
   4. The girls are the ones who are laughing.

b. 1. He who studies learns.
   2. Those who study learn.
   3. He who speaks Spanish will have opportunities.
   4. Those who speak Spanish will have opportunities.

c. 1. What you are doing is easy.
   2. What you are saying is interesting.
   3. What they see is amusing.
   4. What they sell is expensive.

4. Cualquiera *and* dondequiera. Clauses following the indefinite pronoun or adjective **cualquiera** and the indefinite adverb **dondequiera** require the subjunctive.

cualquier ciudad que visitáramos   whatever city we visited
dondequiera que me envíen   wherever they (may) send me

Cualquiera may drop the final **a** before any noun. The plural of **cualquier(a)** is **cualesquier(a).** Notice that **que** introduces the clause following both **cualquier(a)** and **dondequiera.**

■ Práctica

Diga en español.

a. 1. whatever book you read
    2. whatever country you visit
    3. whatever suit you buy
    4. whatever movie you see

b. 1. wherever they go
    2. wherever they are
    3. wherever they live
    4. wherever they eat

E. Writing

Test yourself

1. Don't laugh when Carlos says he is going to be a millionaire.
2. After taking at least two more years of Spanish, he will be well prepared to go to Hispanic America.
3. There are many companies that send representatives there.
4. He will get a job with one of them, and wherever they send him, he will work with great determination.
5. Perhaps he will become president of the company.
6. There are great opportunities in Hispanic America for those who prepare themselves to go there.
7. One must first learn Spanish and then learn the details of a business.
8. We have investments in Mexico of around six hundred millon dollars, which surprised Carlos.
9. In all the countries through which Juan traveled, he noticed great progress.
10. New buildings, factories, and public works are being built everywhere.
11. For all these things Hispanic America needs the machinery, the steel, and other products that we export.
12. Virginia's father says that Hispanic America is the best market for our exports.
13. He who wants the future to smile on him ought to go to Hispanic America.

Composition

Write a composition about the opportunities for employment with American companies in Spanish America. Tell how one should prepare to meet these opportunities. Tell whether or not you would like to get a job in Hispanic America and what you will do if you get one.

CIELITO LINDO

Arranged by EMILIO de TORRE

1. De la Sie - rra Mo - re - na, cie - li - to lin - do, vie -
2. U - na fle - cha en el ai - re, cie - li - to lin - do, lan -
3. E - se lu - nar que tie - nes, cie - li - to lin - do, jun -

\- nen ba - jan - do,_____ un par de o - ji - tos
\- zó Cu - pi - do,_____ y e - sa fle - cha vo -
\- to a la bo - ca,_____ no se lo des a

ne - gros, cie - li - to lin - do, de con - tra - ban - do.___
lan - do, cie - li - to lin - do, bien me ha he - ri - do __
na - die, cie - li - to lin - do, que a mí me to - ca.___

que   can - tan - do se a - le - gran, cie   -   li - to - lin - do, los

co - ra - zo - nes. ____   zo - nes. ____

LESSON 27

A. More orthographic changes in verbs

1. *Verbs in* **-guar.** To preserve the sound of **gu** (= gw) throughout the conjugation, verbs whose infinitive ends in **-guar** require a diaeresis over the **u (ü)** before a personal ending that begins with **e,** that is, in the first person singular of the preterit and throughout the present subjunctive.

averiguar to find out			
PRETERIT		PRESENT SUBJUNCTIVE	
averigüé	averiguamos	averigüe	averigüemos
averiguaste	averiguasteis	averigües	averigüéis
averiguó	averiguaron	averigüe	averigüen

2. *Verbs in* **-uar.** Some verbs whose infinitive ends in **-uar** (except **-guar**) accent the **u** throughout the singular and in the third person plural of both the present indicative and the present subjunctive.

continuar to continue			
PRESENT INDICATIVE		PRESENT SUBJUNCTIVE	
continúo	continuamos	continúe	continuemos
continúas	continuáis	continúes	continuéis
continúa	continúan	continúe	continúen

■ Práctica

Cambie según se indica.

1. Vd. lo averiguó ayer.
   yo / nosotros / tú / vosotros / ellos
2. Prefieren que ellos lo averigüen.
   Vd. / tú / yo / Vd. y yo / vosotros
3. Ella continúa bailando.
   nosotros / yo / vosotros / tú / ellas
4. Sugieren que continuemos buscando.
   tú / Vd. / Vds. / vosotros / yo

B. Listening and speaking

la altitud altitude
angosto narrow
el agua *f.* water
el altiplano plateau
antiguo old
árido arid
central central
el centro center
la civilización civilization
la costa coast
el desierto desert
distinto distinct; different
dividir(se) to divide
entre between; among
el este east
la faja strip
fértil fertile
la ganadería cattle-raising
la gente people
geográfico geographical
hallarse to be
los incas Incas
el indio Indian
la industria industry

el interior interior
el lago lake
largo long
la línea ecuatorial equator
el llano plain
majestuoso majestic
montañoso mountainous
el norte north
el oasis oasis
poseer to possess
el puerto port
la región region
los restos remains
el salitre nitrate
situado situated, located
templado temperate
la tierra land
el valle valley
vasto vast

IDIOMS AND OTHER EXPRESSIONS

el mismo que the same (one) as
el viaje de vuelta return trip

Algo sobre Sudamérica

Esta mañana Juan continúa hablando[1] de su viaje a la América del Sur.

—Cuando enviaron a mi tío a la Argentina—dice—averigüé que sería posible pasar algún tiempo en otros países, porque tendríamos más tiempo para el viaje de vuelta. Fue por eso que decidí acompañarle.

—Como dije, pasamos dos días en Caracas. ¡Ojalá que hubiéramos tenido más tiempo en esa bella ciudad de Venezuela! Al volver, visitamos la capital de Chile, la del Perú, la del Ecuador y la de Colombia. En todos esos países el paisaje es maravilloso. Todos son países montañosos que tienen una estrecha faja de tierra a orillas del Pacífico. Se ven montañas majestuosas en todas partes.

—Chile es un país largo y angosto dividido en tres regiones distintas. Al norte hay un gran desierto, cuyo producto principal es el salitre. Casi nunca llueve en esa región. El centro del país es una región templada, cuyos productos agrícolas son los mismos que los de los Estados Unidos. De Chile se exportan muchas frutas a nuestro país. En el Valle Central se halla la capital, Santiago. Esa ciudad es muy antigua: fue fundada por Pedro de Valdivia en 1541. El sur de Chile es una región de lagos hermosísimos. El² agua de esos lagos es de un azul precioso. Y al este siempre se ven los Andes.

—El Perú es otro país dividido en tres regiones. Al oeste se halla una faja estrecha de tierra como la de Chile. Es bastante árida, pero posee fértiles oasis. El centro es una región montañosa con grandes altiplanos donde vive la gente.³ Entre esas montañas vivían los incas, los restos de cuya civilización se ven en el Cuzco y en Machu Picchu. Al otro lado de los Andes, al este, se halla la selva tropical. Lima, la capital, está cerca de la costa. Fue fundada por Francisco Pizarro en 1535.

—El Ecuador se llama así porque está situado en la línea ecuatorial. Visitamos el gran puerto de Guayaquil y la capital, Quito, situada en el interior, entre montañas, y a una altitud de 9500 pies. El Ecuador es un país muy pintoresco. Como en el interior del Perú, hay indios en todas partes.

—La capital de Colombia, Bogotá, es otra ciudad situada a gran altitud. En efecto su altitud es de 8650 pies. En Colombia los Andes se dividen en tres cordilleras entre las cuales se encuentran importantes valles: el hermoso Valle del Cauca al oeste, y el valle tropical del río Magdalena. Al este de los Andes se halla la vasta región de los llanos de Colombia y de Venezuela, cuya industria principal, como la de la pampa argentina, es la ganadería.

—Un país muy pintoresco que no visité fue Bolivia. Pero en tan pocas semanas de vacaciones nadie puede verlo todo.⁴

■ Preguntas

1. ¿De qué continúa hablando Juan?
2. ¿Qué averiguó Juan?
3. ¿Qué exclama Juan cuando piensa en Caracas?

4. ¿Qué otras capitales visitó Juan?
5. ¿Cómo es el paisaje de los países que visitó Juan?
6. ¿Qué hay a orillas del Pacífico en esos países?
7. ¿Qué se ve en todas partes?
8. ¿Cómo es Chile?
9. ¿Qué hay al norte de Chile?
10. ¿Cuándo y por quién fue fundada Santiago de Chile?
11. ¿Cómo es el sur de Chile?
12. ¿Cómo es el Perú?
13. ¿Dónde se ven los restos de la civilización de los incas?
14. ¿Por quién fue fundada la capital del Perú?
15. ¿Dónde está situada la capital del Ecuador?
16. ¿Cuál es el gran puerto del Ecuador?
17. ¿A qué altitud está Bogotá?
18. ¿Qué se halla en Colombia al este de los Andes?

NOTES

1. **Continuar,** like **seguir,** is followed by the gerund, not the infinitive.

   Juan continúa hablando de su viaje.   Juan continues to talk (continues speaking) of his trip.
   Siguieron divirtiéndose.   They continued to have a good time.

2. The masculine definite article is used with feminine singular nouns beginning with stressed **a** or **ha.**

   el agua   the water   **el hambre**   hunger

3. **La gente** (*people*) is singular and requires a singular verb.

   La gente *vive* en los altiplanos.   The people *live* on the plateaus.
   Esta gente *es* muy trabajadora.   These people *are* very hardworking.

4. The redundant object pronoun **lo** is used with **todo** (*everything*).

   Lo **sabe todo.**   He knows everything.
   No se puede ver*lo* todo.   You can't see everything.

■ Práctica

Diga en español.

1. They know everything.
2. They understand everything.
3. She sees everything.
4. She hears everything.

C. Structure

1. *Relative adjective* **cuyo. Cuyo (cuya, cuyos, cuyas)** is a relative adjective. It never has the interrogative meaning "whose?" Interrogative "whose?" is **¿de quién?** or **¿de quiénes?**

Este es el autor cuyas obras leí.   This is the author whose works I read.

But:
¿De quién es este libro?   Whose book is this?

■ Práctica

Cambie según los modelos.

a. **El muchacho.**
Vi su sombrero.
El muchacho cuyo sombrero vi.

1. El individuo.
     Compré su coche.
2. El alumno.
     Hallé sus libros.
3. Las personas.
     Visité sus casas.
4. El pintor.
     Vendí sus cuadros.

b. **He hallado este sombrero.**
¿De quién es este sombrero?

1. He hallado este reloj.
2. He hallado esta guitarra.
3. He hallado estas raquetas.
4. He hallado estos zapatos.

2. *A fourth demonstrative pronoun.* In addition to **éste, ése,** and **aquél** there is a fourth demonstrative pronoun. It has the same forms as the definite article,—**el, la, los, las,**—and it means *the one, that.* It is always followed by **de** or **que. El (la, etc.) de** means *the one of, that of.* **El (la, etc.) que** means *the one who, that which, etc.* We have already used this pronoun as

a. *A possessive.*

mi casa y *la de mi hermano*   my house and *my brother's* (*that of my brother*)

b. *The first element in the compound relative pronoun.*

El *que* estudia aprende.   *He who* studies learns.
estos libros y *los que* Vd. tiene   these books and *those which* you have

Often **de** has other meanings than *of.*

la *de* los ojos negros   *the one with* the dark eyes
el *del* traje negro   *the one in* the black suit
la *de* los anteojos   *the one with* the glasses

■ Práctica

Diga en español.

a. 1. my car and my sister's
    2. my house and my father's
    3. my horses and the cowboys'
    4. my flowers and my mother's

b. 1. the one in the blue shirt
    2. the one in the white blouse
    3. the ones with the new shoes
    4. the ones with the nylon stockings

3. *Passive voice.*

a. As you know, a reflexive construction is widely used in Spanish instead of the passive voice, when no agent is expressed.

***Se ven* montañas en todas partes.**   Mountains *are seen* everywhere.
Aquí *se publican* muchísimos periódicos.   A great many newspapers *are published* here.

b. Spanish has a true passive voice. It is formed by combining the verb **ser** with the past participle of a transitive verb, just as the English passive is formed by the verb *to be* plus a past participle. It is used chiefly when the agent is named: *by Charles, by her, etc. By* is usually translated **por.** The past participle agrees in gender and number with the subject.

Lima *fue fundada por* Pizarro.   Lima *was founded by* Pizarro.
El libro *fue escrito por* Cervantes.   The book *was written by* Cervantes.
Las ventanas *fueron abiertas por* el alumno.   The windows *were opened by* the student.

c. When a *living being* is the subject and no agent is expressed, Spanish uses the third person plural of the *active* verb instead of either the true passive or the reflexive passive.

Enviaron a mi tío a Buenos Aires.   My uncle *was sent* to Buenos Aires.
(*They sent* my uncle to Buenos Aires.)
Ascendieron al capitán.   The captain *was promoted.* (*They promoted* the captain.)

■ Práctica

Diga en español.

a. 1. Many cities were founded.
    2. Many books were published.
    3. Many compositions were read.
    4. Many exercises were written.

b. 1. The city was founded by Cortés.
    2. The book was published by a Spaniard.
    3. The composition was read by the students.
    4. The exercise was written by the student.

c. 1. He was sent to Mexico.
    2. He was seen in the gymnasium.
    3. I was told that it was the truth.
    4. I was asked if it was the truth.

4. *Estar with past participles.* You have been using **estar** with adjectives and past participles in expressing an accidental or temporary state or condition. Such expressions may sometimes resemble a passive voice, but they must not be confused with the passive.

La puerta está cerrada.   The door is closed.
Las ventanas estaban abiertas.   The windows were open.
El libro está escrito en español.   The book is written in Spanish.

■ Práctica

Conteste según el modelo.

  ¿Cerraron el museo?
  Sí, el museo está cerrado.

1. ¿Abrieron la ventana?
2. ¿Construyeron bien las casas?

3. ¿Publicaron el libro?
4. ¿Escribieron los libros en español?
5. ¿Escribieron bien las composiciones?
6. ¿Cerraron los museos?

D. Writing

Test yourself

1. When his uncle was sent to Argentina, Juan found out that they would have enough time to visit other countries.
2. Oh that he had spent more time in Venezuela!
3. He visited the capitals of Chile and Peru and those of Ecuador and Colombia.
4. In those countries mountains are seen everywhere.
5. The Central Valley of Chile is a temperate region, whose products are the same as those of the United States.
6. Santiago was founded by Pedro de Valdivia in 1541.
7. In the mountainous region of Peru the people live on very high plateaus.
8. Here the Incas lived, and on the other side of the mountain range is the tropical forest.
9. Ecuador is a picturesque country, whose two most important cities are Quito and Guayaquil.
10. To the east of the Andes in Colombia are the vast plains, whose chief industry is cattle-raising.

Composition

Write a composition about the countries on the west coast of South America. Describe their geography. Tell which cities you would like to visit and where they are located.

LESSON 28

A. More orthographic-changes in verbs

1. *Verbs in a consonant* + **-cer, -cir.** To preserve the soft sound of the **c** throughout the conjugation, verbs whose infinitive ends in a consonant + **-cer** or **-cir** change **c** to **z** before a personal ending that begins with **o** or **a,**—that is, in the first person singular of the present indicative and throughout the present subjunctive.

---

convencer   to convince

PRESENT INDICATIVE		PRESENT SUBJUNCTIVE	
convenzo	convencemos	convenza	convenzamos
convences	convencéis	convenzas	convenzáis
convence	convencen	convenza	convenzan

---

2. *Verbs in a vowel* + **-cer, -cir.** You have already studied verbs like **conocer,** whose infinitive ends in a vowel + **-cer** or **-cir** (see Lesson 5). Other verbs conjugated like **conocer** are **parecer,** *to seem,* **agradecer,** *to thank,* **ofrecer,** *to offer,* **merecer,** *to deserve,* **nacer,** *to be born.* You remember that in these verbs **z** is inserted before the **c** in the first person singular of the present indicative and throughout the present subjunctive (**conozco; conozca**). Verbs whose infinitive ends in **-ducir** are conjugated like **conocer** in the present indicative and present subjunctive, but they are irregular in the preterit and the imperfect subjunctive.

303

producir to produce

PRETERIT		IMPERFECT SUBJUNCTIVE
produje	produjimos	produjera, produjeras, etc.
produjiste	produjisteis	
produjo	produjeron	produjese, produjeses, etc.

Other common verbs like **producir** are **traducir**, *to translate,* and **conducir,** *to conduct, to drive.*

■ Práctica

Cambie según se indica.

1. Le convencemos de la verdad.
   yo / vosotros / tú / él / Vds.

2. No es posible que le convenzan.
   ella / tú / vosotros / yo / Vd. y yo.

3. Se lo agradecemos.
   tú / yo / Vd. / vosotros / ellas

4. Esperan que Vd. lo merezca.
   yo / nosotros / Vds. / vosotros / tú

5. Produjeron la materia en España.
   Vd. / yo / tú / nosotros / vosotros

6. Era necesario que él produjera más.
   tú / Vds. / vosotros / yo / Vd. y yo.

B. Listening and speaking

absolutamente absolutely
el azteca Aztec
la campaña campaign
el capítulo chapter
civil civil
la conquista conquest
conquistar to conquer
contemporáneo contemporary
el continente continent
Cristóbal Colón Christopher
  Columbus
cultural cultural
la chiquita little girl

el desarrollo development
descubierto *past part. of*
  descubrir discovered
la dictadura dictatorship
durar to last
la época epoch
la epopeya epic
explorar to explore
frecuente frequent
la guerra war
el héroe hero
la independencia independence
Juanito Johnny

la literatura literature
militar military
la nación nation
la novela novel
ocurrir to occur
pedante pedantic
poquito very little, a tiny bit
la revolución revolution

no seas don't be
el siglo century
el soldado soldier
la tragedia tragedy
vecino neighboring
ven come
verdadero true, real

Un poco de historia

—América—dijo Juan—fue descubierta por Cristóbal Colón el doce de octubre de 1492.

—¡No me digas, Juanito!—exclamó María, riéndose. —No seas tan pedante o me voy.

—No te vayas, chiquita. Ven acá. Quédate aquí con Carlos y Virginia. ¿Cuánto sabes tú de la historia de América?

—Poquito, en verdad.

—La historia de Hispanoamérica es interesantísima. La conquista de América es una verdadera epopeya. En unos cincuenta años los españoles exploraron y conquistaron dos continentes donde hallaron grandes civilizaciones como la de los aztecas en Méjico y la de los incas en el Perú. La literatura de aquellos tiempos contiene libros sobre asuntos históricos que fascinan, absolutamente, como por ejemplo *La verdadera historia de la conquista de la Nueva España,* del viejo soldado, Bernal Díaz del Castillo, la cual describe la campaña de Cortés. Los españoles trajeron a América una rica civilización, construyeron ciudades como Lima y Méjico, que eran grandes centros culturales, y fundaron universidades cien años antes que se fundara la primera universidad de la América del Norte. El período colonial duró más de tres siglos. Luego ocurrió el corto período de las guerras de la independencia, desde 1810 hasta 1826. Esta época también es de gran interés. Las campañas militares de los grandes héroes, Bolívar, San Martín y otros, fueron verdaderamente asombrosas. La historia de los siglos diecinueve y veinte—época del desarrollo de las repúblicas— contiene capítulos llenos de interés, a pesar de la tragedia de las frecuentes guerras civiles. Pongo por ejemplo el período de la dictadura de Rosas en la Argentina y el de la Revolución Mejicana de 1910, que produjo una nación nueva en esa república vecina. La rica literatura de las naciones hispanoamericanas no es menos interesante que su historia y vale la pena de estudiarse—sobre todo la magnífica novela contemporánea que nos permite comprender la vida de aquellos países.

—Juanito, ¡nunca te oí hablar con tanto entusiasmo! Pero no necesito que me convenzas de todo esto. Lo creo, y el año que viene voy a seguir unas asignaturas de historia y de literatura hispanoamericanas.

■ Preguntas

1. ¿Cuál es la fecha del descubrimiento de América?
2. ¿Qué le dice María a su hermano?
3. ¿Cómo responde éste?
4. ¿Qué hicieron los españoles en unos cincuenta años?
5. ¿Qué civilizaciones hallaron en América?
6. ¿Qué trajeron los españoles a América?
7. ¿Qué construyeron y qué fundaron en América?
8. ¿Cuánto tiempo duró el período colonial?
9. ¿Cuáles son las fechas de la independencia en Hispanoamérica?
10. ¿Qué ocurrió en Méjico en 1910?
11. ¿Qué va a hacer María?

C. Structure

1. *Further uses of the infinitive*

a. In Spanish the infinitive is commonly used after verbs of perception (hearing, seeing, etc.), especially when English uses a present participle.

Oigo *cantar* **a Virginia.**   I hear Virginia *singing.*
Vimos *entrar* **al profesor.**   We saw the professor *come in.*

b. A dependent infinitive instead of a noun clause in the subjunctive may be used, even when the subject of the subordinate verb is different from the subject of the main verb, after the following verbs of causation:

mandar   to order   **permitir**   to permit
hacer   to make, have   **impedir**   to prevent
dejar   to let, allow

Hago venir al médico.   I have the doctor come.
Déjele hacerlo.   Let him do it.

■ Práctica

Diga en español.

a. 1. We heard Paquita singing.
   2. We heard José come in.
   3. We saw them leaving.
   4. We saw them return.

b. 1. I had the doctor come.
   2. I had the boys work.
   3. They permitted us to do it.

4. They permitted us to see it.
5. He ordered them to tell it.
6. He ordered them to answer.
7. You allowed me to speak.
8. You allowed me to listen.

2. *The familiar imperative*

a. You learned (Lesson 5) that the familiar imperative, singular, has the same form, for most verbs, as the third person singular, present indicative.

habla (tú)   speak
aprende (tú)   learn
escribe (tú)   write

You also learned that in reflexive verbs the reflexive pronoun **te** follows and is attached to this affirmative form.

siéntate (tú)   sit down
duérmete (tú)   go to sleep

b. For the plural of the familiar imperative, we have been following Spanish-American usage in using the third person plural command with **ustedes.**

siéntense Vds.   sit down
aprendan Vds.   learn
escriban Vds.   write

In Castilian Spanish, however, the plural of the familiar imperative has a special form. For all verbs it is formed by dropping the **-r** of the infinitive and substituting **-d.** The subject, which may be used for emphasis, is **vosotros.**

hablad (vosotros)   speak
aprended   learn
escribid   write

Reflexive verbs add the second person plural reflexive pronoun **os,** after dropping the final **-d.** Note the accented **í** in the third conjugation.

sentaos   sit down
vestíos   get dressed

But in the plural of the verb **irse,** *to go away,* the **-d** is not dropped.

idos   go away

c. The singular imperative of a few common verbs is irregular, but the plural is always regular.

decir	di	decid	salir	sal	salid
hacer	haz	haced	ser	sé	sed
ir	ve	id	tener	ten	tened
poner	pon	poned	venir	ven	venid

d. The familiar imperative is used only in the affirmative. To express a familiar command in the negative, the second persons singular and plural of the present subjunctive are used. The subject pronouns **tú** and **vosotros** may be used for emphasis.

no hables	no habléis	don't speak
no aprendas	no aprendáis	don't learn
no escribas	no escribáis	don't write
no te sientes	no os sentéis	don't sit down
no te vayas	no os vayáis	don't go away

■ Práctica

Conteste según los modelos.

a. **Quiero levantarme.**
   Levántate, pues.

   1. Quiero sentarme.
   2. Quiero bañarme.
   3. Quiero vestirme.
   4. Quiero despedirme.
   5. Quiero acercarme.
   6. Quiero acostarme.
   7. Quiero lavarme.

b. **Queremos hablar.**
   Hablad, pues.

   1. Queremos comer.
   2. Queremos salir.
   3. Queremos escuchar.
   4. Queremos venir.
   5. Queremos acercarnos.
   6. Queremos vestirnos.
   7. Queremos despedirnos.
   8. Queremos irnos.

c. **Quiero salir.**
   Sal, pues.

   1. Quiero venir.
   2. Quiero ir.
   3. Quiero decirlo.
   4. Quiero hacerlo.
   5. Quiero tenerlo.
   6. Quiero serlo.
   7. Quiero ponérmelo.

d. **No quiero bailar.**
   Pues, no bailes.

   1. No quiero leer.
   2. No quiero escribir.
   3. No quiero cantar.
   4. No quiero sentarme.
   5. No quiero irme.
   6. No quiero decirlo
   7. No quiero hacerlo.
   8. No quiero salir.

e. **No queremos volver.**
   Pues, no volváis.

1. No queremos pensar.
2. No queremos venir.
3. No queremos devolverlo.
4. No queremos pedirlo.
5. No queremos irnos.
6. No queremos sentarnos.
7. No queremos dormirnos.
8. No queremos levantarnos.

3. *Diminutives.* Spanish attains great variety of effect by the use of diminutive suffixes, which are added to nouns, adjectives, or adverbs after a final unstressed vowel has been dropped. Diminutives imply small size and may also express affection.

a. **-ito (-ita)** and **-illo (-illa)** are the commonest diminutive suffixes. To many words they are added directly. To others they are added after a final vowel has been dropped.

animal animal	**animalito** little animal
niña girl	**niñita** little girl
perro dog	**perrillo** little dog

b. **-cito (-cita)** and **-cillo (-cilla)** are added to words of two or more syllables ending in **-n** or **-r** and to words ending in **-e**.

canción song	**cancioncita** little song
mujer woman	**mujercita** (dear) little woman
pobre poor man	**pobrecillo** poor little fellow

c. **-ecito (-ecita)** and **-ecillo (-ecilla)** are added to words of one syllable ending in a consonant.

pan bread	**panecillo** roll
flor flower	**florecilla** little flower

Spelling changes are sometimes necessary to preserve the sound of the final consonant of the original word.

amigo friend	**amiguito** little friend
poco little	**poquito** tiny bit
pez fish	**pececito** little fish

Dé el diminutivo de las siguientes palabras.

a. 1. niño
   2. chico
   3. papel
   4. abuela
   5. hija
   6. largo

b. 1. madre
   2. hombre
   3. Ramón
   4. calzón
   5. tambor
   6. sabor

4. **Dates.** Except for **el primero** (*the first*) cardinal numerals are used in expressing dates in Spanish. As in the case of the days of the week, the preposition *on* is not translated. Note the use of **de** before the year.

el primero de junio de 1971   June first, 1971
el dos de mayo de 1808   May second, 1808
el treinta y uno de julio   (on) the thirty-first of July
¿Cuál es la fecha?   What is the date?
¿Qué fecha es hoy?   What is the date today?
Hoy es el veintitrés de enero.   Today is the twenty-third of January.
¿A cuántos estamos (del mes)?   What day of the month is it?
Estamos a diez (de febrero).   It is the tenth (of February).

■ Práctica

Diga en español.

a. 1. January first.
   2. February second.
   3. the fifteenth of November.
   4. the thirty-first of December.

b. 1. June 12, 1969.
   2. July 14, 1971.
   3. August 26, 1972.
   4. September 1, 1974.

c. 1. What is the date today?
   2. What day of the month is it?
   3. It's the eleventh.
   4. It's the twenty-seventh.

D. Writing

Test yourself

1. Juan said that America was discovered by Christopher Columbus on October 12, 1492.
2. María said that if her brother was going to be so pedantic, she was going to leave.
3. "Come here; don't go away," exclaimed Juan.
4. María knows only a tiny bit about the history of Hispanic America.
5. In fifty years the Spaniards explored and conquered two continents.
6. They found great civilizations like those of the Aztecs and the Incas.
7. Great cities were built and universities were founded.
8. The Spanish colonial period lasted three centuries.
9. The Independence Period lasted from 1810 until 1826.
10. Two interesting periods were that of the dictator Rosas in Argentina and that of the Mexican Revolution of 1910.
11. María does not need Juan to convince her that Hispanic-American history and literature are extremely interesting.

MÉJICO
Y
AMÉRICA
CENTRAL

Los Estados Unidos

BAJA CALIFORNIA

Nogales
Ciudad Juarez
Chihuahua
Río Grande
Durango
Mazatlán
Guadalajara
Monterrey
TRÓPICO DE CÁNCER
Tampico
Mérida
SIERRA MADRE OCCIDENTAL
SIERRA MADRE ORIENTAL
Méjico
Veracruz
Acapulco
Oajaca
YUCATÁN
Bélice
HONDURAS BRITÁNICA
HONDURAS
GUATEMALA
Guatemala
EL SALVADOR
Tegucigalpa
Managua
NICARAGUA
COSTA RICA
San José
Panamá

Océano Pacífico

Golfo de Méjico
Océano Atlántico
La Habana
CUBA
ANTILLAS
JAMAICA
Kingston
MAJORES
ISLAS BAHAMAS
HISPANIOLA
Ciudad Trujillo
San Jua
PUERTO RICO
Port-au-Prince
Mar de las Antillas
AMÉRICA DEL SUR

ESCALA
0   600 Millas
0   965 Kilómetros

ESPAÑA

La Coruña
Vigo
Braga
Oporto
Coimbra
Lisboa
Setubal
Faro
Huelva
Cádiz
Tánger

Golfo de Viscaya
FRANCIA
Oviedo
Santander
MTES. CANTÁBRICOS
Bilbao
Burgos
Pamplona
PIRINEOS
ANDORRA
Río Miño
Río Ebro
Valladolid
Río Duero
Zaragoza
Barcelona
Tarragona
Salamanca
GUADARRAMA
SIERRA DE Madrid
Cuenca
Río Tajo
Toledo
Valencia
ISLAS BALEARES
MENO
MALLORCA
IBIZA
FORMENTERA
Río Guadiana
Córdoba
MORENA
Murcia
Alicante
SIERRA Guadalquivir
Sevilla
Jaén
Lorca
Cartagena
Río
Granada
Mar Mediterráneo
Málaga
Almería
SIERRA NEVADA
Gibraltar
Estrecho de Gibraltar
ÁFRICA

PORTUGAL

Atlántico
Océano

ESCALA
0   100 Millas
0   160 Kilómetros

AMÉRICA
DEL SUR

Mar de las Antillas

Caracas
VENEZUELA

Medellín

Bogotá

COLOMBIA

Rio Orinoco

LAS GUAYANAS

(Inglesa)
(Holandesa)
(Francesa)

Océano Atlántico

ECUADOR

Quito
ECUADOR
Guayaquil

Iquitos

PERÚ

Rio Negro

Manaus

Rio Madeira

Amazonas

Rio

Belém

Fortaleza

Rio Tocantins

B R A S I L

Recife

Callao Lima

Cuzco

Lago de
Titicaca

La Paz

BOLIVIA

Sucre

Arequipa

Arica

Iquique

Antofagasta

Cuiabá

Rio São Francisco

Salvador

Belo
Horizonte

TRÓPICO DE CAPRICORNIO

Océano
Pacífico

Tucumán

Córdoba

Rosario

Valparaíso
Santiago

Buenos Aires

Bahía
Blanca

Concepción

Rio Paraguay

PARAGUAY

Asunción

Rio Paraguay

São Paulo

Santos

Rio de Janeiro

Porto
Alegre

URUGUAY

Rio Paraná

Montevideo

Océano Atlántico

ANDES

CORDILLERA DE LOS ANDES

A R G E N T I N A

ESCALA

0   900 Millas

0   1448 Kilómetros

ISLAS
FALKLAND

Estrecho de
Magallanes

Cabo de
Hornos

APPENDIX

A. Verb forms not studied in the text

1. *The preterit perfect tense.* In addition to the pluperfect indicative (for example, **había hablado, había aprendido, había vivido**) Spanish has another form which is equivalent to the English pluperfect. This is the preterit perfect tense, formed by combining the preterit of **haber** with a past participle.

hube hablado   I had spoken
hubiste hablado   you had spoken
Vd. hubo hablado   you had spoken
hubo hablado   he had spoken

hubimos hablado   we had spoken
hubisteis hablado   you had spoken
Vds. hubieron hablado   you had spoken
hubieron hablado   they had spoken

The use of this tense is restricted to dependent clauses introduced by expressions meaning essentially "as soon as."

En cuanto hube comido, fui al cine.   As soon as I had eaten, I went to the movies.
Apenas hubieron llegado, nos dieron los regalos.   They had scarcely arrived when they gave us the gifts.

2. *The future perfect tense.* Spanish, like English, sometimes uses the future perfect tense, which is formed by combining the future of **haber** with a past participle.

Habré estudiado la lección.   I shall have studied the lesson.

The future perfect, like the simple future, sometimes expresses conjecture or probability.

¿Adónde habrán ido?   Where can they have gone?
Habrá llegado.   He probably has arrived.

315

3. *The future subjunctive.* Spanish has a future subjunctive, which is used rarely now except in proverbs and in legal terminology. It is the same in form as the **-ra** imperfect subjunctive except that **-re** is substituted throughout for **-ra.**

> **hablare, hablares, etc.**
> **aprendiere, aprendieres, etc.**
> **viviere, vivieres, etc.**

Adonde fueres, haz lo que vieres. When in Rome, do as the Romans do. (*Literally*, Wherever you go, do what you see.)

B. The passive voice

As you have learned, Spanish has a passive voice, formed by combining the verb **ser** (as in English we combine the verb *to be*) with the past participle of a transitive verb. The past participle functions as an adjective, and thus agrees in gender and number with the subject. The use of the passive voice is normally restricted to statements in which the agent is named. **Por** usually translates English *by.*

> **La ventana fue cerrada por el alumno.** The window was closed by the student.
> **Las cartas fueron escritas por la secretaria.** The letters were written by the secretary.

When no agent is named, the reflexive verb is commonly used instead of the passive, the subject usually following the verb (see page 222).

> **Se bailó el bambuco.** The bambuco was danced.
> **Se estudian las lecciones.** The lessons are studied.
> **Se hará todo lo necesario.** Everything necessary will be done.

But when, in English, a living being is the subject of a passive and no agent is named, Spanish expresses the idea, not by means of the reflexive construction, but by the third person plural active.

> **Asesinaron al presidente.** The President was assassinated. (They assassinated the President.)
> **Ascendieron al capitán.** The captain was promoted. (They promoted the captain.)

C. Summary of the uses of the subjunctive in dependent clauses

1. The subjunctive is used in a noun clause which depends on

a. Verbs of wishing and desiring: **querer** (to wish, want), **desear** (to desire). (See page 187.)

Quiero que Vd. se levante temprano. I want you to get up early.

When there is no change of subject within the sentence, however, the infinitive is used.

No quiero levantarme temprano.   I don't want to get up early.

b. Verbs of commanding and requesting: **mandar** (to command), **decir** (to tell) in the sense of *to command*; **pedir** (to ask, request), **rogar** (to beg) and verbs similar in idea, **hacer** (to make, have), **aconsejar** (to advise), **preferir** (to prefer), **proponer** (to propose, suggest). (See page 198.)

Le pido que venga a mi casa.   I ask him to come to my house.
Mi padre me ha dicho que trabajara mucho.   My father has told me to work hard.
Nos aconsejan que ahorremos dinero.   They advise us to save money.

When there is no change of subject within the sentence, however, the infinitive is used.

No me permito hablar.   I do not permit myself to speak.
Prefieren hacerlo.   They prefer to do so.

Five of these verbs may be followed by an infinitive, whether or not the subject of the sentence changes. They are **mandar, hacer, dejar, permitir, impedir.**

Hago venir al médico.   I have the doctor come.
Nos permiten hacerlo.   They permit us to do it.

c. Verbs of emotion: **esperar** (to hope), **sentir** (to regret, be sorry), **temer** (to fear), **alegrarse de** (to be glad), **extrañar** (to be surprised). (See page 209.)

Me alegro de que Vd. se haya divertido.   I am glad you have had a good time.

Yo sentía que mi amigo estuviera enfermo.   I was sorry that my friend was ill.

When there is no change of subject within the sentence, however, the infinitive is used.

Siento llegar tan tarde.   I am sorry to arrive so late.
Esperan salir aprobados en el curso.   They hope to pass the course.

d. Verbs of doubt, denial, and uncertainty, including verbs of belief used negatively: **dudar** (to doubt), **negar** (to deny), **no creer** (not to believe), **no estar seguro** (not to be sure). (See page 210.)

Dudo que hayan visto esa película.   I doubt that they have seen that picture.
No creían que nosotros hubiéramos estudiado.   They did not believe that we had studied.
No estamos seguros de que él esté aquí.   We are not sure that he is here.

But negative verbs of doubt and denial and positive verbs of belief are followed by the indicative.

No niegan que el libro es interesante. They do not deny that the book is interesting.

Creemos que será un buen presidente. We believe that he will be a good president.

When there is no change of subject within the sentence, however, the infinitive is used.

Niego haber dicho esto. I deny that I said that.
Creo comprenderlo. I believe I understand it.

e. Impersonal expressions *not stating a fact*, but expressing necessity, possibility, probability, advisability, etc.: **es necesario, es preciso** (it is necessary), **es posible** (it is possible), **es probable** (it is probable), **conviene** (it is advisable), **es fácil** (it is likely), **basta** (it is enough), **parece mentira** (it is incredible). (See page 221.)

Es posible que hayan estado aquí. It is possible that they have been here.
Parece mentira que Vd. no sepa esto. It seems incredible that you do not know this.

The infinitive is used, however, when (1) the English sentence does not have a second subject, or (2) when the infinitive of the English sentence has an unemphatic pronoun subject.

(1) **Es necesario hacer eso.** It is necessary to do that.
    Basta decirlo. It is enough to say so.
(2) **Me es imposible hacerlo.** It is impossible for me to do it.

2. The subjunctive is used in an adjective clause which has an indefinite or a negative antecedent. (See page 232.)

Buscamos una secretaria que hable español. We are looking for a secretary who speaks Spanish.

Querían una casa que fuera nueva. They wanted a house that was new.

No había libros que no hubiera leído. There were no books that he had not read.

But when the antecedent is definite, the verb of the adjective clause is in the indicative.

Conocemos a una secretaria que habla español. We know a secretary who speaks Spanish.

Tenían una casa que era nueva. They had a house which was new.

Vendió los libros que había leído. He sold the books which he had read.

3. The use of the subjunctive in an adverb clause depends upon the meaning of the clause.

a. An adverb clause of purpose is always in the subjunctive. It is introduced by **para que, a fin de que** (in order that), **de modo que, de manera que** (so that). (See page 242.)

Le daré el libro para que lo lea.   I shall give you the book in order that you
may read it.

Fuimos al parque de manera que los niños vieran los animales.   We went to
the park so that the children might see the animals.

b. An adverb clause of proviso is always in the subjunctive. It is introduced
by **a menos que** (unless), **con tal que** (provided [that], **en caso de que** (in case).
(See page 243.)

No iré a menos que Vd. vaya también.   I shall not go unless you go, too.

Siempre llevaba paraguas, en caso de que lloviera.   He always carried an um-
brella in case it should rain.

c. An adverb clause of time is in the subjunctive when the time of the clause is
future. It is introduced by **antes (de) que** (before), **después (de) que** (after), **en
cuanto, tan pronto como** (as soon as), **cuando** (when), **mientras (que)** (while),
hasta que (until). (See page 253).

Le veré cuando venga.   I shall see him when he comes.

Tenemos que estudiar hasta que sepamos la lección.   We must study until
we learn the lesson.

Antes que se vaya Vd., quiero conversar un rato.   Before you go, I want to talk
a while.

But when the time of the clause is present, and sometimes when it is past, the
clause is in the indicative.

Cuando estudiamos, aprendemos.   When we study, we learn.

Le vi en cuanto vino.   I saw him as soon as he came.

Después que habíamos estudiado la lección, la sabíamos.   After we had studied
the lesson, we knew it.

When the time of the clause, though past, is future in relation to the time of
the main verb, the subjunctive is used.

No quería esperar hasta que llegaran.   He did not wish to wait until they
arrived.

Dijeron que nos verían después que hubiéramos vuelto.   They said they would
see us after we had returned.

Clauses introduced by **antes (de) que** are always in the subjunctive.

Almorzaron antes de que yo volviera a casa.   They had luncheon before I
returned home.

d. An adverb clause of concession is in the subjunctive when it expresses a
mere possibility. It is introduced by **aunque** (although), **aun cuando** (even though),
a pesar de que (in spite of the fact that). (See page 255.)

Aunque Vd. no quiera, tendrá que hacerlo.   Although you may not want to,
you will have to do it.

Aun cuando esté enfermo, estará en la clase. Even though he may be ill, he will be in class.

But when the concessive clause expresses a fact, it is in the indicative.

Aunque Vd. no quiere, tiene que hacerlo. Although you do not want to, you have to do it.
A pesar de que está enfermo, ha venido a la clase. In spite of the fact that he is ill, he has come to class.

e. An adverb clause of result is regularly in the indicative. It is introduced by **de manera que, de modo que** (so [that]).

Tenían el dinero, de modo que compraron la casa. They had the money; so they bought the house.

But **sin que,** *without,* which introduces a clause of negative result, regularly takes the subjunctive. (See page 266.)

Salió sin que nadie le viera. He went out without anyone's seeing him (without that anyone should see him).

4. The use of the subjunctive in a conditional clause depends upon the kind of condition which the clause expresses.

a. Neutral conditions are regularly in the indicative. Most frequently, the present indicative is used in the conditional clause and the future in the main clause. A simple past tense may be used in both clauses (third example below). But neither the subjunctive nor the future indicative may be used in the *if*-clause. (See page 274.)

Si Vd. estudia, aprenderá. If you study, you will learn.
Si llueve, no iré. If it rains, I shall not go.
Si Vd. estudiaba, aprendía. If you studied, you learned.

b. Conditions contrary to fact take the imperfect subjunctive (or the pluperfect subjunctive) in the conditional clause, and the conditional (or conditional perfect) in the main clause. (See page 274.)

Si tuvieran el dinero, comprarían el automóvil. If they had the money, they would buy the automobile.
Si fuese inteligente, trabajaría. If he were intelligent, he would work.
Si hubieran estado aquí, los habría conocido. If they had been here, I should have met them.

c. Like conditions contrary to fact, conditions expressing uncertainty take the imperfect subjunctive in the conditional clause and the conditional in the main clause. (See page 274.)

Si lloviera mañana, no iría. If it should rain tomorrow, I would not go.
Si llegasen tarde, yo no podría esperarlos. If they should arrive late, I should not be able to wait for them.

D. Numerals

CARDINAL NUMERALS

1 un(o), una	6 seis	11 once
2 dos	7 siete	12 doce
3 tres	8 ocho	13 trece
4 cuatro	9 nueve	14 catorce
5 cinco	10 diez	15 quince

16 diez y seis (dieciséis)	50 cincuenta
17 diez y siete (diecisiete)	60 sesenta
18 diez y ocho (dieciocho)	70 setenta
19 diez y nueve (diecinueve)	80 ochenta
20 veinte	90 noventa
21 veinte y un(o), una	100 ciento (cien)
(veintiuno, -a, veintiún)	101 ciento un(o), una
22 veinte y dos (veintidós)	102 ciento dos
23 veinte y tres (veintitrés)	103 ciento tres
24 veinte y cuatro (veinticuatro)	200 doscientos, -as
25 veinte y cinco (veinticinco)	300 trescientos, -as
26 veinte y seis (veintiséis)	400 cuatrocientos, -as
27 veinte y siete (veintisiete)	500 quinientos, -as
28 veinte y ocho (veintiocho)	600 seiscientos, -as
29 veinte y nueve (veintinueve)	700 setecientos, -as
30 treinta	800 ochocientos, -as
31 treinta y un(o), una	900 novecientos, -as
32 treinta y dos	1000 mil
33 treinta y tres	2000 dos mil
40 cuarenta	1,000,000 un millón
41 cuarenta y un(o), una	2,000,000 dos millones

1946 mil novecientos cuarenta y seis
5794 cinco mil setecientos noventa y cuatro

ORIGINAL NUMERALS

primero (primer), -a first		sexto, -a sixth	
segundo, -a second		séptimo, -a seventh	
tercero (tercer), -a third		octavo, -a eight	
cuarto, -a fourth		noveno, -a ninth	
quinto, -a fifth		décimo, -a tenth	

E. Regular verbs

The simple tenses

INFINITIVE

hablar to speak   **aprender** to learn   **vivir** to live

PRESENT PARTICIPLE

hablando speaking	**aprendiendo** learning	**viviendo** living

INDICATIVE MOOD

Present

I speak (do speak, am speaking) etc.	I learn (do learn, am learning) etc.	I live (do live, am living) etc.
hablo	aprendo	vivo
hablas	aprendes	vives
habla	aprende	vive
hablamos	aprendemos	vivimos
habláis	aprendéis	vivís
hablan	aprenden	viven

Imperfect

I was speaking (used to [would] speak, spoke) etc.	I was learning (used to [would] learn, learned) etc.	I was living (used to [would] live, lived) etc.
hablaba	aprendía	vivía
hablabas	aprendías	vivías
hablaba	aprendía	vivía
hablábamos	aprendíamos	vivíamos
hablabais	aprendíais	vivíais
hablaban	aprendían	vivían

Preterit

I spoke (did speak) etc.	I learned (did learn) etc.	I lived (did live) etc.
hablé	aprendí	viví
hablaste	aprendiste	viviste
habló	aprendió	vivió
hablamos	aprendimos	vivimos
hablasteis	aprendisteis	vivisteis
hablaron	aprendieron	vivieron

Future

I shall (will) speak etc.	I shall (will) learn etc.	I shall (will) live etc.
hablaré	aprenderé	viviré
hablarás	aprenderás	vivirás
hablará	aprenderá	vivirá
hablaremos	aprenderemos	viviremos
hablaréis	aprenderéis	viviréis
hablarán	aprenderán	vivirán

Conditional

I should (would) speak etc.	I should (would) learn etc.	I should (would) live etc.
hablaría	aprendería	viviría
hablarías	aprenderías	vivirías
hablaría	aprendería	viviría
hablaríamos	aprenderíamos	viviríamos
hablaríais	aprenderíais	viviríais
hablarían	aprenderían	vivirían

SUBJUNCTIVE MOOD

Present

(that) I may speak etc.	(that) I may learn etc.	(that) I may live etc.
hable	aprenda	viva
hables	aprendas	vivas
hable	aprenda	viva
hablemos	aprendamos	vivamos
habléis	aprendáis	viváis
hablen	aprendan	vivan

-ra Imperfect

(that) I might speak etc.	(that) I might learn etc.	(that) I might live etc.
hablara	aprendiera	viviera
hablaras	aprendieras	vivieras
hablara	aprendiera	viviera
habláramos	aprendiéramos	viviéramos
hablarais	aprendierais	vivierais
hablaran	aprendieran	vivieran

-se Imperfect*

(that) I might speak etc.	(that) I might learn etc.	(that) I might live etc.
hablase	aprendiese	viviese
hablases	aprendieses	vivieses
hablase	aprendiese	viviese
hablásemos	aprendiésemos	viviésemos
hablaseis	aprendieseis	vivieseis
hablasen	aprendiesen	viviesen

---

* There is also a future subjunctive, rarely used in modern Spanish except in proverbs and in legal terminology. The forms for **hablar** are **hablare, hablares, hablare, habláremos, hablareis, hablaren**; for **aprender, aprendiere etc.**; for **vivir, viviere etc.**

IMPERATIVE MOOD

speak	learn	live
habla (tú)	aprende (tú)	vive (tú)
hablad (vosotros)	aprended (vosotros)	vivid (vosotros)

The perfect tenses

PERFECT INFINITIVE

haber hablado   to have spoken
haber aprendido   to have learned
haber vivido   to have lived

PERFECT PARTICIPLE

habiendo hablado   having spoken
habiendo aprendido   having learned
habiendo vivido   having lived

INDICATIVE MOOD

Present Perfect	*Pluperfect*	*Preterit Perfect*
I have spoken etc.	I had spoken etc.	I had spoken etc.
he hablado	había hablado	hube hablado
has hablado	habías hablado	hubiste hablado
ha hablado	había hablado	hubo hablado
hemos hablado	habíamos hablado	hubimos hablado
habéis hablado	habíais hablado	hubisteis hablado
han hablado	habían hablado	hubieron hablado

Future Perfect	*Conditional Perfect*
I shall have spoken etc.	I should have spoken etc.
habré hablado	habría hablado
habrás hablado	habrías hablado
habrá hablado	habría hablado
habremos hablado	habríamos hablado
habréis hablado	habríais hablado
habrán hablado	habrían hablado

SUBJUNCTIVE MOOD

Present Perfect	*-ra Pluperfect*	*-se Pluperfect*
(that) I may have spoken etc.	(that) I might have spoken etc.	(that) I might have spoken etc.
haya hablado	hubiera hablado	hubiese hablado
hayas hablado	hubieras hablado	hubieses hablado
haya hablado	hubiera hablado	hubiese hablado
hayamos hablado	hubiéramos hablado	hubiésemos hablado
hayáis hablado	hubierais hablado	hubieseis hablado
hayan hablado	hubieran hablado	hubiesen hablado

F. Stem-changing verbs

Class I; *-ar, -er* Verbs. Stem vowel **e** becomes **ie** and stem vowel **o** becomes **ue** when stressed (that is, throughout the singular and in the third person plural of both the present indicative and the present subjunctive, and in the singular of the familiar imperative).

1. pensar to think

Pres. Ind.　**pienso, piensas, piensa,** pensamos, pensáis, **piensan**
Pres. Subj.　**piense, pienses, piense,** pensemos, penséis, **piensen**
Imperative　**piensa** (tú), pensad (vosotros)

Like **pensar: cerrar** to close, **despertar** to awaken, **empezar** to begin, **negar** to deny, **sentar** to seat

2. contar to count

Pres. Ind.　**cuento, cuentas, cuenta,** contamos, contáis, **cuentan**
Pres. Subj.　**cuente, cuentes, cuente,** contemos, contéis, **cuenten**
Imperative　**cuenta** (tú), contad (vosotros)

Like **contar: acordarse** to remember, **acostar** to put to bed, **costar** to cost, **encontrar** to find, **mostrar** to show, **recordar** to recall, **rogar** to beg, **sonar** to sound, **soñar** to dream
Jugar (to play) has this same change, despite the **u.**

Pres. Ind.　**juego, juegas, juega,** jugamos, jugáis, **juegan**
Pres. Subj.　**juegue, juegues, juegue,** juguemos, juguéis, **jueguen**
Imperative　**juega** (tú), jugad (vosotros)

3. perder to lose

Pres. Ind.　**pierdo, pierdes, pierde,** perdemos, perdéis, **pierden**
Pres. Subj.　**pierda, pierdas, pierda,** perdamos, perdáis, **pierdan**
Imperative　**pierde** (tú), perded (vosotros)

Like **perder: atender** to attend, **entender** to understand

4. volver to return

Pres. Ind.　**vuelvo, vuelves, vuelve,** volvemos, volvéis, **vuelven**
Pres. Subj.　**vuelva, vuelvas, vuelva,** volvamos, volváis, **vuelvan**
Imperative　**vuelve** (tú), volved (vosotros)

Like **volver: devolver** to return (give back), **mover** to move, **oler** to smell,* **resolver** to solve, **torcer** to turn

---

* Wherever stem vowel **o** of **oler** is stressed, **o** becomes **hue**, because the diphthong **ue** does not occur at the beginning of a word.

Pres. Ind.　**huelo, hueles, huele,** olemos, oléis, **huelen**
Pres. Subj.　**huela, huelas, huela,** olamos, oláis, **huelan**
Imperative　**huele** (tú), oled (vosotros)

Class II: -ir Verbs. Stem vowel **e** becomes **ie** and stem vowel **o** becomes **ue** when stressed (that is, wherever the same changes occur in Class I, above).

In addition **e** becomes **i** and **o** becomes **u** (1) in the present subjunctive, first and second persons plural; (2) in the preterit, third person singular and plural; (3) throughout the imperfect subjunctive (both forms); (4) in the present participle.

1. sentir to feel, regret

Pres. Part.	**sintiendo**
Past Part.	sentido
Pres. Ind.	**siento, sientes, siente,** sentimos, sentís, **sienten**
Pres. Subj.	**sienta, sientas, sienta,** sintamos, sintáis, **sientan**
Preterit	sentí, sentiste, **sintió,** sentimos, sentisteis, **sintieron**
Imperf. Subj.	**sintiera (sintiese), sintieras (sintieses),** etc.
Imperative	**siente** (tú), sentid (vosotros)

Like **sentir**: **advertir** to warn, advise, **consentir** to consent, **divertir** to amuse, **preferir** to prefer, **referir** to relate, refer

2. dormir to sleep

Pres. Part.	**durmiendo**
Past Part.	dormido
Pres. Ind.	**duermo, duermes, duerme,** dormimos, dormís, **duermen**
Pres. Subj.	**duerma, duermas, duerma, durmamos, durmáis, duerman**
Preterit	dormí, dormiste, **durmió,** dormimos, dormisteis, **durmieron**
Imperf. Subj.	**durmiera (durmiese), durmieras (durmieses),** etc.
Imperative	**duerme** (tú), dormid (vosotros)

Like **dormir: morir** to die (except in the past participle, **muerto**)

Class III: -ir Verbs. Stem vowel **e** becomes **i** when stressed and wherever the **e** of **sentir** becomes **i**.

Pres. Part.	**pidiendo**
Past Part.	pedido
Pres. Ind.	**pido, pides, pide,** pedimos, pedís, **piden**
Pres. Subj.	**pida, pidas, pida, pidamos, pidáis, pidan**
Preterit	pedí, pediste, **pidió,** pedimos, pedisteis, **pidieron**
Imperf. Subj.	**pidiera (pidiese), pidieras (pidieses),** etc.
Imperative	**pide** (tú), pedid (vosotros)

Like **pedir: conseguir** to get, obtain, **despedirse** to say good-by, **impedir** to prevent, **reír** to laugh, **reñir** to scold, quarrel, **repetir** to repeat, **seguir** to follow, continue, **servir** to serve, **sonreír** to smile, **vestir** to dress

G. Verbs with orthographic changes

1. Verbs whose infinitive ends in **-car** change **c** to **qu** before **e**.

buscar to look for

Preterit   **busqué,** buscaste, buscó, buscamos, buscasteis, buscaron
Pres. Subj.   **busque, busques, busque, busquemos, busquéis, busquen**

Like **buscar**: **acercarse** to approach, **equivocarse** to be mistaken, **explicar** to explain, **indicar** to indicate, **sacar** to take out, **tocar** to touch, play

2. Verbs whose infinitive ends in **-gar** change **g** to **gu** before **e**.

pagar to pay

Preterit   **pagué,** pagaste, pagó, pagamos, pagasteis, pagaron
Pres. Subj.   **pague, pagues, pague, paguemos, paguéis, paguen**

Like **pagar**: **llegar** to arrive, **obligar** to oblige, **negar (ie)** to deny, **jugar (ue)** to play

3. Verbs whose infinitive ends in **-zar** change **z** to **c** before **e**.

cruzar to cross

Preterit   **crucé,** cruzaste, cruzó, cruzamos, cruzasteis, cruzaron
Pres. Subj.   **cruce, cruces, cruce, crucemos, crucéis, crucen**

Like **cruzar**: **alcanzar** to overtake, **almorzar (ue)** to lunch, **comenzar (ie)** to commence, **gozar** to enjoy, **empezar (ie)** to begin

4. Verbs whose infinitive ends in **-guar** change **gu** to **gü** before **e**.

averiguar to find out

Preterit   **averigüé,** averiguaste, averiguó, averiguamos, averiguasteis, averiguaron
Pres. Subj.   **averigüe, averigües, averigüe, averigüemos, averigüéis, averigüen**

5. Verbs whose infinitive ends in **-ger** or **-gir** change **g** to **j** before **a** and **o**.

coger to catch

Pres. Ind.   **cojo,** coges, coge, cogemos, cogéis, cogen
Pres. Subj.   **coja, cojas, coja, cojamos, cojáis, cojan**

Like **coger**: **dirigir** to direct, **elegir (i)** to elect, **escoger** to select, **recoger** to pick up

6. Verbs whose infinitive ends in **-guir** change **gu** to **g** before **a** and **o**.

distinguir to distinguish

Pres. Ind.   **distingo,** distingues, distingue, distinguimos, distinguís, distinguen
Pres. Subj.   **distinga, distingas, distinga, distingamos, distingáis, distingan**

Like **distinguir: conseguir (i)** to get, **seguir (i)** to follow, continue

7. Verbs whose infinitive ends in consonant + **-cer,** or consonant + **-cir,** change **c** to **z** before **o** and **a.**

convencer to convince

Pres. Ind.   **convenzo,** convences, convence, convencemos, convencéis, convencen
Pres. Subj.   **convenza, convenzas, convenza, convenzamos, convenzáis, convenzan**

Like **convencer: vencer** to conquer

8. Verbs whose infinitive ends in vowel + **-cer,** or vowel + **-cir,** insert **z** before **co** and **ca.**

conocer to know

Pres. Ind.   **conozco,** conoces, conoce, conocemos, conocéis, conocen
Pres. Subj.   **conozca, conozcas, conozca, conozcamos, conozcáis, conozcan**

Like **conocer: agradecer** to thank, be grateful for, **conducir** to conduct, **nacer** to be born, **merecer** to deserve, **ofrecer** to offer, **parecer** to seem, appear, **producir** to produce, **traducir** to translate, **conducir** to conduct, drive

Verbs in **-ducir** have a further irregularity, in the preterit and in the imperfect subjunctive:

Preterit   **conduje, condujiste, condujo, condujimos, condujisteis, condujeron**
Imperf. Subj. **condujera (condujese), condujeras (condujeses), etc.**

9. Verbs whose infinitive ends in **-uir** (except **-guir** and **-quir**) insert **y** before the ending (except before **i**) and change unstressed **i** to **y** between vowels.

huir to flee

Pres. Part.   **huyendo**
Past. Part.   **huido**
Pres. Ind.   **huyo, huyes, huye,** huimos, huís, **huyen**
Preterit   huí, huiste, **huyó,** huimos, huisteis, **huyeron**
Pres. Subj.   **huya, huyas, huya, huyamos, huyáis, huyan**
Imperf. Subj. **huyera (huyese), huyeras (huyeses), etc.**
Imperative   **huye** (tú), huid (vosotros)

Like **huir: concluir** to conclude, **construir** to construct, **incluir** to include

10. Verbs whose infinitive ends in vowel + **-er,** or vowel + **-ir** (except **-eír**), change unstressed **i** to **y** between vowels. An accent on the stressed **i** of the ending is necessary to prevent a diphthong.

leer to read

Pres. Part.	**leyendo**
Past. Part.	**leído**
Preterit	**leí, leíste, leyó, leímos, leísteis, leyeron**
Imperf. Subj.	**leyera (leyese), leyeras (leyeses), etc.**

Like **leer: caer** to fall, **creer** to believe, **oír** to hear. But **caer** and **oír** have other irregularities: see Irregular Verbs, p. 330.

11. Verbs whose infinitive ends in **-eír** are Class III stem-changing verbs. They bear a written accent over the stressed **i**. Two contiguous **i**'s are reduced to one.

reír (i) to laugh

Pres. Part.	**riendo**
Past Part.	**reído**
Pres. Ind.	**río, ríes, ríe, reímos, reís, ríen**
Pres. Subj.	**ría, rías, ría, riamos, riáis, rían**
Preterit	**reí, reíste, rió, reímos, reísteis, rieron**
Imperf. Subj.	**riera (riese), rieras (rieses), etc.**
Imperative	**ríe (tú), reíd (vosotros)**

Like **reír: sonreír** to smile, **freír** to fry (past part.: **frito**)

12. Some verbs whose infinitive ends in **-iar** bear a written accent on the **i** throughout the singular and in the third person plural of both the present indicative and the present subjunctive, and in the imperative singular.

enviar to send

Pres. Ind.	**envío, envías, envía, enviamos, enviáis, envían**
Pres. Subj.	**envíe, envíes, envíe, enviemos, enviéis, envíen**
Imperative	**envía (tú), enviad (vosotros)**

Like **enviar: confiar** to confide, **fiarse** to confide, trust
But other **-iar** verbs used in this book are regular: **estudiar** to study, **cambiar** to change.

13. Verbs whose infinitive ends in **-uar** (except **-guar**) bear a written accent on the **u** throughout the singular and in the third person plural of both the present indicative and the present subjunctive, and in the imperative singular.

continuar to continue

Pres. Ind.	**continúo, continúas, continúa, continuamos, continuáis, continúan**
Pres. Subj.	**continúe, continúes, continúe, continuemos, continuéis, continúen**
Imperative	**continúa (tú), continuad (vosotros)**

Like **continuar: actuar** to act, **conceptuar** to judge, think

H. Irregular verbs

Infinitive	Participles Imperative	Present Indicative	Imperfect Indicative	Preterit
andar to go	andando andado	ando	andaba	anduve anduviste anduvo
	anda andad			anduvimos anduvisteis anduvieron
caer to fall	cayendo caído	caigo caes cae	caía	caí caíste cayó
	cae caed	caemos caéis caen		caímos caísteis cayeron
dar to give	dando dado	doy das da	daba	di diste dio
	da dad	damos dais dan		dimos disteis dieron
decir to say	diciendo dicho	digo dices dice	decía	dije dijiste dijo
	di decid	decimos decís dicen		dijimos dijisteis dijeron
estar to be	estando estado	estoy estás está	estaba	estuve estuviste estuvo
	está estad	estamos estáis están		estuvimos estuvisteis estuvieron

Irregular verbs

Future	Conditional	Present Subjunctive	Imperfect Subjunctive	
andaré	andaría	ande	anduviera	anduviese
			anduvieras	anduvieses
			anduviera	anduviese
			anduviéramos	anduviésemos
			anduvierais	anduvieseis
			anduvieran	anduviesen
caeré	caería	caiga	cayera	cayese
		caigas	cayeras	cayeses
		caiga	cayera	cayese
		caigamos	cayéramos	cayésemos
		caigáis	cayerais	cayeseis
		caigan	cayeran	cayesen
daré	daría	dé	diera	diese
		des	dieras	dieses
		dé	diera	diese
		demos	diéramos	diésemos
		deis	dierais	dieseis
		den	dieran	diesen
diré	diría	diga	dijera	dijese
dirás	dirías	digas	dijeras	dijeses
dirá	diría	diga	dijera	dijese
diremos	diríamos	digamos	dijéramos	dijésemos
diréis	diríais	digáis	dijerais	dijeseis
dirán	dirían	digan	dijeran	dijesen
estaré	estaria	esté	estuviera	estuviese
		estés	estuvieras	estuvieses
		esté	estuviera	estuviese
		estemos	estuviéramos	estuviésemos
		estéis	estuvierais	estuvieseis
		estén	estuvieran	estuviesen

Irregular verbs

Infinitive	Participles Imperative	Present Indicative	Imperfect Indicative	Preterit
haber to have	habiendo habido	he has ha hemos habéis han	había	hube hubiste hubo hubimos hubisteis hubieron
hacer to do, make	haciendo hecho haz haced	hago haces hace hacemos hacéis hacen	hacía	hice hiciste hizo hicimos hicisteis hicieron
ir to go	yendo ido ve id	voy vas va vamos vais van	iba ibas iba íbamos ibais iban	fui fuiste fue fuimos fuisteis fueron
oír to hear	oyendo oído oye oíd	oigo oyes oye oímos oís oyen	oía	oí oíste oyó oímos oísteis oyeron
poder to be able	pudiendo podido	puedo puedes puede podemos podéis pueden	podía	pude pudiste pudo pudimos pudisteis pudieron

Irregular verbs

Future	Conditional	Present Subjunctive	Imperfect Subjunctive	
habré	habría	haya	hubiera	hubiese
habrás	habrías	hayas	hubieras	hubieses
habrá	habría	haya	hubiera	hubiese
habremos	habríamos	hayamos	hubiéramos	hubiésemos
habréis	habríais	hayáis	hubierais	hubieseis
habrán	habrían	hayan	hubieran	hubiesen
haré	haría	haga	hiciera	hiciese
harás	harías	hagas	hicieras	hiciese
hará	haría	haga	hiciera	hiciese
haremos	haríamos	hagamos	hiciéramos	hiciésemos
haréis	haríais	hagáis	hicierais	hicieseis
harán	harían	hagan	hicieran	hiciesen
iré	iría	vaya	fuera	fuese
		vayas	fueras	fueses
		vaya	fuera	fuese
		vayamos	fuéramos	fuésemos
		vayáis	fuerais	fueseis
		vayan	fueran	fuesen
oiré	oiría	oiga	oyera	oyese
		oigas	oyeras	oyeses
		oiga	oyera	oyese
		oigamos	oyéramos	oyésemos
		oigáis	oyerais	oyeseis
		oigan	oyeran	oyesen
podré	podría	pueda	pudiera	pudiese
podrás	podrías	puedas	pudieras	pudieses
podrá	podría	pueda	pudiera	pudiese
podremos	podríamos	podamos	pudiéramos	pudiésemos
podréis	podríais	podáis	pudierais	pudieseis
podrán	podrían	puedan	pudieran	pudiesen

Irregular verbs

Infinitive	Participles Imperative	Present Indicative	Imperfect Indicative	Preterit
poner to put	poniendo puesto	pongo pones pone	ponía	puse pusiste puso
	pon poned	ponemos ponéis ponen		pusimos pusisteis pusieron
querer to wish	queriendo querido	quiero quieres quiere	quería	quise quisiste quiso
	quiere quered	queremos queréis quieren		quisimos quisisteis quisieron
saber to know	sabiendo sabido	sé sabes sabe	sabía	supe supiste supo
	sabe sabed	sabemos sabéis saben		supimos supisteis supieron
salir to go out	saliendo salido	salgo sales sale	salía	salí
	sal salid	salimos salís salen		
ser to be	siendo sido	soy eres es	era eras era	fui fuiste fue
	sé sed	somos sois son	éramos erais eran	fuimos fuisteis fueron

Irregular verbs

Future	Conditional	Present Subjunctive	Imperfect Subjunctive	
pondré	pondría	ponga	pusiera	pusiese
pondrás	pondrías	pongas	pusieras	pusieses
pondrá	pondría	ponga	pusiera	pusiese
pondremos	pondríamos	pongamos	pusiéramos	pusiésemos
pondréis	pondríais	pongáis	pusierais	pusieseis
pondrán	pondrían	pongan	pusieran	pusiesen
querré	querría	quiera	quisiera	quisiese
querrás	querrías	quieras	quisieras	quisieses
querrá	querría	quiera	quisiera	quisiese
querremos	querríamos	queramos	quisiéramos	quisiésemos
querréis	querríais	queráis	quisierais	quisieseis
querrán	querrían	quieran	quisieran	quisiesen
sabré	sabría	sepa	supiera	supiese
sabrás	sabrías	sepas	supieras	supieses
sabrá	sabría	sepa	supiera	supiese
sabremos	sabríamos	sepamos	supiéramos	supiésemos
sabréis	sabríais	sepáis	supierais	supieseis
sabrán	sabrían	sepan	supieran	supiesen
saldré	saldría	salga	saliera	saliese
saldrás	saldrías	salgas		
saldrá	saldría	salga		
saldremos	saldríamos	salgamos		
saldréis	saldríais	salgáis		
saldrán	saldrían	salgan		
seré	sería	sea	fuera	fuese
		seas	fueras	fueses
		sea	fuera	fuese
		seamos	fuéramos	fuésemos
		seáis	fuerais	fueseis
		sean	fueran	fuesen

Irregular verbs

Infinitive	Participles Imperative	Present Indicative	Imperfect Indicative	Preterit
tener to have	teniendo tenido	tengo tienes tiene	tenía	tuve tuviste tuvo
	ten tened	tenemos tenéis tienen		tuvimos tuvisteis tuvieron
traer to bring	trayendo traído	traigo traes trae	traía	traje trajiste trajo
	trae traed	traemos traéis traen		trajimos trajisteis trajeron
valer to be worth	valiendo valido	valgo vales vale	valía	valí
	val valed	valemos valéis valen		
venir to come	viniendo venido	vengo vienes viene	venía	vine viniste vino
	ven venid	venimos venís vienen		vinimos vinisteis vinieron
ver to see	viendo visto	veo ves ve	veía veías veía	vi viste vio
	ve ved	vemos veis ven	veíamos veíais veían	vimos visteis vieron

Irregular verbs

Future	Conditional	Present Subjunctive	Imperfect Subjunctive	
tendré	tendría	tenga	tuviera	tuviese
tendrás	tendrías	tengas	tuvieras	tuvieses
tendrá	tendría	tenga	tuviera	tuviese
tendremos	tendríamos	tengamos	tuviéramos	tuviésemos
tendréis	tendríais	tengáis	tuvierais	tuvieseis
tendrán	tendrían	tengan	tuvieran	tuviesen
traeré	traería	traiga	trajera	trajese
		traigas	trajeras	trajeses
		traiga	trajera	trajese
		traigamos	trajéramos	trajésemos
		traigáis	trajerais	trajeseis
		traigan	trajeran	trajesen
valdré	valdría	valga	valiera	valiese
valdrás	valdrías	valgas		
valdrá	valdría	valga		
valdremos	valdríamos	valgamos		
valdréis	valdríais	valgáis		
valdrán	valdrían	valgan		
vendré	vendría	venga	viniera	viniese
vendrás	vendrías	vengas	vinieras	vinieses
vendrá	vendría	venga	viniera	viniese
vendremos	vendríamos	vengamos	viniéramos	viniésemos
vendréis	vendríais	vengáis	vinierais	vinieseis
vendrán	vendrían	vengan	vinieran	viniesen
veré	vería	vea	viera	viese
		veas		
		vea		
		veamos		
		veáis		
		vean		

SPANISH-ENGLISH VOCABULARY

The following abbreviations are used in the vocabularies:

abbr. = abbreviation	*indef.* = indefinite	*plu.* = plural
adj. = adjective	*indir. obj.* = indirect object	*poss.* = possessive
adv. = adverb	*inf.* = infinitive	*prep.* = preposition
conj. = conjunction	*int.* = interrogative	*pres. part.* = present participle
def. = definite	*invar.* = invariable	*pron.* = pronoun
demonstr. = demonstrative	*m.* = masculine	*reflex.* = reflexive
dir. obj. = direct object	*n.* = neuter	*rel.* = relative
f. = feminine	*past part.* = past participle	*subj.* = subject

The sign — means a repetition of the word printed in black type at the beginning of the paragraph; thus, — **mismo** under **ahora** means **ahora mismo**. When the word is a noun preceded by its article, the sign — stands for the noun alone.

a to; at
abierto open
el abogado lawyer
el abrigo overcoat; shelter
abril *m.* April
abrir to open
absolutamente absolutely
la abuela grandmother
el abuelo grandfather
acá here
acabar to finish; — **de** + *inf.* to have just + *past part.*
aceptar to accept
acerca de about, concerning
acercarse (a) to draw near (to), approach
el acero steel
acompañar to accompany, go with

aconsejar to advise
acordarse (ue) (de) to remember
acostarse (ue) to go to bed
acostumbrado accustomed
el actor actor
la actriz actress
acudir to attend; to go; to come
además *adv.* besides; — **de** *prep.* besides
adiós good-by
¿adónde? where?
la aduana customs
aéreo *adj.* air; **la línea aérea** airline
el aeropuerto airport
agosto *m.* August
agradable agreeable
agradecido grateful
agrícola agricultural

el agua *f.* water
ahora now; — **mismo** right now;
   ¡— **lo oigo!** this is the first time
   I've heard about it!
el aire air; **al** — **libre** in the open air
al (a + el) to the; — + *inf.* upon +
   pres. part
alegrarse (de) to be glad; to rejoice,
   grow merry
alegre happy, gay
alejarse to withdraw
algo something, anything
alguien someone, somebody, anybody
alguno, algún some, any, someone,
   anyone
el alma *f.* soul
almorzar (ue) to lunch
alrededor de about, around
el alrededor vicinity; *usually plu.*
   los —es outskirts
la alteña highland girl
el altiplano plateau
la altitud altitude
alto tall
el alumno student
allá there, back there
allí there
amable kind
la amapola poppy
amar to love
América *f.* America; **la** — **del Norte**
   North America; **la** — **del Sur**
   South America
la amiga friend *f.*
el amigo friend *m.*
el amor love
Andalucía Andalusia
andaluz Andalusian
angosto narrow
angustiado sorrowful
el animal animal
la animación animation; bustle,
   movement
anoche last night
antaño long ago
anteayer day before yesterday
antes *adv.* before; — **de** *prep.* before;
   — **(de) que** *conj.* before; **cuanto** —
   as soon as possible
antiguo old

anunciar to announce
añadir to add
el año year; **el** — **pasado** last year;
   tener (veinte) —s to be (twenty)
   years old; **¿cuántos —s tiene Vd.?**
   how old are you?
el apartamento apartment
aprender to learn
aprobado: salir — to pass (*a course*)
aprovechar to take advantage of
el apuro difficulty, predicament
aquel, aquella, aquellos, aquellas
   demonstr. adj. that, those; the
   former
aquél, aquélla, aquéllos, aquéllas
   demonstr. pron. that, those; the
   former
aquí here; — **(lo) tiene Vd.** here (it)
   is; **de** — **en (cuatro días)** (four
   days) from now; **por** — this way
el árbol tree
la Argentina Argentina
argentino Argentine
árido arid
arriba above; **río** — up the river
el arroz rice
el arte art
el artículo article
el asado roast; — **de vaca** roast beef
el ascensor elevator
así thus, so
la asignatura course
asistir (a) to attend
asombroso astonishing, amazing
el asunto matter
la atención attention; **prestar** —
   to pay attention
aun, aún even, yet, still
aun cuando even though
aunque although
la ausencia absence
el automóvil automobile
el ave *f.* bird
averiguar to find out
el avión plane, airplane; **en** — by
   plane
avisar to inform, let know
ay oh
ayer yesterday
el azteca Aztec

azul blue
el azulejo colored tile

bailar to dance
bajar to go down; — de to get out
of, off (*a vehicle*)
bajo short
bañarse to bathe
barato cheap
la barra gang
bastante enough, sufficient; rather,
quite; a good deal
bastar to be enough, be sufficient
el béisbol baseball
bello beautiful
la biblioteca library
bien well; very; está — all right
el bistec steak, beefsteak
blanco white
la blusa blouse
la boca mouth
bonito pretty
bordo: a — on board
el Brasil Brazil
el bridge bridge (*card game*)
brillante brilliant
la broma joke; en — jokingly
bueno, buen good; — pues all right
then, well then; —s días good
morning
la busca search
buscar to look for

el caballero gentleman
el caballo horse; (montado) a —
on horseback
la cabeza head
el Cabildo Town Hall
cada *invar. adj.* each, every
caer to fall; ya caigo now I get it;
—se de to fall out of
el café coffee; café
los calcetines socks
caliente hot
California California
el calor heat; hace — it is warm,
hot; tener — to be warm (*of
living beings*)
los calzones breeches
la calle street

la cama bed
el camarero waiter
cambiar to change, exchange
caminar to walk
el camino road, way
la camisa shirt
la campaña campaign
el campeón champion
el campeonato championship
el campo country
la canción song
la cancha court (*tennis, etc.*)
cansado tired
cantar to sing
el canto singing; — flamenco
flamenco
la cantidad quantity
la capital capital
el capítulo chapter
la cara face
¡ caramba! confound it! gracious!
Carlos Charles
caro dear, expensive
la carta letter
la casa house, home; a — (to)
home; en — at home
casarse con to marry
casi nearly, almost
el caso case; en — de que in case
el catalán Catalan
Cataluña Catalonia
la catedral cathedral
catorce fourteen
célebre famous, celebrated
celoso jealous
el cenicero ashtray
el centavo cent (*Spanish America*)
el céntimo cent (*Spain*)
central central
el centro center
cerca de near
cerquita de *diminutive of* cerca de
close to
cerrar (ie) to close
certificar to register
el cielo sky
ciento, cien a (one) hundred
cierto (a) certain
cinco five
cincuenta fifty

el **cine** movies
la **cinta** tape
citado: estar — con to have an
  appointment, date, with
la **ciudad** city
civil civil
la **civilización** civilization
¡ **claro!** of course! sure!
la **clase** class; kind
clásico classic
el **cliente** client
el **clima** climate
la **clínica** hospital
el **coche** car
coger to catch, pick up
la **colección** collection
Colombia Colombia
colonial colonial
colorado red
la **comedia** comedy
el **comedor** dining room, dining salon
comenzar (ie) to begin
comer to eat; **—se** to eat up; **—se**
  las eses to swallow the letter *s*
la **comida** dinner, meal; **la hora de**
  la — dinner time
la **comisión** commission
como like, as; **— si** as if
¿ **cómo?** how? ¿ **a — se vende?** how
  is it sold? what is the price? ¡ **— no!**
  of course!
cómodo comfortable
el **compañero** companion
la **compañía** company
completamente completely
la **composición** composition
la **compra** purchase; **ir de —s** to
  go shopping
comprar to buy
comprender to understand
el **compromiso** engagement,
  appointment
con with; **— tal que** provided that
concentrar to concentrate; **— la**
  atención en to concentrate on
conducir to lead, conduct
confidencial confidential
conmigo with me
conocer to know; to meet, make
  the acquaintance of

conocido well-known
la **conquista** conquest
conquistar to conquer
conseguir (i) to get, obtain
el **consejero** adviser
el **consejo** (piece of) advice
consigo with himself, with herself,
  with yourself, etc.
construir to build, construct
el **consultorio** doctor's office
el **contacto** contact
contar (ue) to count, tell
contemporáneo contemporary
contener to contain
contento happy
contestar (a) to answer
el **continente** continent
continuar to continue
contra against
el **contrabando** contraband; **venir**
  de — to come by stealth
contrario: al — on the contrary
el **contrato** contract
convencer to convince
conversar to converse, talk
el **convidado** guest
conviene it is advisable
la **copa** wine glass
el **coral** coral
el **corazón** heart
la **corbata** tie, necktie
el **cordero** lamb
la **cordillera** mountain range
Córdoba Cordova
el **correo** mail; **— aéreo** air mail
correr to run
cortés polite
la **cosa** thing
la **costa** coast
la **costumbre** custom
creer to believe, think
la **criada** servant, maid
el **cuadro** picture, painting
el **cual, la cual, los cuales, las cuales**
  rel. pron. that, which, who, whom;
  lo — *n.* which
¿ **cuál?** which (one)? what?
la **cualidad** quality
cualquier(a) any(one), whichever,
  whatever

cuando when; **aun —** even though
¿ **cuándo?** when?
cuanto all that; **— antes** as soon as
possible; **en —** *conj.* as soon as;
unos —s a few
¿ **cuánto?** how much? ¿ **a —?** at
how much? at what price? ¿ **—s?**
how many?
cuarenta forty
cuarto fourth
el cuarto room; quarter; **las diez
menos —** a quarter to ten
cuatro four
cuatrocientos four hundred
cubano Cuban
la cubierta deck
cubierto *past part. of* **cubrir** covered
cubrir to cover
la cuenta bill, check; **darse — de** to
realize
el cuidado care; **pierda Vd. —**
don't worry
cultural cultural
la cuna cradle
cursar to take, study (*a course*)
cuyo whose, of which

la chaparrita rosy-cheeked girl
chapeteado rosy-cheeked
charlar to chat
chico small
Chile *m.* Chile
chileno Chilean
la chiquita little girl
el chiste joke
el chocolate chocolate
la chuleta chop

dar to give; to show (*a movie*);
— con to meet, run into; **—se
cuenta de** to realize; **—se prisa**
to hurry
de of, from; **más — dos** more than
two; **el alumno más inteligente —
la clase** the most intelligent
student in the class; **el —** the one
of, the one with
deber to owe; ought, should, must
decidir to decide
décimo tenth

decir to say, tell; **— que sí (no)**
to say yes (no); **oír — que** to hear
that; **querer —** to mean; **¡ diga!**
hello! (*on the telephone*)
dejar to leave; to let, allow
del (de + el) of the, from the
delante de in front of
delgado thin
demasiado too, too much
dentro de within
el deporte sport
la derecha right hand; **a la —** to
(at, on) the right
derecho right; straight
el desarrollo development
el desayuno breakfast
descansar to rest
describir to describe
descubierto *past part. of* **descubrir**
discovered
el descubrimiento discovery
descubrir to discover
desde from, since
desear to desire
el desierto desert
desgraciado unfortunate
desocupado unoccupied
despacio slowly
el despacho de billetes ticket office
despedirse (i) to take one's leave
despertarse (ie) to wake up, awaken
después *adv.* afterwards; **— de** *prep.*
after; **— (de) que** *conj.* after
el destierro exile
el destino destiny
el detalle detail
detrás de behind
devolver (ue) to return, give back
el día day; **¡ buenos días!** good
morning! **todos los —s** every day
diciembre *m.* December
el dictador dictator
la dictadura dictatorship
dicho *past part. of* **decir** said
diecinueve nineteen
dieciocho eighteen
dieciséis sixteen
diecisiete seventeen
el diente tooth
diez ten

difícil difficult
el dineral large amount of money
el dinero money
Dios God; ¡ — **mío!** my goodness!
¡ **por** —! for heaven's sake! **quiera**
— God grant; ¡ **vaya Vd. con** —!
off with you! good-by!
dirigir to direct; —**se a** to address,
speak to; to go toward
discutir to discuss
disfrutar to enjoy
distinto distinct, different
divertido amusing
divertirse (ie) to amuse oneself,
have a good time
dividir, —**se** to divide
doce twelve
la docena dozen
el doctor doctor
el documento document
el dólar dollar
doler (ue) to ache, pain, hurt
el domingo (on) Sunday
don (*abbr.* **D.**) Mr., Don (*title used
with first names only*)
donde where
¿ **dónde?** where? ¿ **a** —? where?
dondequiera wherever
doña (*abbr.* **Da.**) Mrs., Miss, Doña
(*title used with first names only*)
dormir (ue) to sleep; —**se** to go to sleep
dos two
doscientos two hundred
el dramaturgo playwright
dudar to doubt
la dueña mistress
el dueño owner
durante during
durar to last

ebrio intoxicated
la economía economy
ecuatorial equatorial; **la línea** —
equator
la edad age ¿ **qué** — **tiene?** how old
is he?
el edificio building
efecto: en — in fact
el ejemplo example; **poner por** —
to take for example

el ejercicio exercise
el *m.* the; — **de** that of, the one of;
— **que** he who, the one who
(which), that which
él he; *after prep.* him, it (*m.*)
ella she; *after prep.* her, it (*f.*)
ellas they (*f.*); *after prep.* them (*f.*)
ello it (*n.*); — **es que** the fact is that
ellos they (*m.*); *after prep.* them (*m.*)
embargo: sin — nevertheless, however
empezar (ie) to begin
el empleado employee, clerk
el empleo job
emprender to undertake
en in, into, on
enamorado in love
el enamorado sweetheart
encantar to charm, enchant
encima de on top of
encontrar (ue) to find
enero *m.* January
enfermar to become ill, get sick
enfermo ill, sick
enojado angry
enorme enormous
la ensalada salad
enseñar to teach; to show
entender (ie) to understand
entonces then
entrar (en) to enter, go in (to)
entre between, among
entregar to hand over
entretanto meanwhile
entretener to entertain
el entusiasmo enthusiasm
enviar to send
la época epoch
la epopeya epic
el equipaje baggage
el equipo team
errante errant, wandering
escribir to write
escrito *past part. of* **escribir** written
escuchar to listen (to)
ese, esa, esos, esas *demonstr. adj.*
that, those
ése, ésa, ésos, ésas *demonstr. pron.*
that (one), those
la ese (letter) *s*; **comerse las** —**s** to
swallow the (letter) *s*

eso *n. demonstr. pron.* that; — **de**
that matter of; **por** — therefore,
for that reason, that's why
España *f.* Spain
español, -ola Spanish; **el** —
Spanish, Spaniard
especial special
especialmente especially
esperar to wait; to hope
la esposa wife
el esposo husband
esquiar to ski
la esquina corner
la estación station; season
estacionar to park
el estadio stadium
el estado state
los Estados Unidos United States
estar to be; — **para** to be about to;
está bien all right
este, esta, estos, estas *demonstr. adj.*
this, these
éste, ésta, éstos, éstas *demonstr.*
pron. this (one), these; the latter
el este east
esto *n. demonstr. pron.* this
estrechar to press
estrecho narrow
la estrella star
el estudiante student
estudiar to study
el estudio study
Europa *f.* Europe
el examen examination
examinar to examine
exclamar to exclaim
la excursión excursion, trip; — **de**
estudio field trip; **hacer una** —
to take, go on, a trip, excursion
explicar to explain
la exportación export
exportar to export
el extranjero foreigner
extrañar to surprise
extraño strange
extraviado strayed

la fábrica factory
fabricar to manufacture
fácil easy

facturar to check
la faja strip
la falda skirt
la falta lack; **me hace** — I need
la familia family
famoso famous
la farra spree
fascinar to fascinate
fastidiado annoyed
el fastidio boredom
fatigado tired
el favor favor; **por** — please;
haga Vd. el — **de . . .** please . . .
febrero *m.* February
la fecha date
feliz happy
el ferrocarril railroad
fértil fertile
la fiebre fever
la fiesta holiday; celebration
la filosofía philosophy
el fin end; **al** — finally; **por** —
finally, at last; **a** — **de que** in
order that
la finca farm
el flan custard
la flecha arrow
la flor flower
la fortuna fortune
francés, -a French; **el** — French,
Frenchman
Francia *f.* France
franco frank
el frío cold; **hace** — it is cold;
tener — to be cold (*of living*
beings)
frito fried
la fruta fruit
fuerte strong
la función performance, show
funcionar to work, run
fundar to found
el fútbol football

la ganadería cattle-raising
ganar to win; to earn
la ganga bargain
la gardenia gardenia
la garganta throat
el gasto expense

generoso generous
la gente people
la geografía geography
geográfico geographical
la geología geology
el gimnasio gymnasium
la golondrina swallow
gordo fat
¡gracias! thank you! thanks!
  ¡muchas —! thank you very much!
grande, gran large, big; great
grave serious
guardar to keep; **— cama** to stay in bed
la guerra war
el guisante pea
el guitarrista guitarist
gustar (a) to be pleasing (to); **me gusta** I like it; **me gustan** I like them; **me gusta más** I like it better
el gusto pleasure; **con mucho —** with pleasure, gladly; **¡cuánto — de verle!** how pleased (I am) to see you! **mucho — de verle** (I am) very pleased to see you; **tanto — de conocerle** so pleased to meet you; how do you do?

haber to have (*auxiliary*); **— de +** *inf.* to be to, be supposed to, must; **hay** there is, there are; **había** there was, there were; **habrá** there will be; **hay que** it is necessary, one must; **no hay de qué** you're welcome, don't mention it
la habichuela string bean
el habitante inhabitant
hablar to speak; **— para sí** to talk to oneself
hacer to do, make; **— la maleta** to pack one's suitcase; **— una excursión** to go on an excursion; **— una pregunta** to ask a question; **— un viaje** to take a trip; **hace calor, frío, etc.** it is warm, cold, etc.; **hace buen tiempo** the weather is good; **hace una semana** a week ago; **hace tres meses que estudio** I have been studying for

three months; **hacía mucho tiempo que esperaban** they had been waiting for a long time; **se hace tarde** it is becoming late
hallar to find; **—se** to be
el hambre *f.* hunger; **tener —** to be hungry
hasta until; even; **— luego** until later, see you later; **— que** *conj.* until
hay *see* **haber**
hecho *past part. of* **hacer** done, made
el helado ice cream
herir (ie) to wound
la hermana sister
el hermano brother
hermosísimo most (very, exceedingly) beautiful
hermoso beautiful
el héroe hero
el hierro iron; **—s** bars
la hija daughter
el hijo son
Hispanoamérica *f.* Hispanic America
hispanoamericano Hispanic American
la historia history
histórico historical
el hockey hockey
hola hello
el hombre man
el honor honor
honrado honest
la hora hour; **la — de la comida** dinner time; **a estas —s** at this time
el hotel hotel
hoy today
el huaso cowboy (Chilean)
el huevo egg
huir to flee
hundir to sink

la idea idea
la identidad identity
el idioma language
idolatrar to idolize
impaciente impatient
impedir (i) to prevent
importante important

importar to matter; **no importa** it doesn't matter
imposible impossible
la impresión impression
impresionante impressive
impresionar to impress
el inca Inca
el inconveniente objection
la independencia independence
el indio Indian
el individuo individual, person
la industria industry
industrial industrial
el ingeniero engineer
Inglaterra *f.* England
inglés, -esa English; **el —** English, Englishman
ingrato ungrateful
inmediatamente immediately
insistir to insist
inteligente intelligent
el interés interest
interesante interesting
interesar to interest; **—se por (en)** to be interested in
el interior interior
interrumpir to interrupt
la inversión investment
el invierno winter
la invitación invitation
invitar to invite
ir to go; **— de compras** to go shopping; **—se** to go off, go away
Italia *f.* Italy
el italiano Italian
la izquierda left hand; **a la —** to (at, on) the left

jamás never, not . . . ever; ever
joven young; **el —** young man
Juan John
Juanito Johnny
el jueves (on) Thursday
la jugada play (*in a game*)
jugar (ue) to play
el jugo juice
julio *m.* July
junio *m.* June
junto a next to, beside

la *f.* the; *pron.* her, you, it; **— de** that of, the one of, the one with; **— que** she who, the one who (which), that which
el lado side; **al — de** beside; **(la cancha) de al —** the next (court)
el lago lake
la lana wool
lanzar to throw, fling
largo long
la lástima pity; **es —** it's a pity; **¡qué —!** what a pity!
lavar to wash; **—se** to wash, get washed
le him, you; to him, to her, to it, to you
la lección lesson
la leche milk
el lecho bed
leer to read
la legumbre vegetable
lejos far, distant
la lengua language
lentamente slowly
la lenteja lentil
levantarse to get up, rise
libre free; **al aire —** in the open air
el libro book
ligero light
limpiar to clean
limpio clean
lindo pretty
la línea line; **— aérea** airline; **— ecuatorial** equator
la lista (de platos) menu
listo ready
la literatura literature
lo *n. def. article* the; *pron.* it, so; **— de** that of; **— que** that which, what
la Lonja Exchange
luego then; **hasta —** until later, see you later
la luna moon; **a la luz de la —** by moonlight
el lunar mole; beauty spot
el lunes (on) Monday
la luz light

llamar to call; **—se** to be called;
   me llamo my name is; **¿cómo se
   llama?** what is his name?
el llano plain
la llegada arrival
llegar to arrive; **— a** to arrive at,
   reach; **— a ser** to become
lleno full
llevar to take; to wear
llorar to weep
llover (ue) to rain
la lluvia rain

la madre mother
magnífico magnificent
majestuoso majestic
mal badly; **salir —** to flunk, fail
la maleta suitcase; **hacer la —** to
   pack one's suitcase
malo bad; ill, sick
la mamá mother, mamma
la manera manner, way; **de — que**
   so (that)
la mano hand
la mansión abode
manso gentle
mañana *adv.* tomorrow; **— por la
   mañana** tomorrow morning;
   pasado — day after tomorrow
la mañana morning; **por la —** in
   the morning; **a las diez de la —**
   at ten o'clock in the morning
la maquinaria machinery
maravilloso marvellous
María Mary
el martes (on) Tuesday
marzo *m.* March
más more, most; **— que** more than;
   no . . . — que only; **¡qué vestido —
   bonito!** what a pretty dress!
   sin — ni — just like that, without
   more ado
las matemáticas mathematics
el material rodante rolling stock
mayo *m.* May
mayor older, oldest; greater
me me; to me, myself
la medianoche midnight
las medias stockings
el médico doctor

medio *adj.* half; **media docena (de)**
   half a dozen; **a las dos y media** at
   half past two, at two-thirty
el mediodía noon
mejicano Mexican
Méjico *m.* Mexico
mejor better, best
mejorarse to get better, recover
menor younger, youngest
menos less, least; fewer, fewest;
   a — que unless; **al —** at least;
   las diez — cuarto a quarter to
   ten
la mentira lie; **parece —** it seems
   incredible
el mercado market
la merienda light lunch, picnic lunch
el mes month
la mesa table
la mezquita mosque
mi, mis *poss. adj.* my
mí *after prep.* me, myself
el miedo fear; **tener —** to be afraid
mientras (que) while
el miércoles (on) Wednesday
mil a (one) thousand
militar military
el millón million
el millonario millionaire
mío *poss. adj.* my; of mine; **el —**
   poss. pron. mine
mirar to look (at)
mismo same, self; **el — que** the same
   (one) as
la mitad half
moderno modern
el modo way, manner; **de — que**
   so (that); **de todos —s** at any rate
molestar to bother
el momento moment
mono cute
la montaña mountain
montar a caballo to ride horseback,
   go (horseback) riding; **montados
   a caballo** on horseback
el monumento monument
moreno dark, brunet
morir (ue) to die
mostrar (ue) to show
el movimiento movement

el **mozo** young man; **buen** —
good-looking
la **muchacha** girl
la **muchachada** group of boys
el **muchacho** boy
muchísimo very much, a very great deal
mucho *adj.* much, a great deal of;
plu. many; *adv.* much, a great deal,
a lot, hard, very
la **mujer** woman
el **mundo** world; **todo el** —
everybody
el **museo** museum
la **música** music
muy very

nacer to be born
la **nación** nation
nada nothing; *adv.* not at all; **de** —
you're welcome, don't mention it
nadar to swim
nadie nobody, no one, not . . .
anybody
la **naranja** orange
natural natural
necesario necessary
la **necesidad** necessity
necesitar to need
negar (ie) to deny
negociar to negotiate
el **negocio** business
negro black
nevar (ie) to snow
ni nor, (not) . . . or; — . . . —
neither . . . nor
la **nieve** snow
el **nilón** (*usually pronounced as if
spelled* **nailon**)
ninguno, ningún none, no one, no,
not . . . any
la **niña** girl
el **niño** child, boy
no not, no
la **noche** night; **esta** — tonight;
a las once de la — at eleven
o'clock at night; **¡buenas noches!**
good night! good evening!
Norte América *f.* North America
norteamericano (North) American;
el — American

nos us, to us; ourselves
nosotros we; *after prep.* us, ourselves
notar to notice
novecientos nine hundred
la **novela** novel
noveno ninth
noventa ninety
la **novia** sweetheart
noviembre *m.* November
el **novio** sweetheart
nublado cloudy
nuestro *poss. adj.* our, of ours; **el** —
poss. pron. ours
Nueva York New York
nueve nine
nuevo new
el **número** number
nunca never, not . . . ever

o or
el **oasis** oasis
la **obra** work (*of art*)
observar to observe
el **ocio** idleness
octavo eighth
octubre *m.* October
ocupado busy
ocurrir to occur
ochenta eighty
ocho eight
ochocientos eight hundred
el **oeste** west
la **oficina** office
ofrecerse a to offer
oír to hear; — **decir que** to hear
that, hear it said that; **¡ahora lo
oigo!** this is the first time I've
heard it! **¡oiga Vd.!** listen!
¡ojalá! oh that! would that! I
wish that . . . !
el **ojo** eye
once eleven
la **onda** wave
la **ópera** opera
la **oportunidad** opportunity
la **orilla** bank, shore; **a** —**s de**
beside
la **orquesta** orchestra
os *dir. and indir. obj. pron.* you, to
you, yourselves

el **otoño** autumn
otro other, another

el **Pacífico** Pacific (*Ocean*)
el **padre** father; los —s father and
　mother, parents
pagar to pay
el **país** country
el **paisaje** landscape
el **pájaro** bird
la **palabra** word
el **palacio** palace
la **pampa** pampa(s)
el **pan** bread
el **panecillo** roll
las **papas** potatoes; **puré de** —
　mashed potatoes
el **par** pair, couple
para to, in order to, for; — **que** in
　order that; ¿— **qué?** for what
　reason? **estar** — to be about to;
　dijo — **sí** he said to himself
parecer to seem, appear; ¿ **qué le**
　parece ...? how do you like ...?
el **parecer** opinion
la **pared** wall
la **parte** part; la **mayor** — **de** most
　of; en **todas** —s everywhere
particular private
el **partido** game (*match*)
partir to start, leave
pasado past, last; — **mañana** day
　after tomorrow; el **verano** —
　last summer
el **pasaje** passage
el **pasaporte** passport
pasar to pass, spend; to go in;
　pase Vd. come in
pasearse to stroll
el **paseo** walk, stroll, promenade;
　dar un — to take a walk
patinar to skate
la **patria** native land
pedante pedantic
pedir (i) to ask (for), request; to
　order (*in a restaurant*)
peinarse to comb
la **película** moving picture, film
el **pelo** hair
el **pendiente** earring

pensar (ie) to think; — **en** to think
　of; — + *inf.* to intend
peor worse, worst
pequeño small—
perder (ie) to lose; **pierda Vd.**
　cuidado don't worry
el **peregrino** pilgrim
perezoso lazy
el **periódico** newspaper
el **período** period
permanecer to remain
permitir to permit, allow
pero but
la **persona** person
el **Perú** Peru
pesar: a — **de** in spite of; **a** — **de**
　que in spite of the fact that
el **pescado** fish
pescar to fish
la **peseta** peseta (*monetary unit of*
　Spain)
el **peso** weight; peso
el **pie** foot; **a** — on foot
el **pintor** painter
pintoresco picturesque
la **pintura** paint
la **pirámide** pyramid
el **piso** floor; — **bajo** ground floor;
　— **principal** main floor
el **placer** pleasure
la **plata** silver
el **plato** plate, dish; — **del día**
　day's speciality; **lista de** —s menu
la **playa** beach
la **plaza** square
pobre poor
poco *adj. and pron.* little; —s few;
　adv. little, a bit
poder to be able
el **político** politician
el **pollo** chicken; **arroz con** —
　chicken with rice
poner to put, place; — **por ejemplo**
　to take for example; — **un**
　telegrama to send a telegram; — **se**
　to put on; to become
popular popular
poquito very little, a tiny bit
por for, by, through, along, around,
　on behalf of, in exchange for, for

the sake of, on account of; — **eso**
therefore, for that reason, that's
why; — **favor** please; — **fin**
finally; — **supuesto** of course;
¡— **Dios**! for heaven's sake! — **la
tarde** in the afternoon; — **ser**
because he (it) is
¿ **por qué**? why?
porque because
el portugués Portuguese
el porvenir future
poseer to possess
la posesión possession
posible possible
el postre dessert
el precio price
precioso pretty, beautiful; precious
precisamente just at this moment
preciso necessary
predilecto favorite
preferir (ie) to prefer
la pregunta question
preguntar to ask
preparar to prepare
la presentación introduction
presentar to introduce
el presidente president
prestar to lend; — **atención** to pay
attention
la prima cousin
la primavera spring
primero, primer first
el primo cousin
el primor beauty; excellence
principal principal
el principio beginning; **al —** at
first
la prisa haste; **darse —** to hurry
probable probable
producir to produce
el producto product
el profesor professor, teacher
el programa program
progresista progessive
el progreso progress
prometer to promise
pronto soon; **de —** suddenly; **tan —
como** as soon as
propio own
proponer to propose, suggest

próximo next
la psicología psychology
público public
la puerta door
el puerto port
pues as, for, since; well, then;
bueno, — well then, all right then
la pulmonía pneumonia
el punto point; **las tres en —**
three o'clock sharp
puntual punctual
el puré: — de papas mashed
potatoes

que *rel. pron.* who, whom, that,
which; *conj.* that; than; **el —**
rel. pron. who, whom, that, which,
he who, the one who, the one
which; **lo —** *rel. pron. n.* that
which, what
¿**qué**? *int. pron. and adj.* what?
which?
¡**qué**! what a . . . ! how . . . !
quedar to remain; — **agradecido** to
be grateful; —**se** to remain, stay;
—**se con** to take
la queja complaint; lament
querer to wish, want; — **a** to like,
love; — **decir** to mean; **quiera
Dios** God grant
quien who, whom; he who
¿**quién**? who? ¿ **de —**? whose?
quince fifteen
quinientos five hundred
quinto fifth
quizá, quizás perhaps

la rambla boulevard
la radio radio
la rancherita little ranch girl
el rancho ranch
la raqueta racket
el rato while; **largo —** a long while
el ratón mouse
la razón right; **tener —** to be right
la realidad reality
realizar to realize, carry out, fulfill
rebajar to lower
recibir to receive
recientemente recently

recobrar to recover
recoger to pick up
recomendar (ie) to recommend
recordar (ue) to remember
los recuerdos regards
el refresco refreshment; **tomar un
— to** have (get) something to
drink
regalar to give (*as a gift*)
el regalo gift
la región region
la regla rule; **estar en —** to be in
order
reír (i) to laugh; **—se de** to laugh at
la reja grating
el reloj clock, watch
la remolacha beet
repetir (i) to repeat
el representante representative
la república republic
reservar to reserve
el resfriado cold
resistir to resist; to stand
responder (a) to answer
el restaurante restaurant
el resto rest; **los —s** remains
resultar to result, turn out to be
la retirada withdrawal, retreat
revisar to inspect
la revolución revolution
rezar to pray
rico rich
el río river; **— arriba** up the river
el rodeo roundup
rogar (ue) to beg
rojo red
la ropa clothing, clothes
rosado pink
rubio blond

el sábado (on) Saturday
saber to know; to learn, find out;
— + inf. to know how to
sabroso delicious
sacar to take out
la sala room; **— de clase** classroom
salir (de) to leave, go out (of);
—aprobado to pass (*a course*);
— mal to fail, flunk (*a course*)
el salitre nitrate

la salud health; **estar bien de —**
to be in good health
saludar to greet
el salvaje savage
el santo saint; **San, Santo** Saint
santo *adj.* saintly
se himself, herself, yourself, etc.;
each other
la secretaría de policía police
headquarters
la sed thirst; **tener —** to be thirsty
la seda silk
seguida: en — at once
seguir (i) to follow; to continue
segundo second
seis six
seiscientos six hundred
la selva forest
el sello stamp
la semana week; **la — que viene**
next week
sentado seated, sitting
sentarse (ie) to sit down
sentir (ie) to regret, be sorry; **lo
siento mucho** I am very sorry;
—se to feel
señalar to indicate, point out
señor (*abbr.* **Sr.**) Mr., sir; **el —**
gentleman; **el Señor** the Lord
señora (*abbr.* **Sra.**) Mrs., madam;
la — lady
señorita (*abbr.* **Srta.**) Miss; **la —**
young lady, miss
septiembre *m.* September
ser to be; **es que** the fact is that;
llegar a — become
servir (i) to serve; **no — para nada**
to be of no use, to be good for
nothing
sesenta sixty
setecientos seven hundred
Sevilla Seville
sexto sixth
si if, whether
sí yes; **yo —** I am (did, was, etc.)
sí *after prep.* himself, herself,
yourself, etc.; **dijo para —** he
said to himself
siempre always; **lo de —** the same
old thing

la **Sierra Morena** range of mountains in Spain
siete seven
el **siglo** century
simpático nice, congenial
simple simple
sin without; — **que** *conj.* without; — **embargo** however
sino but
la **situación** situation
situado situated, located
sobre on, upon; — **todo** especially
el **sol** sun; **hace** — it is sunny
el **soldado** soldier
solicitar to apply for
solo alone
sólo only
el **sombrero** hat
sonar (ue) to sound; to ring
sonreír (i) to smile
soñar (ue) to dream; — **con** to dream of
la **sopa** soup
sorprender to surprise
su, sus *poss. adj.* his, her, its, your, their
subir (a) to go up; to get in, get on
Sudamérica South America
el **suelo** ground
el **sueño** dream
la **suerte** luck
sugerir (ie) to suggest
sumamente extremely, exceedingly
supuesto: por — of course
el **sur** south
suyo *poss. adj.* his, her, your, their; of his (hers, yours, theirs); el — *poss. pron.* his, hers, yours, theirs

tacaño stingy
tal such, such a; — **vez** perhaps; **con** — **que** provided (that)
tallar to deal (*cards*)
también also, too
tampoco neither, not . . . either
tan *adv.* as, so; such; — . . . **como** as . . . as; — **pronto como** as soon as; ¡**qué flores** — **lindas!** what pretty flowers!
tanto as much, so much

el **tanto** point (*in a game*)
tardar en to be long in, take (time) to
tarde late; **se hace** — it is becoming late
la **tarde** afternoon, evening; ¡**buenas** —**s!** good afternoon!
la **tarjeta** card; — **de identidad** identification card
el **taxi** taxi
la **taza** cup
te you, to you; yourself
el **teatro** theater
le **técnica** technique
Tejas *m.* Texas
el **tejido** textile
telefonear to telephone
el **teléfono** telephone
el **telegrama** telegram; **poner un** — to send a telegram
la **televisión** television
el **tema** theme
temer to fear
templado temperate
el **templo** temple
temprano early
tener to have; — **que** to have to; — **calor, etc.** to be warm, etc.; ¿**qué tengo?** what is the matter with me? **aquí lo tiene Vd.** here it is; ¿**cuántos años tiene Juan?** how old is John?
el **tenis** tennis
Tepa *short for* **Tepatitlán**
Tepatitlán a city in Mexico
tercero, tercer third
terminar to finish
ti *after prep.* you, yourself
la **tía** aunt
el **tiempo** time; weather; **a** — in, on time; ¿**cuánto** —? how long? **más** — longer; **hace buen** — the weather is good; ¿**qué** — **hace?** what kind of weather is it, how is the weather?
la **tienda** shop, store
tierno tender
la **tierra** land
el **timbre** bell
el **tío** uncle

típico typical
tocar to play (*an instrument, song*)
todavía still, yet
todo all; every; — **el mundo**
    everybody; **sobre** — especially;
    —**s los días** every day; **toda la**
    lección all the lesson, the whole
    lesson
tomar to take; to have (*with liquids*);
    — **un refresco** to have something
    to drink
Tomás Thomas
las tostadas toast
el total total
trabajar to work
el trabajo work
traer to bring
la tragedia tragedy
el traje suit; — **de baño** bathing suit
tranquilo calm
trece thirteen
treinta thirty
el tren train
tres three
trescientos three hundred
triste sad
tropical tropical
tu, tus *poss. adj.* your
tú you
tuyo *poss. adj.* your, of yours; **el —**
    poss. pron. yours

último last
un, una a (an); one
único only
la universidad university
uno, un, una one
unos some
urgente urgent
urgir to be urgent
usar to use
usted you

la vaca cow; **asado de —** roast beef
las vacaciones vacation
valer to be worth; **vale la pena** it —
    is worth while
el valle valley
vamos let's go; — **a estudiar** let's
    study

el vapor steamer, boat
el vaquero cowboy
varios several
el vaso glass
vasto vast
vecino neighboring
veinte twenty
veloz swift
vender to sell
venir to come; **la semana que**
    viene next week
la ventanilla window (*of a bank, etc.*)
ver to see
el verano summer
la verdad truth; **es —** it is true;
    ¿ —? ¿ **no es** —? isn't he? doesn't
    it? don't you? etc.
verdadero true
la vergüenza shame; **me da —**
    it makes me ashamed
el vestido dress
vestirse (i) to dress, get dressed
la vez time; **en — de** instead of;
    otra — again; **por primera —** for
    the first time; **tal —** perhaps
la vía way; **por — aérea** by air
viajar to travel
el viaje trip; — **de vuelta** return trip;
    hacer un — to take a trip
la vida life
viejo old
el viento wind; **hace —** it is windy
el viernes (on) Friday
el vino wine
la virgen virgin
Virginia Virginia
la visita visit
visitar to visit
visto *past part. of* **ver** seen
vivir to live
volar (ue) to fly
volver (ue) to return, go back;
    — **a** + *inf.* to (do) again
vosotros you, yourselves
la voz voice
la vuelta return; **el viaje de —**
    return trip
vuelto *past part. of* **volver** returned
vuestro *poss. adj.* your, of yours;
    el — *poss. pron.* yours

any alguno; cualquier(a); **if there are —** si los hay
anybody alguien
anyone alguien
anything algo
apartment el apartamento
appear parecer; presentarse
appetite el apetito
apply for solicitar
appointment el compromiso; **to have an — with** estar citado con
approach acercarse a
April abril *m.*
Argentina la Argentina
Argentine argentino
arid árido
around por; alrededor de
arrival la llegada
arrive llegar (a)
art el arte
as como; tan; **— good —** tan bueno como; **— for** en cuanto a; **— if** como si; **— much —** tanto como; **— soon —** en cuanto, tan pronto como
ashamed: to be — tener vergüenza; **it makes me —** me da vergüenza
ashtray el cenicero
ask preguntar; **— a question** hacer una pregunta; **— for** pedir (i)
astonishing asombroso
at en, a
attend asistir (a)
attention: to pay — to prestar atención a
August agosto *m.*
aunt la tía
auto el coche, el automóvil
automobile el automóvil
autumn el otoño
awaken despertarse (ie)
Aztec el azteca

back: to be — estar de vuelta
bad malo; **it's too —** es lástima
badly mal
baggage el equipaje
bank el banco
baseball el béisbol
bathe bañarse

be ser, estar, hallarse; **to — about to** estar para; **to — to, — supposed to** haber + *inf.*; **there is, there are** hay; **there was, there were** había
beach la playa
beautiful bello, hermoso; precioso
because porque; **— of** a causa de
become llegar a ser; ponerse
bed la cama; **to go to —** acostarse (ue); **to stay in —** guardar cama
beefsteak el bistec
before antes de *prep.*; antes (de) que *conj.*
beg rogar (ue)
begin empezar (ie), comenzar (ie), echar(se) a + *inf.*
behind detrás de
believe creer
bell el timbre
beside al lado de; a orillas de
besides además
best mejor
better mejor; **to get —** mejorarse
between entre
big grande
bill la cuenta
bird el pájaro
bit: a — algo; **not a —** nada
black negro
blond rubio
blouse la blusa
blue azul
board: on — a bordo (de)
boat el vapor
book el libro
boredom el fastidio
borrow pedir (i) prestado
boulevard la rambla (*in Barcelona*)
boy el muchacho
Brazil el Brasil
bread el pan
break romper (*past part.* roto)
breakfast el desayuno
bridge (*card game*) el bridge
brilliant brillante
bring traer
brother el hermano
brunet moreno
build construir
building el edificio

business el negocio
bustle la animación
busy ocupado
but pero; sino
buy comprar
by por; — ten o'clock para las diez

café el café
California California
call llamar; to be called llamarse
calm tranquilo
campaign la campaña
can poder (ue)
capital la capital
car el coche, el auto
carry llevar
case: in — en caso de que
Catalan el catalán
Catalonia Cataluña
catch coger
cathedral la catedral
cattle-raising la ganadería
celebrated célebre
celebration la fiesta
cent el centavo (*Spanish America*),
  el céntimo (*Spain*)
center el centro
central central
century el siglo
certain cierto
champion el campeón
championship el campeonato
chapter el capítulo
Charles Carlos
cheap barato
check la cuenta
chicken el pollo; — with rice el
  arroz con pollo
child el niño
Chile Chile
church la iglesia
city la ciudad
civil civil
civilization la civilización
class la clase; in — en la clase
classic clásico
classroom la sala de clase
clean limpio; to — limpiar
client el cliente
climate el clima

clock el reloj
close cerrar (ie)
cloudy nublado
coast la costa
coffee el café
cold el frío; el resfriado; *adj.* frío;
  to be — (*living beings*) tener frío;
  it is cold (*weather*) hace frío
collection la colección
Colombia Colombia
colonial colonial
comb peinar; to — one's hair
  peinarse
come venir; come in! ¡pase Vd.!
comedy la comedia
comfortable cómodo
commercial comercial
commission la comisión
company la compañía
composition la composición
concentrate concentrar; to — on
  concentrar la atención en
confidential confidencial
confound it! ¡caramba!
congenial simpático
conquer conquistar
conquest la conquista
construct construir
contact el contacto
contain contener
contemporary contemporáneo
continent el continente
continue continuar, seguir (i)
contract el contrato
contrary el contrario; on the — al
  contrario
conversation la conversación
converse conversar
convince convencer
Cordova Córdoba
corner la esquina
count contar (ue)
country el país; el campo
couple el par
course la asignatura; of — claro
  (que), ¡cómo no! por supuesto,
  desde luego
court (*tennis*) la cancha
cousin el primo, la prima
cow la vaca

cowboy el vaquero
cradle la cuna
Cuban cubano
cultural cultural
cup la taza
custard el flan
custom la costumbre
cute mono

dance el baile; bailar
dark moreno
date la fecha; to have a — with
estar citado con
daughter la hija
day el día; — after tomorrow
pasado mañana; — before
yesterday anteayer; all — todo
el día; every — todos los días
deal: a good — bastante; a great —
mucho; a very great — muchísimo
December diciembre m.
decide decidir
deck la cubierta
delicious sabroso
deny negar (ie)
describe describir
desert el desierto
desire desear
dessert el postre
detail el detalle
development el desarrollo
dictator el dictador
dictatorship la dictadura
die morir (ue)
different distinto
difficult difícil
dining room el comedor
dinner la comida; — time la hora
de la comida
direct dirigir
discover descubrir
discovered descubierto
discuss discutir
dish el plato
distant lejos
divide dividir(se)
do hacer
doctor el médico, el doctor
document el documento
dollar el dólar

done hecho (*past part. of* hacer)
door la puerta
doubt dudar
down: to go — bajar
dream soñar; to — of soñar con
dress el vestido; to — vestirse
drink beber; to have (get)
something to — tomar un refresco
during durante

each cada; — one cada uno; to
speak to — other hablarse
early temprano
earn ganar
east el este
easy fácil
eat comer
economy la economía
Ecuador el Ecuador
egg el huevo
eight ocho
eight hundred ochocientos
eighteen diez y ocho, dieciocho
eighth octavo
eighty ochenta
elevator el ascensor
eleven once
end el fin
engagement el compromiso
engineer el ingeniero
England Inglaterra
English inglés; el inglés
Englishman el inglés
enormous enorme
enough bastante
enter entrar (en)
entertain entretener
enthusiasm el entusiasmo
entire entero
epic la epopeya
epoch la época
equator la línea ecuatorial
especially especialmente
Europe Europa
even aun, aún; hasta; — though
aun cuando
evening la tarde; good — ¡buenas
noches! in the — por la noche;
this — esta noche
ever jamás

every cada; todo; — **day** todos los días
everybody todo el mundo
everything todo
everywhere en (a) todas partes
examination el examen
examine examinar
example el ejemplo; **for** — por ejemplo; **to take for** — poner por ejemplo
exceedingly sumamente
exchange cambiar
exclaim exclamar
excursion la excursión
excuse dispensar
exercise el ejercicio
exile el destierro
expense el gasto
expensive caro
explain explicar
export la exportación; exportar
extremely sumamente

face la cara
fact: in — en efecto; **the** — **is that** (ello) es que
factory la fábrica
fail (*a course*) salir mal
fall (*season*) el otoño; **to** — caer; — **out of** caerse de
family la familia
famous famoso, célebre
far lejos
farm la finca
fascinate fascinar
fat gordo
father el padre
favor el favor
favorite predilecto
fear el miedo; temer
February febrero *m.*
feel sentir (ie), sentirse (ie)
fertile fértil
fever la fiebre
few pocos; **a** — unos, unos cuantos
fewer, fewest menos
field trip la excursión de estudio
fifteen quince
fifth quinto
fifty cincuenta

film la película
finally al fin, por fin
find hallar, encontrar (ue); — **out** averiguar, saber
finish terminar, acabar
first primero, primer; **at** — al principio
fish el pescado; pescar
five cinco
five hundred quinientos
flamenco el canto flamenco
flee huir
floor el piso; **ground** — el piso bajo; **main** — el piso principal
flower la flor
flunk (*a course*) salir mal
follow seguir (i)
foot el pie; **on** — a pie
football el fútbol
for por, para *prep.*; pues *conj.*; **as** — en cuanto a
foreigner el extranjero
forest la selva
forget olvidar
forty cuarenta
found fundar
four cuatro
four hundred cuatrocientos
fourteen catorce
fourth cuarto
France Francia
frank franco
free libre; desocupado
French francés; el francés
Frenchman el francés
frequently con frecuencia
Friday viernes *m.*
fried frito
friend el amigo, la amiga
from de; desde
front: in — **of** delante de
fruit la fruta
full lleno
future el porvenir

game el partido
gardenia la gardenia
gay alegre
generous generoso
gentle manso

gentleman el caballero
geographical geográfico
geography la geografía
geology la geología
get conseguir (i); buscar; — **in, on**
  subir (a); — **off** bajar (de); — **up**
  levantarse; **now I** — **it** ya caigo
gift el regalo
girl la muchacha; **little** — la
  chiquita
give dar; (*as a gift*) regalar; — **back**
  devolver (ue)
glad: to be — alegrarse (de); **I am**
  very — **to meet you** tengo mucho
  gusto en conocerle
glass el vaso; **wine** — la copa
go ir; — **away,** — **off** irse; — **back**
  volver (ue); — **down** bajar;
  — **horseback riding** montar a
  caballo; — **in** entrar; — **out** salir;
  — **shopping** ir de compras; — **to**
  bed acostarse (ue); — **toward**
  dirigirse a; — **up** subir; — **with**
  acompañar; **let's go** vamos
God Dios; — **grant** quiera Dios
good bueno, buen; —**-looking** buen
  mozo; **to be** — **for nothing** no
  servir (i) para nada
good-by adiós; **to say** — **to** despedirse
  (i) de
goodness: my —! ¡Dios mío!
grandfather el abuelo
grateful agradecido; **to be** —
  quedar agradecido
great grande, gran
greet saludar
ground el suelo
guest el convidado
guitarist el guitarrista
gymnasium el gimnasio

hair el cabello, el pelo
half medio; la mitad; — **past one**
  la una y media
hand la mano; **to** — **over** entregar
happy contento
hat el sombrero
have tener; haber (*with past part.*);
  to — **to** tener que; — **a good time**
  divertirse (ie); **to** — **just** acabar

+ *inf.*; — **something to drink**
  tomar algo
he él; — **who** el que
head la cabeza
health la salud; **to be in good** —
  estar bien de salud
hear oír; **to** — **that** oír decir que;
  this is the first time I've heard
  about it ahora lo oigo
heat el calor
heaven el cielo; **for** —**'s sake** ¡por Dios!
hello hola
help ayudar
her su, sus *poss. adj.*; la *dir. obj.*;
  le *indir. obj.*; ella *after prep.*
here aquí; acá; — **is** he aquí, aquí
  (lo) tiene Vd.
hero el héroe
hers el suyo, etc., *poss. pron.*; el
  (la, los, las) de ella; **of** —
  suyo *poss. adj.*
herself se; sí *after prep.*
him le *dir. and indir. obj.*; él *after*
  prep.; **with** — consigo *reflex.*
himself se; sí *after prep.*; **he says**
  to — dice para sí
his su, sus *poss. adj.*; el suyo *poss.*
  pron.; el (la, los, las) de él; el
  suyo *poss. adj.*
Hispanic America Hispanoamérica
Hispanic American hispanoamericano
historical histórico
history la historia
hockey el hockey
home la casa; **at** — en casa; **to go**
  — ir a casa
honest honrado
hope esperar
horse el caballo
horseback: to ride — montar a caballo
hospital la clínica
hot: to be — (*living beings*) tener
  calor; **it is** — (*weather*) hace calor;
  caliente *adj.*
hotel el hotel
hour la hora
house la casa
how? ¿cómo? — **long?** ¿cuánto
  tiempo? — **much?** ¿cuánto?
  — **many?** ¿cuántos?

how ... ! ¡qué ... !
hundred ciento, cien
hunger el hambre *f.*
hungry: to be — tener hambre
hurry darse prisa
hurt doler (ue)
husband el esposo

I yo
idleness el ocio
if si; **as —** como si
ill enfermo; **to become —** enfermar
immediately inmediatamente
impatient impaciente
important importante
impossible imposible
impress impresionar
impression la impresión
impressive impresionante
in en; **— the morning** por la mañana;
    at ten o'clock — the morning a las
    diez de la mañana
Inca el inca
incredible: it seems — parece mentira
independence la independencia
Indian el indio
indicate señalar
individual el individuo
industrial industrial
industry la industria
inform avisar
inhabitant el habitante
insist (on) insistir (en)
instead of en vez de
intelligent inteligente
intend pensar en + *inf.*
interest el interés; interesar
interested: to be — in interesarse
    por (en)
interesting interesante
interior el interior
interrupt interrumpir
introduce presentar
investment la inversión
invitation la invitación
invite invitar
it lo, la *dir. obj.*; le *indir. obj.*; él,
    ella, ello *after prep.*
Italian el italiano
Italy Italia

January enero *m.*
job el empleo
John Juan
Johnny Juanito
joke el chiste
jokingly en broma
juice el jugo
July julio *m.*
June junio *m.*
just: to have — acabar de + *inf.*;
    — at this moment precisamente

kind amable *adj.*; la clase
kindness la bondad; **have the — to**
    tenga Vd. la bondad de
know saber; conocer; **to let —**
    avisar

lack la falta; faltar
lady la señora; **young —** la señorita
lake el lago
land la tierra
landscape el paisaje
language la lengua, el idioma
large grande
last último; **to —** durar;
    — summer el verano pasado;
    — night anoche
late tarde; **it is becoming —** se
    hace tarde
later: till —, see you — hasta
    luego
laugh reír; **to — at** reírse de
lawyer el abogado
lazy perezoso
lead conducir
learn aprender; saber
least menos; **at —** al menos
leave salir (de); dejar; partir;
    to take one's — despedirse (i)
left la izquierda
lend prestar
less menos
lesson la lección
let dejar, permitir; **to — know**
    avisar; **let's go** vamos; **let's study**
    vamos a estudiar
letter la carta
library la biblioteca
life la vida

light la luz; ligero *adj.*
like como *prep.*; gustar a; — **that**
   así; **just — that** sin más ni más;
   how do you —? ¿qué le parece?
   I — it better me gusta más; **I**
   should — quisiera
likely: it is — es fácil
list la lista
listen escuchar
literature la literatura
little pequeño; poco; **a —** un poco;
   a very — un poquito
live vivir
located situado
long largo; (*time*) mucho tiempo;
   how —? ¿cuánto tiempo?
longer más tiempo; **any —** más;
   no — ya no
look: — for buscar; **— at** mirar
lose perder (ie)
lot: a — mucho
love querer a; **to be in —** estar
   enamorado
lower (*a price*) rebajar
luck la suerte
lunch almorzar (ue); **light —,**
   picnic — la merienda

machinery la maquinaria
made hecho (*past part. of* **hacer**)
Madrid Madrid
magnificent magnífico —
maid la criada
majestic majestuoso
mamma mamá
man el hombre
manner la manera
manufacture fabricar
many muchos
March marzo *m.*
market el mercado
marry casarse con
marvelous maravilloso
Mary María
mathematics las matemáticas
matter el asunto; importar; **it**
   doesn't — no importa; **that — of**
   eso de; **what's the — with you?**
   ¿qué tiene Vd.?
May mayo *m.*

me me *dir. and indir. obj.*; mí *after*
   prep.; **with —** conmigo
meal la comida
mean querer decir
meanwhile entretanto
meet encontrar (ue); conocer; dar
   con
Mexican mejicano
Mexico Méjico
midnight la medianoche
military militar
milk la leche
million el millón
millionaire el millonario
mine mío; el mío; **of —** mío
minute el minuto
Miss señorita
modern moderno
moment el momento; **just at this —**
   precisamente
Monday lunes *m.*
money el dinero; **large amount of —**
   el dineral
month el mes
monument el monumento
moon la luna
moonlight: by — a la luz de la luna
more más; **— than** más que, más de
morning la mañana; **good morning**
   buenos días; **in the —** por la
   mañana
mosque la mezquita
most más; **— of** la mayor parte de
mother la madre; la mamá
mountain la montaña; **— range** la
   cordillera
movies el cine
moving picture la película
Mr. señor
Mrs. señora
much mucho; **as (so) —** tanto;
   how —? ¿cuánto? **very —**
   muchísimo
museum el museo
music la música
must deber; tener que; **one —** hay que
my mi; mío

name el nombre; **his — is** se llama;
   what is his —? ¿cómo se llama?

narrow angosto, estrecho
nation la nación
natural natural
near cerca de
nearly casi
necessary necesario, preciso; **it is —**
es necesario, es preciso, hay que +
inf.
necessity la necesidad
necktie la corbata
need necesitar
neighboring vecino
negotiate negociar
neither tampoco; ni; **— . . . nor**
ni . . . ni
never nunca, jamás
nevertheless sin embargo
new nuevo
newspaper el periódico
New York Nueva York
next próximo; **— week** la semana
que viene; **— court** la cancha de
al lado
nice simpático
night la noche; **good —** buenas
noches; **last —** anoche
nine nueve
nine hundred novecientos
nineteen diez y nueve, diecinueve
ninety noventa
ninth noveno
nitrate el salitre
no no *adv.*; ninguno, ningún *adj.*;
— longer ya no; **— one** nadie;
to say — decir que no
nobody nadie
none ninguno
noon el mediodía
nor ni
north el norte
North America la América del
Norte
North American norteamericano
nothing nada: **to be good for —**
no servir (i) para nada
notice notar
novel la novela
November noviembre *m.*
now ahora; ya; **from — on** de aquí
en adelante; **(four days) from —**

de aquí en (cuatro días); **right —**
ahora mismo
nylon el nilón

oasis el oasis
objection el inconveniente
observe observar
obtain conseguir (i)
occur ocurrir
o'clock: one — la una; **two —** las
dos
October octubre *m.*
of de
offer ofrecerse a
office la oficina; **doctor's —** el
consultorio
often a menudo, muchas veces
oh oh, ay
old viejo; antiguo; **to be twenty
years —** tener veinte años; **how
— is he?** ¿cuántos años tiene?
older, oldest mayor
on en, sobre; **— entering** al entrar;
— Saturday el sábado; **— time** a
tiempo
once una vez; **at —** en seguida
one uno, un, una; se *indef. subj.
pron.*; **the — of (with)** el (la) de;
the (—s) who (which) el (la, los,
las) que; **it is — o'clock** es la una;
no — nadie; **some—** alguien
oneself se *dir. and indir. obj.*; sí
after prep.; **to talk to —** hablar
para sí
only único *adj.*; sólo, **no . . . más
que**; **the — thing** lo único
open abrir
opera la ópera
opinion la opinión, el parecer
opportunity la oportunidad
or o
orange la naranja
orchestra la orquesta
order mandar; (*in a restaurant*)
pedir; **in — to** para; **in — that**
para que, a fin de que; **to be in —**
estar en regla
other otro
ought deber
our nuestro

ours el nuestro; **of —** nuestro
out: get — of (*a vehicle*) bajar de;
go **— (of)** salir (de)
overcoat el abrigo
owe deber
own propio

Pacific (*Ocean*) el Pacífico
pack (*a suitcase*) hacer (*una
maleta*)
paint la pintura
painter el pintor
painting el cuadro
pair el par
palace el palacio
pampas la pampa
parents los padres
pardon dispensar, perdonar
park (*a car*) estacionar (*un coche*)
part la parte; **the greater —** la
mayor parte
pass pasar; (*a course*) salir
aprobado
passage el pasaje
passport el pasaporte
pay pagar; **— attention to** prestar
atención a
pedantic pedante
people la gente
performance la función
perhaps quizá(s), tal vez
period el período
permit permitir
person la persona, el individuo
Peru el Perú
philosophy la filosofía
pick up coger; recoger
picnic lunch la merienda
picture el cuadro; **moving —** la
película
picturesque pintoresco
pink rosado
pity: it's a — es lástima
plain el llano
plane el avión; **by —** en avión
plateau el altiplano
play jugar (ue); (*an instrument*)
tocar; (*in a game*) la jugada
player el jugador
playwright el dramaturgo

please gustar a; por favor; haga
Vd. el favor de . . . ; tenga Vd. la
bondad de . . .
pleased: how — (I am) to see you!
¡cuánto gusto de verle! **so pleased
to meet you!** ¡tanto gusto de
conocerle!
pleasure el gusto; **with —** con
mucho gusto; **the — is mine** el
gusto es mío
pneumonia la pulmonía
point el punto; (*in a game*) el tanto;
— at señalar
polite cortés
politician el político
poor pobre
popular popular
port el puerto
Portuguese el portugués
possess poseer
possible posible; **as soon as —**
cuanto antes
potatoes las papas
prefer preferir (ie)
prepare preparar
president el presidente
pretty bonito, lindo, precioso
prevent impedir (i)
price el precio; **what is the — of?**
¿a cómo se vende? ¿cuál es el
precio de . . . ? **at what —?**
¿a cuánto?
principal principal
private particular
probable probable
produce producir
product el producto
professor el profesor
program el programa
progressive progresista
progress el progreso
promise prometer
propose proponer
provided (that) con tal que
psychology la psicología
public público
punctual puntual
purchase la compra
put poner; **— on** ponerse
pyramid la pirámide

quarter el cuarto; **it is a — to five** son las cinco menos cuarto
question la pregunta; **ask a —** hacer una pregunta
quickly pronto
quite bastante

racket la raqueta
radio la radio; **— (set)** el radio
railroad el ferrocarril
rain la lluvia; llover (ue)
raise levantar
ranch el rancho
rate: at any — de todos modos
rather bastante
reach llegar (a)
read leer
ready listo
reality la realidad
realize darse cuenta de
reason la razón; **for that —** por eso; **for what —? ¿**para qué?
receive recibir
recommend recomendar (ie)
recover mejorarse; recobrar
red rojo, colorado
refreshment el refresco
region la región
regret sentir (ie)
relative el pariente
remain quedarse
remains los restos
remember recordar (ue), acordarse (ue) (de)
repeat repetir (i)
representative el representante
republic la república
request pedir (i)
reserve reservar
resist resistir
rest descansar
restaurant el restaurante
result resultar
return la vuelta; volver (ue); (*give back*) devolver (ue); **— trip** el viaje de vuelta
revolution la revolución
rice el arroz
rich rico

ride montar; **— horseback** montar a caballo
right la razón; (*hand*) la derecha; **— now** ahora mismo; **all —** está bien; **all —, then** bueno pues; **to be —** tener razón
ring sonar (ue)
rise levantarse
river el río; **up the —** río arriba
rolling stock el material rodante
room la sala, el cuarto
roundup el rodeo
run correr; funcionar; **— into** dar con

s la ese
sad triste
said dicho (*past part. of* **decir**)
saint Santo, San; el santo
salad la ensalada
salesgirl la vendedora
same mismo; **the same (one) as** el mismo que
Saturday sábado *m.*
say decir
season la estación
second segundo
see ver
seem parecer
seen visto (*past part. of* **ver**)
sell vender
send enviar; **— a telegram** poner un telegrama
September septiembre *m.*
serious grave
servant la criada
serve servir (i)
seven siete
seven hundred setecientos
seventeen diez y siete, diecisiete
seventh séptimo
seventy setenta
several varios
Seville Sevilla
shame la vergüenza
sharp: three o'clock — las tres en punto
she ella
shirt la camisa
shoe el zapato

shop la tienda
shopping: to go — ir de compras
short bajo
show mostrar (ue); enseñar; (*a movie*) dar
sick enfermo; **to become —** enfermar
side el lado
silk la seda
simple simple
since desde; como; pues; ya que
sing cantar
sister la hermana
sit down sentarse (ie)
sitting sentado
six seis
six hundred seiscientos
sixteen diez y seis, dieciséis
sixth sexto
sixty sesenta
skate patinar
ski esquiar
skirt la falda
sky el cielo
sleep dormir (ue); **to go to —** dormirse (ue)
slowly lentamente
small pequeño, chico
smile sonreír
snow la nieve; nevar (ie)
so así; tan (*with adj. or adv.*); **— much** tanto; **— that** de modo que, de manera que
socks los calcetines
soldier el soldado
some alguno, algún; unos
somebody, someone alguien
something algo
sometimes a veces, algunas veces
somewhat algo
son el hijo
song la canción
soon pronto; **as — as** en cuanto, tan pronto como; **as — as possible** cuanto antes
sorry: to be — sentir (ie); **I am very — lo** siento mucho
sound sonar (ue)
soup la sopa
south el sur

South America Sudamérica, la América del Sur
Spain España
Spaniard el español
Spanish español; el español
speak hablar
spend gastar; (*time*) pasar
spite: in — of a pesar de; **in — of the fact that** a pesar de que
sport el deporte
spring la primavera
square la plaza
stadium el estadio
stand (*resist*) resistir
star la estrella
start partir
state el estado
station la estación
stay quedarse
steak el bistec
steamer el vapor
steel el acero
still todavía, aun, aún
stingy tacaño
stockings las medias
store la tienda
straight derecho
strange extraño
street la calle
strip la faja
stroll pasearse
strong fuerte
student el alumno, el estudiante
study estudiar; el estudio
such tan *adv.*; **— a** tal *adj.*
suddenly de pronto
suffer sufrir
sufficient bastante, suficiente; **to be —** bastar
suggest proponer, sugerir (ie)
suit el traje; **bathing —** el traje de baño
suitcase la maleta
summer el verano
sun el sol
Sunday domingo *m.*
sunny: it is — hace sol
surprise sorprender, extrañar
swallow: to — the (letter) *s* comerse las eses

sweetheart el novio, la novia, el enamorado
swim nadar

table la mesa
take tomar; llevar; llevarse; (*a course*) cursar; — **a trip (an excursion)** hacer un viaje (una excursión); — **for example** poner por ejemplo
talk conversar
tall alto
tape la cinta
taxi el taxi
tea el té
teacher el profesor, la profesora; **Spanish —** el profesor de español
team el equipo
technique la técnica
teeth los dientes
telegram el telegrama
telephone el teléfono; telefonear
television la televisión
tell decir; contar (ue)
temperate templado
ten diez
tennis el tenis; — **court** la cancha de tenis
tenth décimo
Texas Tejas
textile el tejido
than que; **more — ten** más de diez
thank dar las gracias a; —**s!** ¡gracias! — **you very much** ¡muchas gracias!
that que *conj. and rel. pron.*; el cual, el que *rel. pron.*; ese, esa, aquel, aquella *demonstr. adj.*; ése, ésa, eso, aquél, aquélla, aquello *demonstr. pron.*; — **of** el (la, lo) de; — **which** lo que; **all — which** todo lo que, cuanto; **oh, —; would —** ojalá
the el, la, los, las
theater el teatro
their su, sus, de ellos
theirs el suyo, el de ellos; **of —** suyo, de ellos
them los, las *dir. obj.*; les *indir. obj.*; ellos, ellas *after prep.*; **with them** consigo *reflex.*

themselves se; sí *after prep.*
then entonces; luego, después; pues; **all right —, well —** bueno pues
there allí; allá; **back —** allá; — **is, — are** hay; — **was, — were** había; **if — are any** si los hay
therefore por eso; por consiguiente
these estos, estas *demonstr. adj.*; éstos, éstas *demonstr. pron.*
they ellos, ellas
thin delgado
thing la cosa; **the same old —** lo de siempre
think pensar (ie); creer; **to — of** pensar en
third tercero, tercer
thirst la sed
thirsty: to be — tener sed
thirteen trece
thirty treinta
this este, esta *demonstr. adj.*; — **(one)** éste, éste, ésta, esto *demonstr. pron.*
Thomas Tomás
those esos, esas, aquellos, aquellas *demonstr. adj.*; ésos, ésas, aquéllos, aquéllas *demonstr. pron.*; — **who (which)** los (las) que; — **of** los (las) de
though: even — aun cuando
thousand: a (one) — mil
three tres
three hundred trescientos
throat la garganta
through por
Thursday jueves *m.*
thus así
tile: colored — el azulejo
tie la corbata
time el tiempo; la vez; la hora; **at this —** a estas horas; **at the same —** a la vez; **dinner —** la hora de la comida; **in (on) —** a tiempo; **for the first —** por primera vez; **this is the first — I've heard about it** ahora lo oigo; **to have a good —** divertirse (ie); **at what —?** ¿a qué hora? **what — is it?** ¿qué hora es?

tired cansado
to a, para; **in order —** para; **a
quarter — nine** las nueve menos
cuarto
toast las tostadas
today hoy
tomorrow mañana; **— morning**
mañana por la mañana; **day after
—** pasado mañana
too también; demasiado; **— much**
demasiado
tooth el diente
total el total
tourist el turista
tragedy la tragedia
train el tren
travel viajar
tree el árbol
trip el viaje; la excursión; **return —**
el viaje de vuelta; **to take a —**
hacer un viaje
tropical tropical
true verdadero; **it is —** es verdad
truth la verdad
try pretender, tratar de
Tuesday martes *m.*
turn: — out to be resultar
twelve doce
twenty veinte
two dos
two hundred doscientos
typical típico

uncle el tío
understand comprender, entender (ie)
United States los Estados Unidos
university la universidad
unless a menos que
unoccupied desocupado
until hasta *prep.*; hasta que *conj.*
up arriba; **— the river** río arriba
upon: — leaving al salir
Uruguay el Uruguay
urgent urgente; **to be —** urgir
us nos *dir. and indir. obj.*; nosotros
after prep.
use usar; **to be of no —** no servir
(i) para nada

vacation las vacaciones

valley el valle
various varios
vast vasto
very muy; bien
view la vista
Virginia Virginia
visit la visita; visitar

wait esperar
waiter el camarero
walk caminar
wall la pared
want querer
war la guerra
warm: to be — tener calor
(*living beings*); **it is —** hace calor
(*weather*)
wash lavar(se)
washed: to get — lavarse
watch el reloj
water el agua *f.*
way la manera; el camino; **this —**
por aquí
we nosotros, nosotras
wear llevar
weather el tiempo; **the — is good**
hace buen tiempo
Wednesday miércoles *m.*
week la semana
weigh pesar
welcome: you're — no hay de qué;
de nada
well bien; pues; **— then** bueno
pues; **to get —** mejorarse
well-known conocido
west el oeste
what lo que *rel. pron.*; **—?** ¿qué?
¿cuál? **— a . . . !** ¡qué . . . ! **what a
beautiful dress!** ¡qué vestido más
hermoso!
whatever cualquier(a)
when cuando; **—?** ¿cuándo?
where donde; *int.* ¿dónde? ¿adónde?
wherever dondequiera
whether si
which que, el cual, el que, lo cual
rel. pron.; **—?** ¿qué? ¿cuál?
those — los (las) que
while el rato; **a long —** largo rato;
mientras (que) *conj.*

white blanco
who que, quien, el cual, el que *rel. pron.*; —? ¿quién? **the one** —, **he (she)** — el (la) que
whole entero; **the** — **lesson** toda la lección
whom que, a quien, al cual, al que *rel. pron.*; —? ¿a quién?
whose cuyo *rel. adj.*; —? ¿de quién?
why? ¿por qué?
wife la esposa
win ganar
window la ventana
wind el viento
windy: it is — hace viento
wine el vino
winter el invierno
wish querer
with con
within dentro de
without sin *prep.*; sin que *conj.*
woman la mujer
wool la lana
woolen de lana
word la palabra
work el trabajo; (*of art*) la obra; trabajar; funcionar
world el mundo
worry: don't — pierda Vd. cuidado
worse peor
worst peor
worth: to be — valer; **it's** — **while** vale la pena (de)

would that! ¡ojalá!
write escribir
written escrito (*past part. of* escribir)

Yankee el yanqui
year el año; **last** — el año pasado
yes sí; — **I am (was, did,** *etc*) yo sí; **to say** — decir que sí
yesterday ayer; — **afternoon** ayer por la tarde; **day before** — anteayer
yet todavía, aun, aún; **not** — todavía no
you usted (Vd.), ustedes (Vds.) *subj. and after prep.*; le, la lo, los, las *dir. obj.*; le, les *indir. obj.*; *familiar forms:* tú, vosotros *subj. pron.*; te, os *dir. and indir. obj.*; ti, vosotros *after prep.*
young joven; — **man** el joven; — **lady** la joven, la señorita; — **people** los jóvenes
younger menor
youngest menor
your su, sus, de Vd., de Vds.; tu, tus (*familiar*); vuestro (*familiar plu.*)
yours el suyo, el de Vd. (Vds.); el tuyo, el vuestro (*familiar*); **of** — suyo, de Vd. (Vds.); tuyo, vuestro (*familiar*)

INDEX